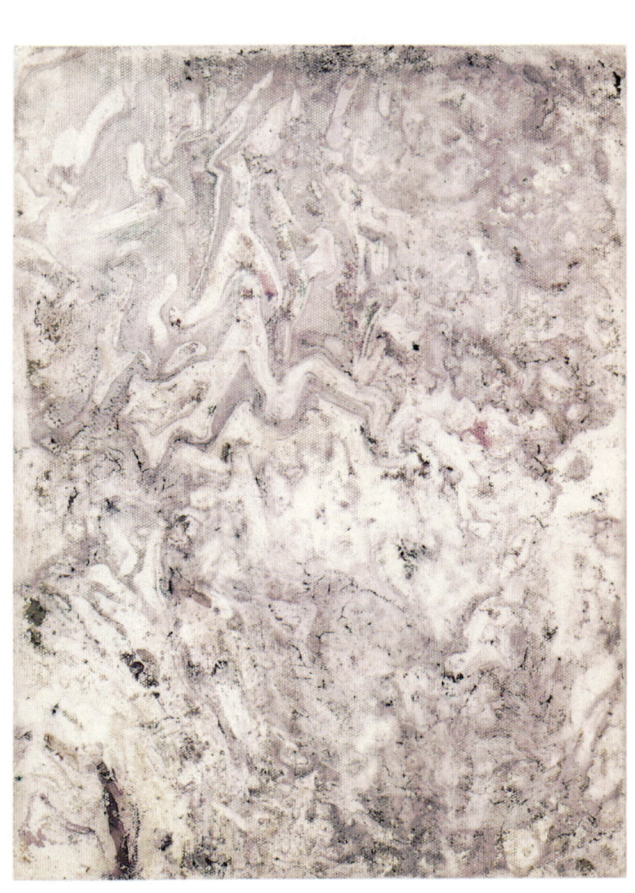

春の修学旅行〜国会にて〜 昭和12年4月

津波、写真、
Tsunami, Photographs, and LOST & FOUND PROJECT
Family Photos swept away

それから

Then

by 3.11 East Japan Tsunami

はじめに

人はなぜ、ことあるごとに写真を撮るんだろうかとずっと思っていた。東京の動物園にパンダが来たとき、一日中パンダのところにいて写真を撮るという仕事をしたことがある。日本に来たばかりのパンダはとても人気で、お客さんは２時間以上じっと並んで自分の番が来るのを待っていた。そして自分の番が来るとすぐに携帯を取り出し、記念写真を撮ると満足そうにその場を離れた。そんな写真はインターネットにいくらでもありそうなものなのに。地震が起きてからもう３年が経った。その間ぼくは写真について考え続け、失望し、やがてこれだけ写真というものがぼくらの人生に密着している意味を知った。世界中の人が日々似たような写真を撮り続けていることにも、同じ理由が当てはまるかと思う。書ききれなかったことも多くあるけれど、ぼくが写真というものにどう関わり、そのなかでどんなことが見えてきたのかがみなさんに伝わるといいなと思う。

Foreward

Why are people always taking photographs? I am constantly faced with this recurring question. I was once assigned a job to photograph zoo visitors who had come to see a panda which had just arrived in Tokyo. It had been getting a lot of media attention and so people would patiently wait in line for more than two hours for their turn to come. When they finally reached the cage, they would photograph the panda with their cell phones and leave satisfied. At the time, I thought to myself why would they take photographs there were already so many similar images of pandas on the internet. Two years have now passed since the earthquake and for that entire time I have been thinking about photography. I felt let down by its powerlessness, yet gradually I started to appreciate how it could be a part of our lives. I think that is the reason why so many photographs - many of which look interchangeable - are taken everyday around the world. With this account, I hope the readers get the idea of how I coped with the photographic media, and what I experienced and saw as a photographer. So many things have happened over the past two years, of which this is only a fraction.

2011.3.11 1日目

大きな地震が起きた。東京にあるぼくの家も数分にわたり揺れ続けた。何が起きたのかとテレビをつけると、そのなかで事態はどんどん大きくなっていった。津波が港にやってきて町を沈め、人を呑み込んでいた。それからというもの、毎日ネットや新聞には様々な写真が掲載されていった。津波が去ったあとの風景や、捜索の様子や悲しむ人の顔や遺体安置所など。被災地で何が起きているのかを伝えているかに見えた。しかしその写真たちも、数日を過ぎると似たような写真の繰り返しになった。そして気づいたことがある。写真は何の役にも立っていない。電気ガス水道のライフラインが止まり、食べ物がなく、ガソリンがなく、暖をとるための燃料もないなかで写真にできることは何もない。ただ酷い場所の姿を、酷くないところにいるぼくらに届けているだけに見えた。自分がずっと学んで仕事にもしてきた写真というものは、いざというときこんなにも役に立たないということを知り、ずいぶんと無駄に生きてきてしまったと思った。

2011.3.11 Day 1

A big earthquake hit Japan. My apartment in Tokyo was shaking for minutes. I turned on the television to see what was going on. The things got worse and worse and as the tsunami hit the coast, small harbor towns sank and people drowned. Soon after, tons of photographs appeared in the newspapers and web media: landscapes devastated after the tsunami; officials searching for survivors; makeshift mortuaries; and the faces of people in despair. They seemed to show us what was happening in the affected regions, yet after a few days they became somewhat repetitive. It was then that I realized that photographs were not helping the victims. When the lifelines - electricity, gas and water - had stopped, when there was no food or fuel, and no way to keep warm, there was nothing photography could do to help them. The photographs just seemed to be documenting and delivering the scenes of the horrific event to the people in safe places. Photography, which I had studied and made my living from, was so powerless in the face of such a catastrophe and I couldn't help but feel that I had wasted my entire life.

2011.4.26　46日目

そのうちに東京の街も少し落ち着き、カメラマンとしての仕事も再開した。そしてある日、取材先の人がこんなことを言った。「今できることがなくても、現地に行けるようになったら観光に行ってお金を使ってくれば、それも十分応援になるんだよ」 確かにそれもそうだと思い、ちょうどその頃テレビでやっていた、被害が少なくホテルもいち早く再開したという宮城県の松島へと友達を誘って行くことにした。インターネットで調べると、すんなりとホテルの予約をとることができた。東京から5時間ほど車に乗り、ホテルに着く頃には夜になっていた。お金を使うべく町にごはんを食べに出たのだけれど、メインストリートであるはずの駅前の道はほとんど真っ暗で、しばらく歩いてもやっている店はチェーンのレストランと地元のおじさんが集まっている、小舟という飲み屋だけだった。その飲み屋は他に客の姿もなく、いかにも仲間が集まっている感じで少し入りづらかった。どちらにしようか迷ったものの「ここまで来てチェーン店に入ったんじゃ何しに来たんだかわからないよね」と話して小舟の方に入った。扉を開けると、中で飲んでいた5人のおじさんのうちのひとりに話しかけられた。「なんだお前ら、ボランティアか？」どう答えたものかと考えていたら、友達がすかさず「違います、来てみました」と答えた。「そうかそうか、お前らちゃんと見ておけよ」とそのおじさんが言ってくれた。「野次馬に来てんじゃねえ、バカヤロー帰れ！」なんて展開も想像していたので、ぼくらはその言葉でホッとして店に入ることができた。小舟は、おじさんたちが集まって飲む場所が欲しいということで、みんなで協力してい

ち早く瓦礫を片付けた店だった。東京でカメラマンの仕事をしていると言うと、「なんだもっと早く来ればよかったのになー、家の上に船が乗ってたりしておもしろかったんだぞ」なんてことを冗談めかして言っていた。おじさんたちはみんな明るかった。酒飲んで冗談で笑い飛ばして、悲しいことは落ち着いてからゆっくり考えるのだろうかと思った。夕方からずっと飲んでいたというおじさんたちが帰ると、お店のママが津波に流されたときのことを話してくれた。車で逃げる途中で小道に入り、そこで津波に追いつかれたこと、車は水が来るとスッと浮くこと、そこから脱出しずぶ濡れになりながら近くの建物までたどり着いたこと、とても寒い夜で見上げるとものすごい星空だったこと。「自分は生かされたんだから頑張らないと」と言っていた。

2011.4.26 Day 46

As Tokyo gradually regained a sense of routine, I got back into my daily photographic work. One day at a shoot someone said to me, "Even if there is nothing you can do now, you can still visit the affected areas and spend some money, that would be of great support." That made sense. I called my friend and suggested that we go to a hotel which I had seen on television. It was in the less-damaged Matsushima area of Miyagi prefecture, and had reopened right after the earthquake. I checked the hotel's website and reserved a room, and everything went very smoothly. After a five-hour drive from Tokyo, we reached the hotel in the evening. We went out to spend some money, but the main street leading to the train station was almost pitch black. We walked for a while and the only places we found open were a chain restaurant and a pub called Kobune (small boat), in which a group of local men were having drinks. The pub seemed less inviting as the men obviously knew each other and seemed content. We hesitated, but it would have been crazy if we went to the chain restaurant and so we decided to check out Kobune. Shortly after we entered, one of the five men who were drinking inside asked us, "Are you guys volunteers?" I wasn't sure how to respond, but my friend quickly said, "No, we're just visiting." The man replied earnestly, "Alright, alright. Don't forget what you see here." I was expecting something like, "Go away! Leave us alone!" but his words relieved us and we felt accepted being there. They went on to tell us that after the earthquake they wanted to have a place to gather and drink, and so they had got together to clean up Kobune, and it was the first pub in the area to reopen. I told them that I worked as a photographer in Tokyo, to which one of them replied half-jokingly, "Really? You should've come sooner. It was crazy, you could have seen a huge ship on top of a house." The men were in good spirits, although maybe they were drunk and laughing at the situation because they

knew that when they sobered up they'd have to face the reality of what needed to be done. Having drunk since sunset, the men left and the pub owner started to tell us about her experience of being taken by the tsunami. She had been escaping by car, but the tsunami caught her when she made turn down a narrow alley. At first, her car floated in the water and so she quickly got out and took refuge in a nearby building. Desperate and soaking wet, it was a very cold night, but the sky was full of stars. "My life has been spared: I've got to stick with it," she said.

2011.4.27　47日目

次の朝、小舟に寄ってママに挨拶をしてから、前日におじさんに教えてもらった道を進んだ。どこも自衛隊の車が走っていた。海の方に向けて道を曲がり少し進むと、急に視界が開けた。海の近くにあったものはほとんど流され、平らになった場所が延々と続いていた。そこら中に潰れた車やガードレールや木や、いろんなものが転がっていた。津波はかぶったものの、流されずに残った家にはみな、何かを探す人の姿があった。天気は穏やかで、とても静かだった。カメラは持って行ったものの、その光景を前にすると自分が写真を撮る意味が全く見出せなかった。記録をしておかねばと思いシャッターを押すけれど、それが何のため誰のための記録だというのだろう。ファインダー越しに見える風景は、多少の違いこそあれ自分がネットで見た、役に立たないと思った写真にそっくりだった。この風景を忘れてはいけない、そんなことを思うのは生まれて初めてだった。それから海沿いを北上し、いくつかの町のいくつかの壊滅を見た。ぼくらにできることは何もなかった。

2011.4.27　Day 47

The next morning, after stopping by Kobune to say hello to the owner, we headed to a place that one of the men had told us about the night before. The SDF (Self Defense Forces) vehicles were everywhere and as we turned down a street to get closer to the sea, the view suddenly cleared. Everything that once stood near the sea had been swept away; there was the vast flat land scattered with flattened cars, guard rails and broken trees. Residents were trying to salvage their belongings from the debris of the houses that had survived the tsunami. The weather was calm; everything was very quiet. I had a camera with me, and although I kept pressing the shutter release to document what I was seeing, I couldn't justify myself photographing; I didn't know for whom or for what purpose I was taking photographs. What I saw through the viewfinder was more or less the same as the images I had seen on the web and thought were so useless. However for the first time in my life, I felt that I had to remember what I was seeing. Later, we drove further north along the coast. We saw several towns and devastated areas but there was nothing we could do.

2011.5.4　54日目

ある日こんなツイートがまわってきた。「【RT希望】被災地の傷んだ写真と思い出を取り戻す、写真補正ボランティアやります。現地では自衛隊回収の写真を、富士フイルムの指導でボラが洗浄スキャン中。参加希望者はぜひご連絡下さい」これならば自分でも手伝えるなと思い、すぐにツイートをしていた大妻女子大学の柴田先生に連絡をした。これが、津波で流された写真を洗浄し持ち主の手に返す思い出サルベージプロジェクトに関わるきっかけだった。ボランティアの活動は柴田先生の働く大学の一室で行われていた。ぼくが到着すると、洗浄された写真をデータ化するために、スキャンではなく複写をしたいのでやり方を教えてほしいと言われた。現地ではあまり電気が使えないので、自然光で撮る方法が必要だった。基本的なやり方と必要な機材について話しているうちに、次の日に現地に行くということだったのでぼくもついて行くことにした。現場を見なければできることとできないことの判断はつかない。それからすぐに写真学校時代の先生や友達に連絡をして、ぼくの家にあったものと合わせてカメラ、三脚、レフ板など最低限の機材をそろえた。この時点では自分がどこへ行くのかちゃんと理解していなかった。

2011.5.4 Day 54

One day, I came across a tweet which said: Volunteers needed. We clean photographs salvaged in the tsunami-stricken areas to bring the memories back to people. Volunteers are currently cleaning & scanning the photographs salvaged by the SDF, under the supervision of FUJIFILM Corporation. Please let me know if you can help. That, I could do. I contacted Prof. Shibata from Otsuma Women's University who posted the original tweet, and that was how I got involved with "Memory Salvage", the project to return the photographs that were salvaged in tsunami affected areas to their owners. The volunteers were working in a room at the university where Prof. Shibata worked. When I arrived, they asked me how to digitalize existing photographs without using scanners. They needed to digitalize the images so that people could search for their photographs on computers, but the supply of electricity was scant and irregular, meaning that they needed a way to digitalize them without depending on the inconsistent power supply: they needed to use digital cameras. As I began giving basic instructions on duplicating photos using digital cameras, they mentioned that they were going to the affected area the next day, and so I decided to go along. I couldn't figure out what I could do without having seen the damage for myself. Later that day, I contacted friends and teachers from the photography school I attended, and was able to gather minimum numbers of tools; several cameras, tripods, reflection boards and other equipment. At the time, I still had no idea what I was getting myself into.

柴田先生

人はできそうにないことはすぐ諦める。柴田先生は写真洗浄の知識も、複写の知識も、ボランティアの集め方も何も知らなかった。だけど写真を返そうという思いだけはあった。そして多くの人を巻き込み一人ではとてもできないことを達成してしまった。無謀に挑むチャレンジャーが居ることで、始まることがあるということを教えてもらった。

Prof. Shibata

People tend to feel limited by their capabilities. Prof. Shibata didn't have any knowledge of photo cleaning and digitalization, or even how to gather volunteers but nonetheless he was so enthusiastic about returning the photographs to their owners, and in the end he was able to accomplish something miraculous. So many people gave him a hand and it taught me that sometimes, even a reckless challenger can move things forward.

2011.5.5　55日目　午前

次の朝早く、北へと向かう新幹線の中で気になっていたことを柴田先生に聞いた。なぜ全てが流され生活もままならない状況なのに、写真なんて役に立たないものが欲しいんですか、と。それに対する答えはこんなふうだった。「全てが流され、何も残っていないからこそ、何かひとつでも戻るものがあるととても喜ばれるんです。それは戻るということの象徴なんです」その思いは、そのときのぼくにはちゃんとは理解できないものだった。けれど求める人がいるならばしっかり手伝おうと決めた。仙台駅で電車を乗り換え、途中からは車で移動した。ぼくらが着いたのは宮城県の一番南、福島との県境にある山元町という町だった。自衛隊の車がそこら中に走っていることをのぞけば、日本のどこにでもあるようなのんびりした田舎町という印象だった。このときはこんなに付き合いが長くなる場所だとは思っていなかった。山元町に着くと柴田先生は、津波の被害にあった小学校へ連れて行ってくれた。そこにはひとりも子供の姿はなく、海が近くて立ち入り禁止地域になっていることもあり自衛隊が管理する場所になっていた。体育館の入り口に立っている自衛官さんに挨拶して中に入ると、ずらりと何列もケースが並べられていて、その中にはアルバムやバラバラになって流された写真が入れられていた。ステージの上には遺影や位牌や卒塔婆が並べられていた。ランドセルやトロフィーなどもあった。そこは自衛隊や警察や消防やいろんな人が瓦礫の中

から生存者を捜す過程で発見された、誰かの思い出の品が集められる場所になっていた。柴田先生はズラッと並んだ写真を前に、「これを全部データ化したいんです」と言った。ぼくは、いくらなんでもこの量は無理だろうと思いながら、「がんばりましょう」と応えた。それからまた車に乗り、洗浄とデータ化をやっている場所に行った。そこは病院の一角にある旧看護学校兼寮という場所だった。数人の大学生とボランティアさんがいて、黙々と作業をしていた。大学生たちはみんな明るく、でも全く手を抜かずに作業していた。休みの日なのにデートも飲み会もせずに泥だらけになりながら頑張っている姿を見て、これは自分も負けてられないなぁと強く思ったことをよく覚えている。

2011.5.5 Day 55 Morning

Early the next morning, as headed north on the Shinkansen, I asked Prof. Shibata something that I had been wanting to know: why he thought the photographs were so important, when considering the situation, where everything had been swept away and so many lives were in crisis, they seemed so useless. His answer was something like, "For people who lost everything in the tsunami and now nothing remains, anything they can have returned is so precious. However trite that thing was, it signifies the return of their lives." I wasn't sure that I fully understood what he said, but decided to assist him if some people were in need of help. At Sendai Station we transferred to a local train, and arriving at a small station we took a car to a town called Yamamoto-cho, in the southernmost area of Miyagi prefecture, close to the border with Fukushima. It felt like just another peaceful Japanese country town, except that there were SDF officials everywhere in sight. At the time I had no idea that I would become so attached to the town. When we arrived in Yamamoto-cho, Prof. Shibata took me to an elementary school that was damaged by the tsunami. There were no children in sight, and as the school was in a restricted area close to the sea, it was under the supervision of the SDF. We were greeted by a SDF official at the entrance and then went to the gym where rows of cases containing countless numbers of photographs and albums washed away by the tsunami. On the stage they had put portraits of the deceased, memorial tablets and wooden grave markers, and I could also see children's school backpacks and trophies. The place was filled with people's memories that had been salvaged by the SDF officials, police officers, firefighters and volunteers during their search for survivors. Facing the photographs, Prof. Shibata said to me, "I want to digitalize them all." I thought that would be impossible. It seemed like there were simply too many, but I said that I would try my best. We got back into the car, and headed to the workshop where they were working on cleaning and digitalizing the photographs. It was a former nursing school-cum-dormitory within a grounds of a hospital.

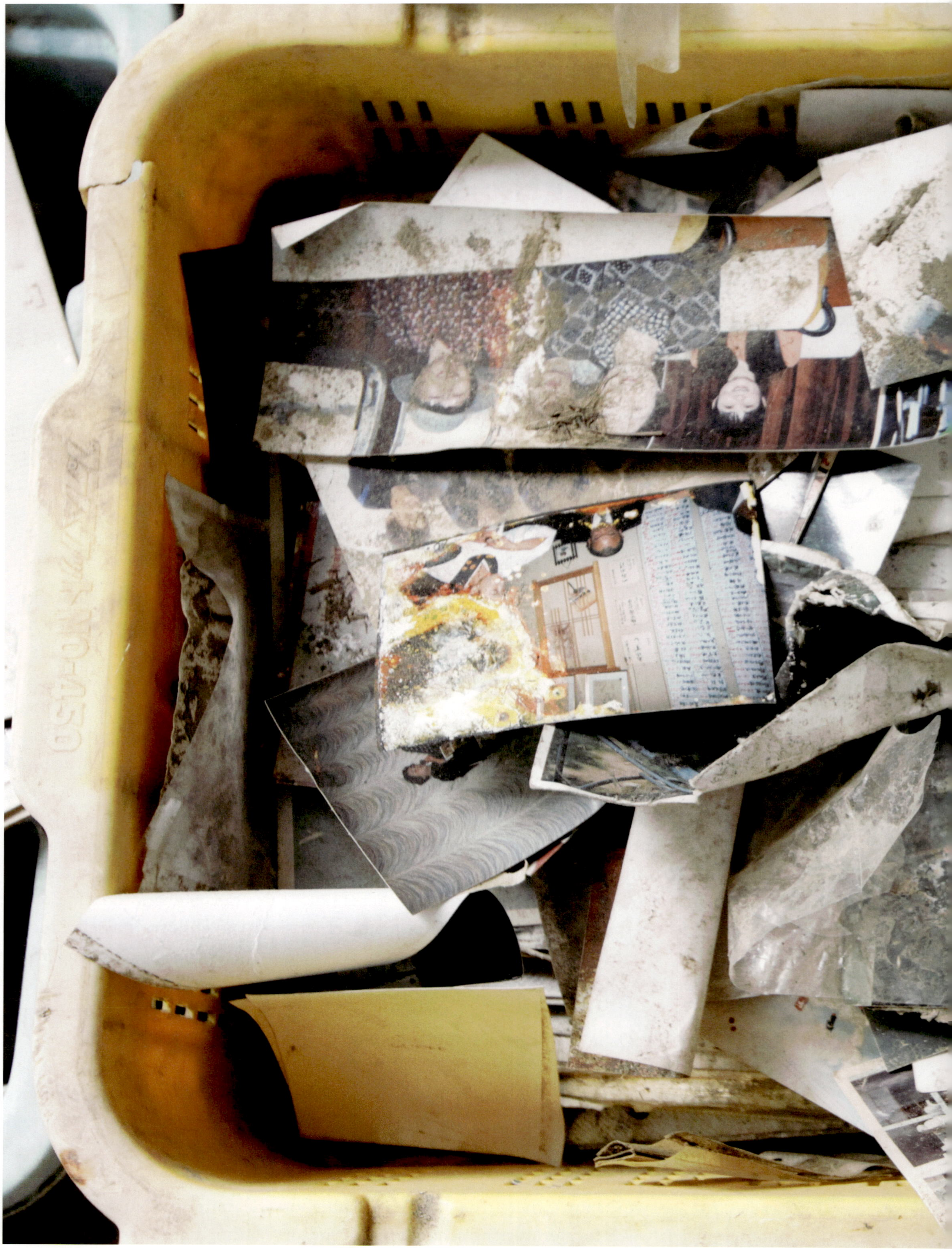

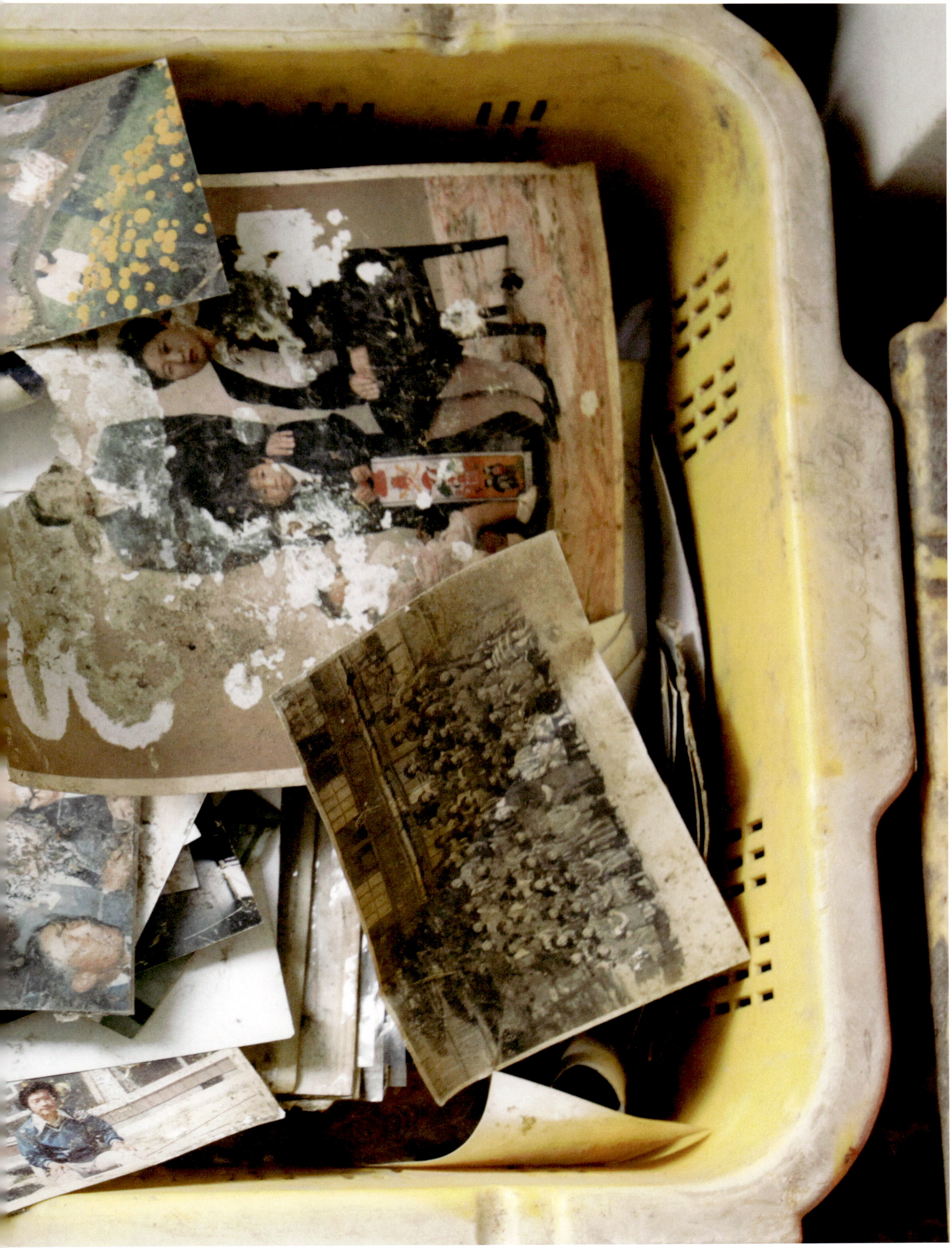

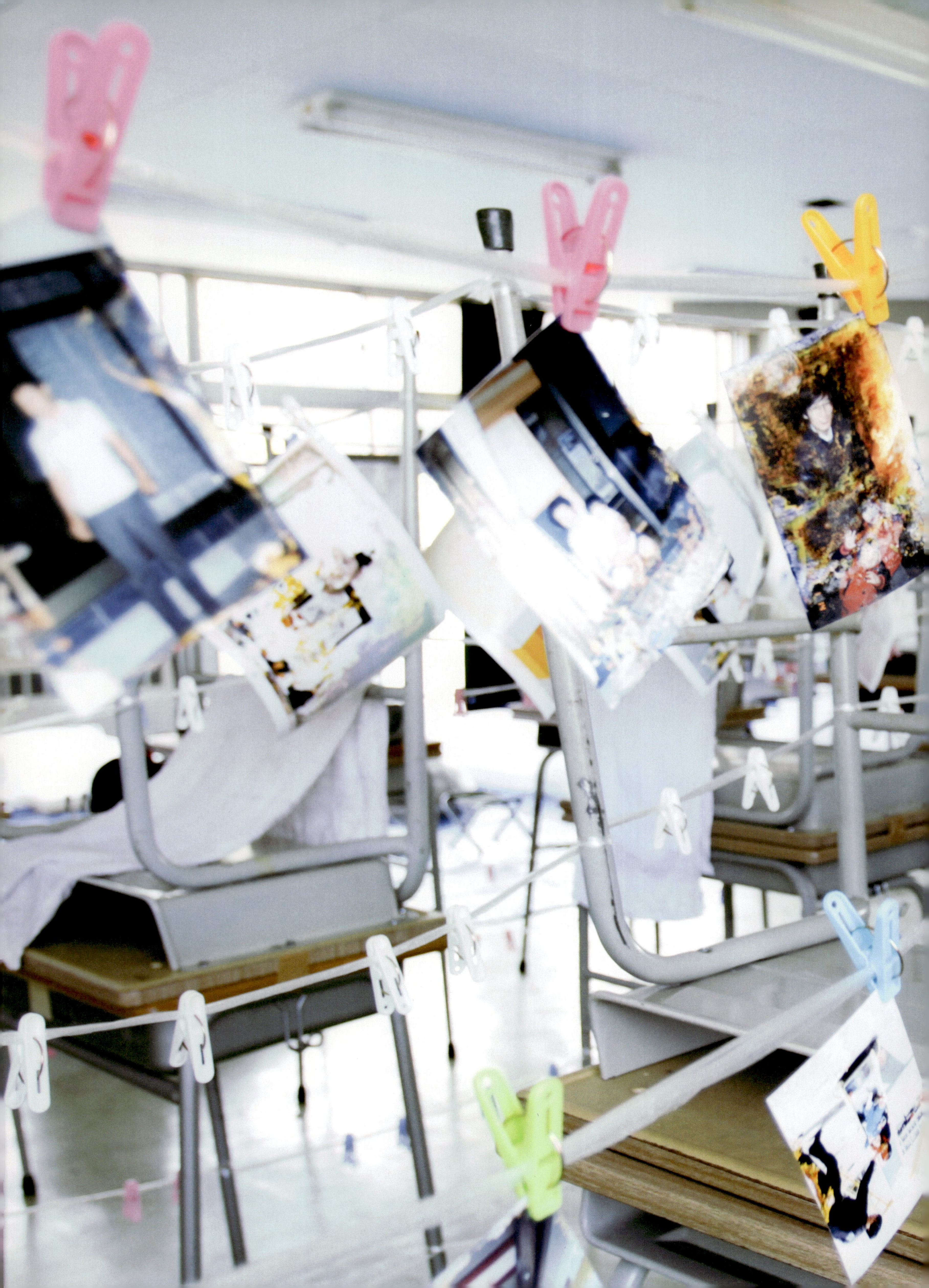

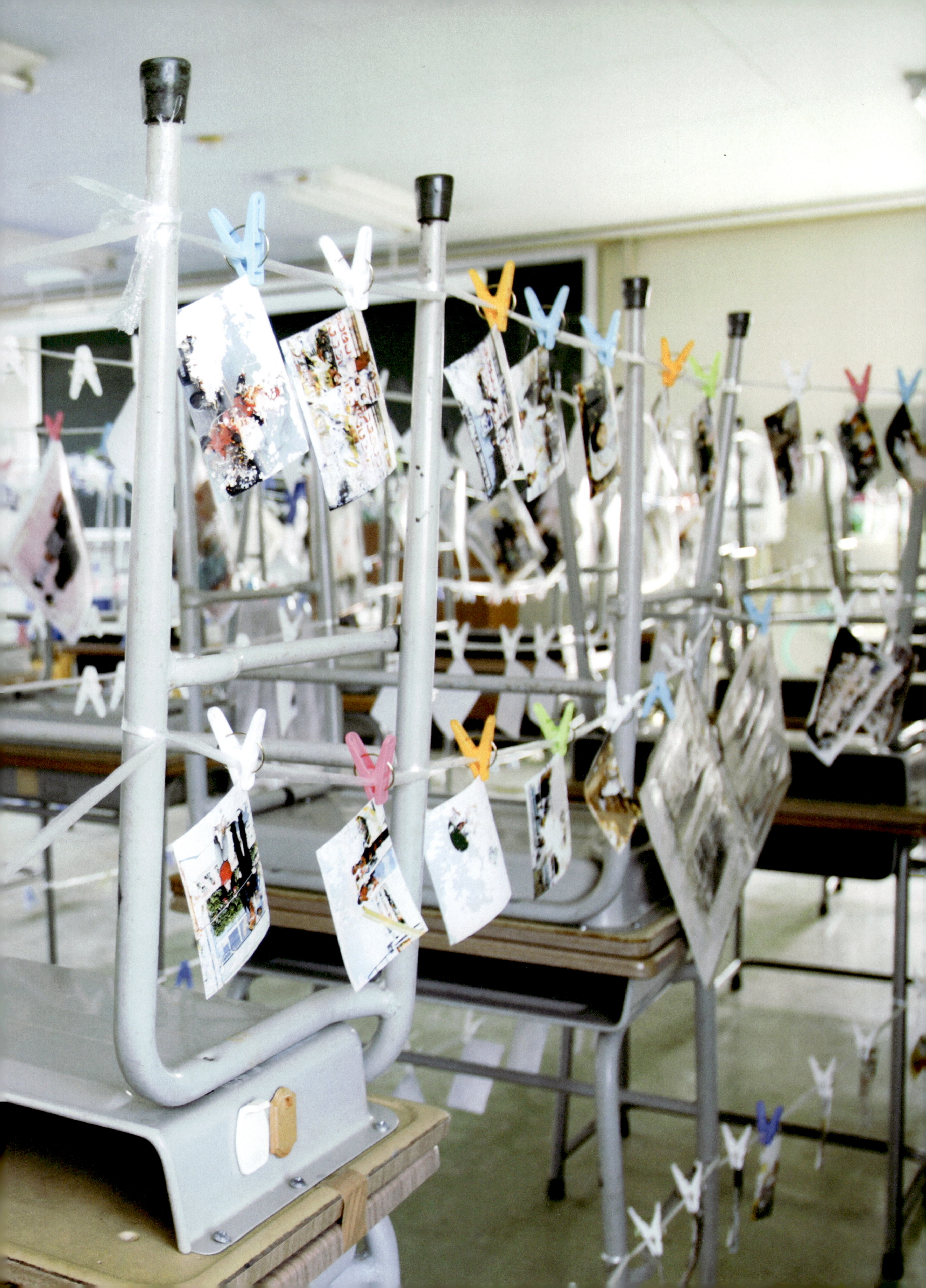

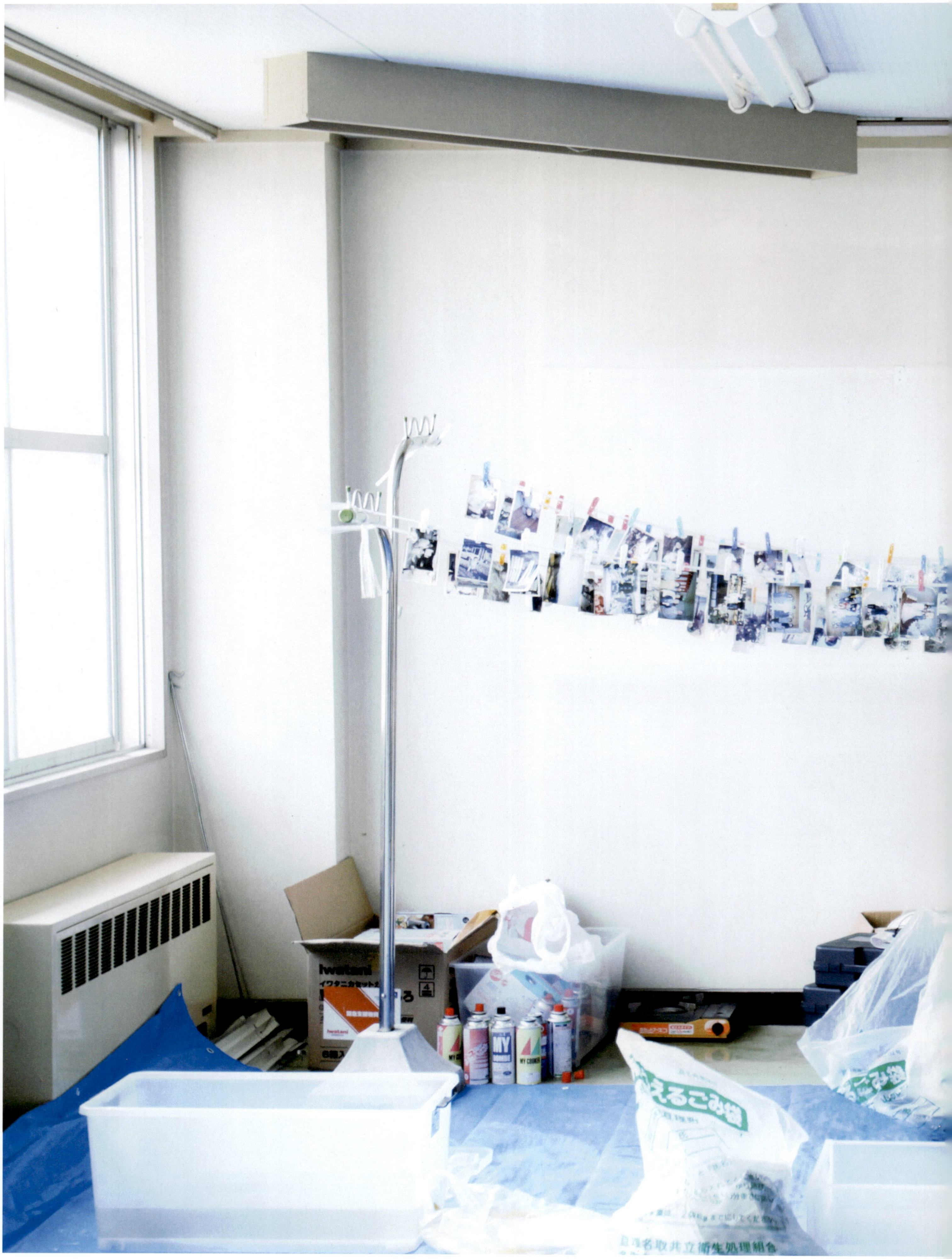
Iwatani
MY

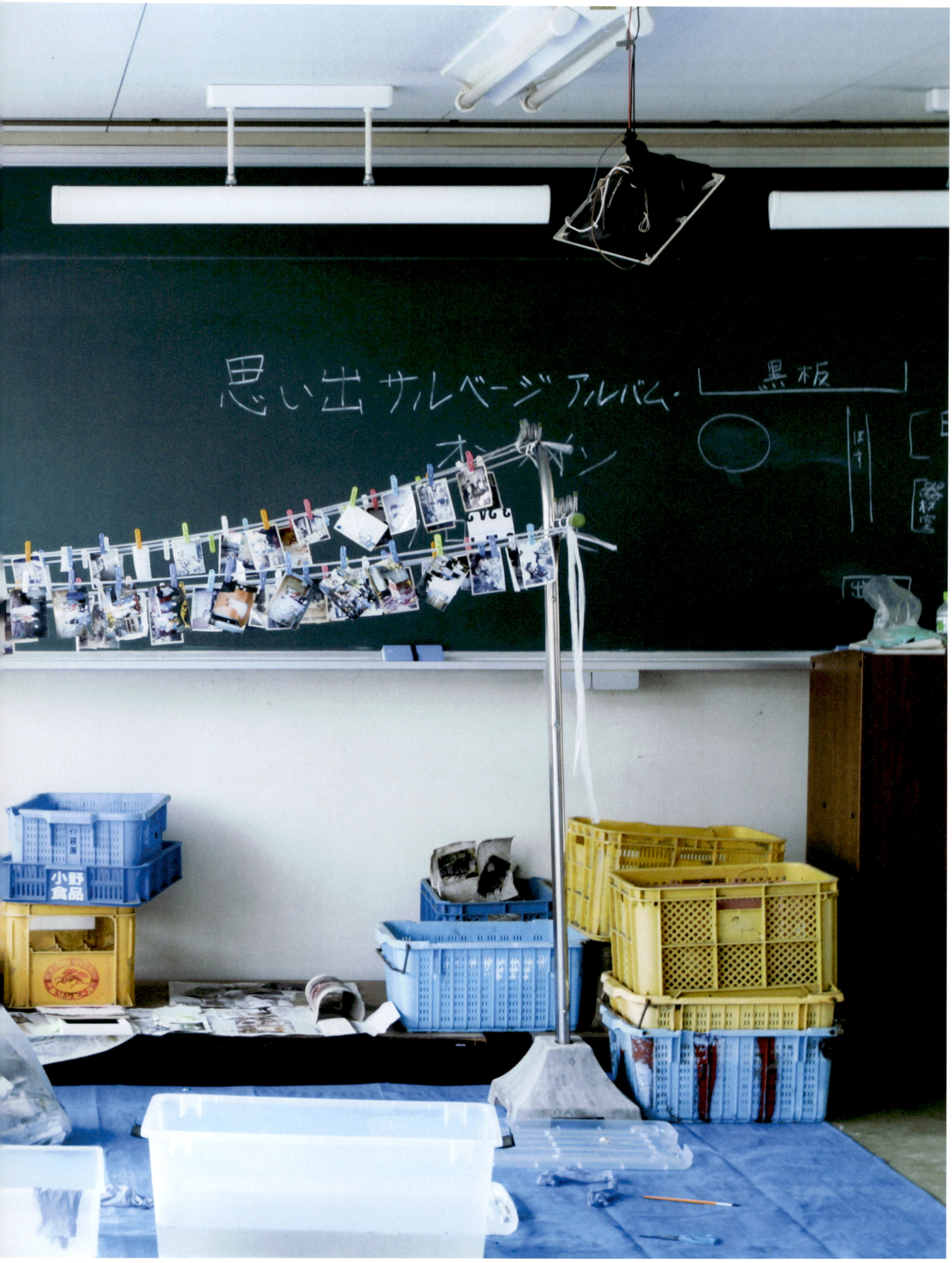
思い出サルベージアルバム・
黒板
小野食品

Several college students and volunteers were inside, in good spirits but working hard and not taking shortcuts. They were covered with mud, and worked hard even on weekends when they should've been out on a date or drinking with their friends. I remember making the decision that I had to respond to their commitment.

溝口くん

作業場を案内してくれたのは、溝口くんという青年だった。彼は京都大学の院生で、震災の少し後からずっと町に滞在していろいろと作業をしていたようだった。彼はなかなか変わった人間で、大量のごはんを食べ無尽蔵の体力をもち、自分の決めたことは延々とひとりでもやり続ける、そしてコミュニケーション能力だけが少し欠落しているものの、全国模試では何度か一位になったことのある頭脳の持ち主だった。彼が定期的に、かなり長期的に滞在していたおかげで写真の返却は滞ることなく継続していった。それは2年が経過した今も続いている。彼はこんなに山元町に来ていて、ちゃんと就職できるのだろうかとみんな心配していたのだが、今では無事に大学院を修了し研究員としてお給料ももらえるようになった。

Mizoguchi-kun

A young man called Mizoguchi-kun gave me a tour of the workshop. He was a graduate student at Kyoto University, and had been staying in the town to help people after the earthquake. He was such a strange guy: he ate an unbelievable amount of food; his physical strength was unparalleled; and he had the ability to continue with what he was determined to do. He may have had a slight communication problem, but was intelligent enough to have come first in the national exams several times. The project of returning photographs to their owners went smoothly, largely thanks to him staying on for such a long time, and even now, some two years later, t is still continuing now. He was in Yamamoto-cho so much that everyone was worried about him being able to graduate, but he successfully finished his graduate program and is now working as a researcher.

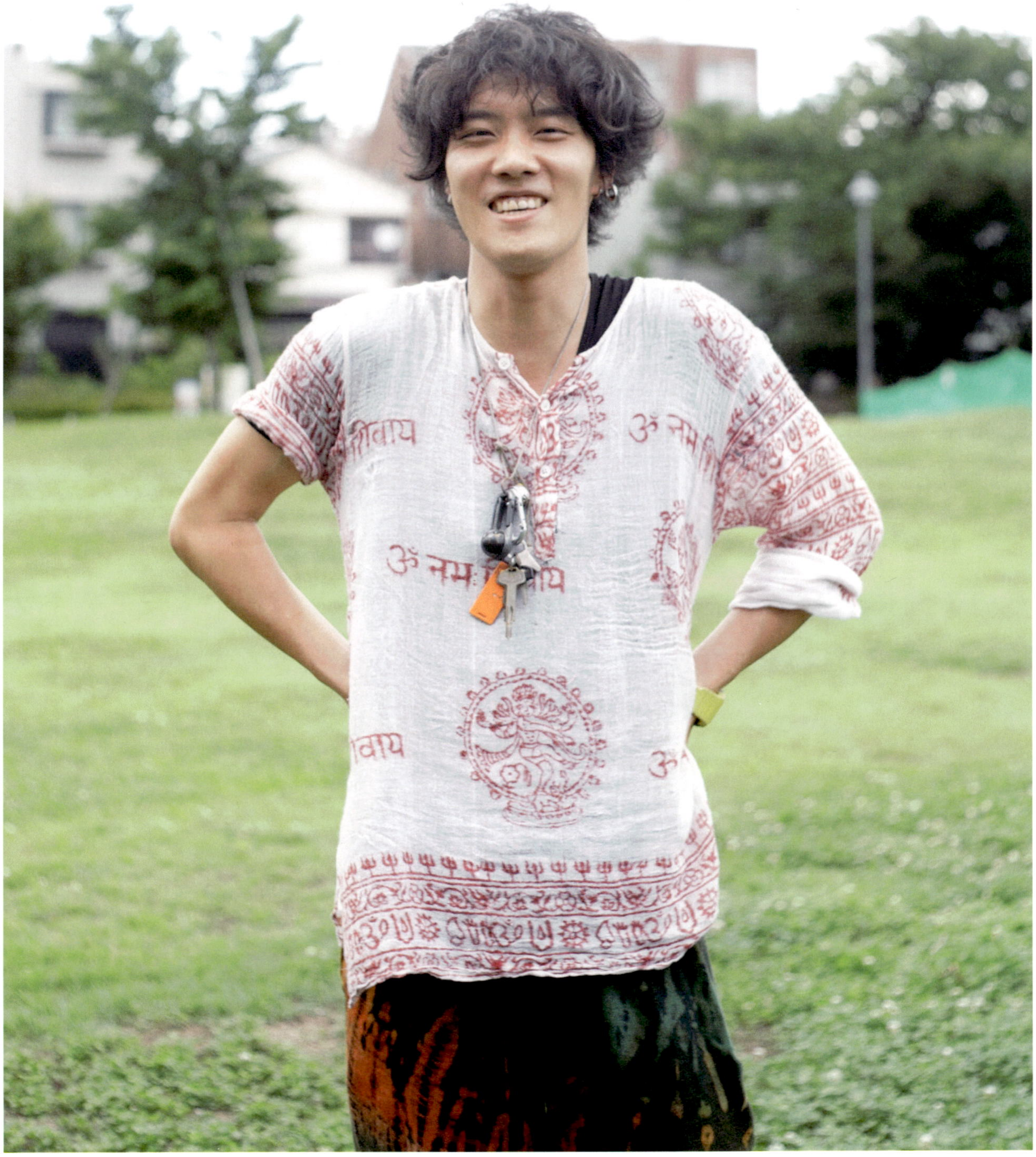

2011.5.5　55日目　午後

まずは現状のデータ化のやり方を見せてもらい、それから持っていった機材を使ってテストをして、うまくいくことが確認できたので複写の方法の説明をした。光を物質と考えて、どこから入って被写体に反射してカメラに届くのか、その方向を見ることでアルバムの表面のビニールへの写り込みを極力避けるという方法だった。次の問題は機材だった。さっき見た膨大な量の写真をデータ化するには機材も人手も全然足りていなかった。とにかくカメラと三脚が必要だった。まずは友達や先輩のカメラマンの家に眠るカメラを狙うことにした。カメラマンというのはだいたい仕事のメインで使うカメラとは別に、予備のサブカメラを持っている。さてどうやって口説くべきか。そんなことを考えながら、帰りの新幹線の中で予告としてツイッターに書き込んだ。東京に戻ったら、知り合いひとりひとりに連絡するつもりだった。思い出の写真を持ち主の手に帰すためにカメラと三脚が必要なこと、現場は津波によるヘドロが乾燥した細かいチリが酷くカメラには最悪の環境であること、なので借りるというわけにはいかないこと、だからくれ！！という感じで。このツイートは東京に着くまでの２時間くらいの間にどんどん広まり、何人もの会ったことのない人たちからカメラや三脚の提供の申し出があった。友達も先生もみんな協力してくれた。多くの人が何か機会があれば手伝いたいと思っていた時期だった。カメラが１０台以上、三脚が７台ほど集まり体制は整ったものの、今度は別の問題も浮上してきた。いろんな人がくれたいろんなカメラは、もちろんメーカーも機種もバラバラだった。一眼レフを使ったことのない大学生ボランティア達にカメラの使い方を教えたり、マニュアルを作るためにはある程度の数の同じカメラが必要だった。

2011.5.5 Day 55 Afternoon

At the workshop, I asked the volunteers to show me their method of digitalization, after which we did several experiments with the equipment I had brought along. They went well, and so I taught the volunteers how to do photo duplications, telling them that they had to think of light as a material and consider where it came from and how it was reflected before reaching the lens. This knowledge was important to minimize the reflection on the surface of the photographs. However another problem soon arose: a shortage of equipment. We obviously didn't have enough equipment to duplicate all the photos in the gym - we needed more people, more cameras and more tripods. I began to seek out unused cameras from my friends and colleagues. I knew that photographers usually had cameras in addition to their main, work cameras, I just had to work out how to convince them to let me have them. On the Shinkansen back to Tokyo, I tweeted about the project and made a plan to personally contact each and every one of my possible helpers. I tweeted that I needed a considerable number of cameras and tripods in order to return photographic memories to their original owners in the affected areas. The working environment would be contaminated, with the air full of tiny dust particles from the dry sludge, and therefore would not be very good for cameras. This meant that I couldn't borrow the cameras, and so I had to plead them to give me the cameras... for free! The tweet went somewhat viral over the course of the two-hour train ride, with many people, some of whom I'd never even met, offering me their cameras. My friends and former teachers contributed as well, and it was a time when everyone wanted to help out as best they could. We got more than ten cameras and seven tripods, and whilst we seemed well prepared, another problem came up: having come from different people, the cameras were, of course, different brands and models. In order to teach the volunteers how to use the camera and to create a manual for future volunteers, we needed a quantity of the same camera.

2011.5.17　67日目

ぼくは２００２年に写真新世紀というキヤノンが主催している新人賞でデビューし、その後コンパクトカメラのホームページに登場したこともあって、キヤノンには何人かの知り合いがいた。きっとキヤノンの社員ならみんなカメラをいっぱい持ってるんじゃないだろうか、という安直な思いつきで電話をかけて事情を説明し、社内でカメラをくれる人を個人的に募ってみてもらえないだろうかとお願いしてみた。久しぶりに連絡してカメラくれじゃあ嫌われるかもしれないな、とも思ったけれど、可能性があるならば何でもやらないといけない、とい

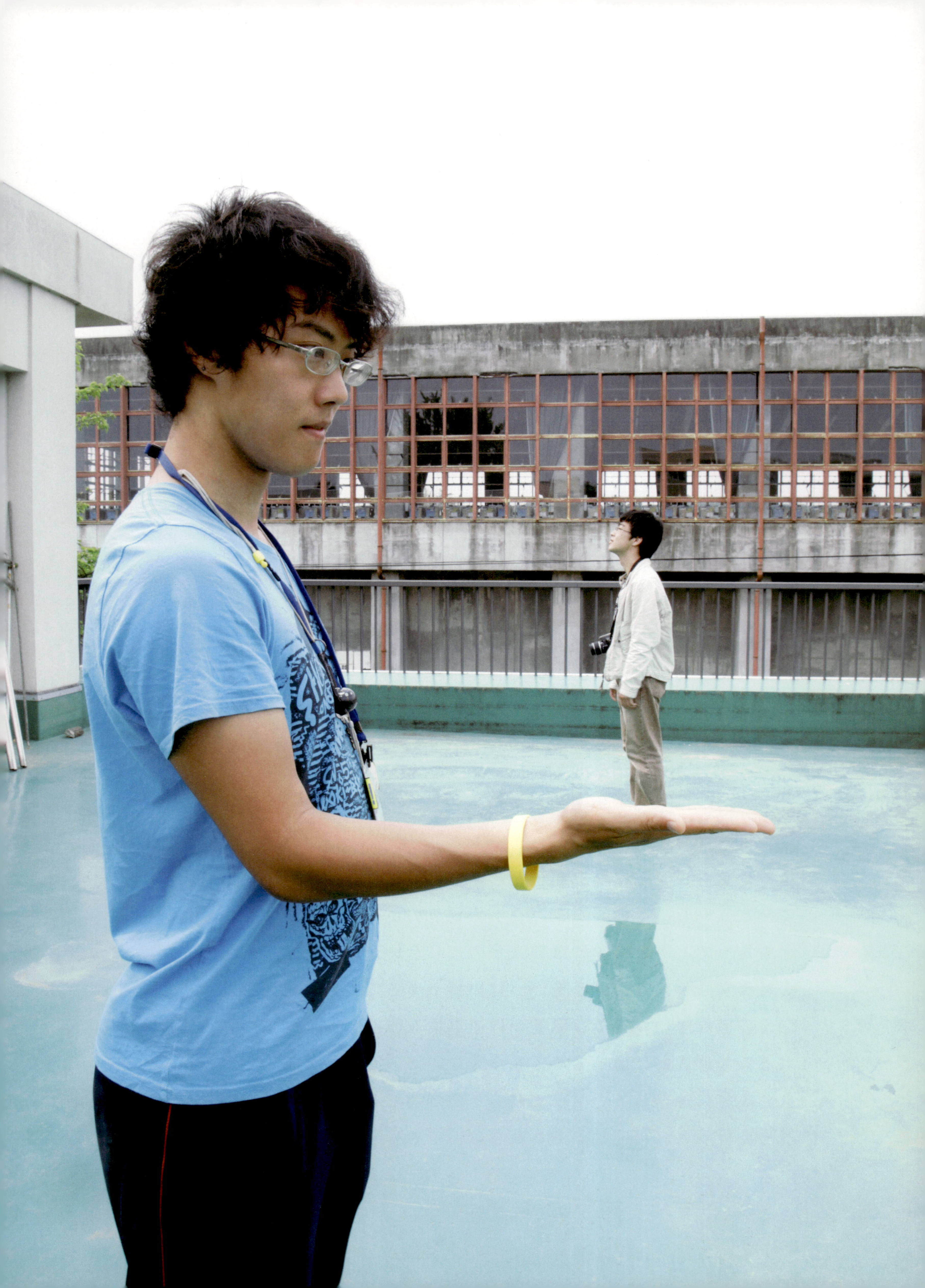

う気持ちだった。普段とてもよくしてくれる人たちだから、きっと協力してくれるだろうという期待もあった。結果的にはこれがマーケティング部の部長さんの耳に届き、EOS Kissを5台提供してもらうことができた。これでマニュアルを作ることもできたし、このカメラ達は2年が経った今も山元町で活躍している。

2011.5.17 Day 67

I began my career as a photographer after winning the New Cosmos of Photography, an annual award organized by Canon, and had also appeared in an advertisement for their compact camera which meant that I knew a few people at the company. I thought that the people there should have at least a few Canon cameras each… and so I called them to explain the situation and ask if they could collect their colleague's extra cameras. It had been a while since I had talked to them, and so was a bit anxious that they would hate me for asking after all those years of silence, but I was desperate for any tiny possibility. At the same time I was optimistic, as they had been always good to me. As a result, the word reached the manager of company's marketing department, and they generously offered us five EOS Kiss (EOS Digital Rebel) cameras. This meant that we could complete the manual successfully, and those cameras are still working after two years in Yamamoto-cho.

写真部

マニュアル作成と同時に写真部も作った。定期的に山元町にボランティアに来ていた大学生達にカメラの使い方を覚えてもらうべく、朝1時間早く起きて絞りとシャッタースピードとISOの関係や、順光、逆光、サイド光の違いなどを教えていった。合言葉は、「いい写真が撮れるとモテる！」少ない時間でみんなどんどん腕を上げ、そして写真を撮ることを好きになってくれた。

Photo Club

As we worked on creating the manual, we formed a Photo Club with the regular volunteers in Yamamoto-cho. Our slogan was, "Being a good photographer makes you popular!" and we woke up an hour early every morning to learn the basics of photography: aperture, shutter speed, ISO, direct lighting, back lighting, side lighting, and so on. Our time was limited, but everyone's skills improved dramatically, and they all fell in love with photography.

2011.5.21 71日目

こうやって準備を進めると同時にボランティアを募り、毎週末２０〜８０人が山元町に集まるようになった。ぼくと同じように、何かできることがあれば手伝いたいと思っている人は多く、たくさんの応募が寄せられた。半数は写真の洗浄、半数は複写に分かれ、作業は少しずつ確実に進んでいった。ある程度人数が増えると、旅日記という旅行会社に協力してもらいバスツアーを組んだり、山元町の近くの白石にある温泉旅館に格安で泊めてもらったりした。学生、写真関係者、町の写真屋さん、手を貸したいというボランティアさんなど、本当に多くの人が力を合わせて作業を進めていった。この頃になると、写真を持ち主に返そうという考えに共感する人のあまりの多さに、ハッキリとではないけれど写真の意味を感じるようになっていた。

2011. 5. 21 Day 71

We recruited volunteers as we continued the project and soon, 20 to 80 volunteers began coming to Yamamoto-cho every weekend. There were a lot of people like myself who were willing to help if there was something they could do, and we had tremendous numbers of applications. The volunteers were divided into two: a photo cleaning team and a duplication team. Slowly and surely, the project started to move. As the number of volunteers increased, we asked a travel agency named TABI-NIKKI to organize a bus tour, and we made a deal with an onsen ryokan near Yamamoto-cho so that people could stay for a reduced rate. The project moved forward with the support of so many students, local photographers, people working in the photographic industry, and volunteers. As people who saw our project commented on its worth, I began to realize the potential of photography, although in a very vague sense.

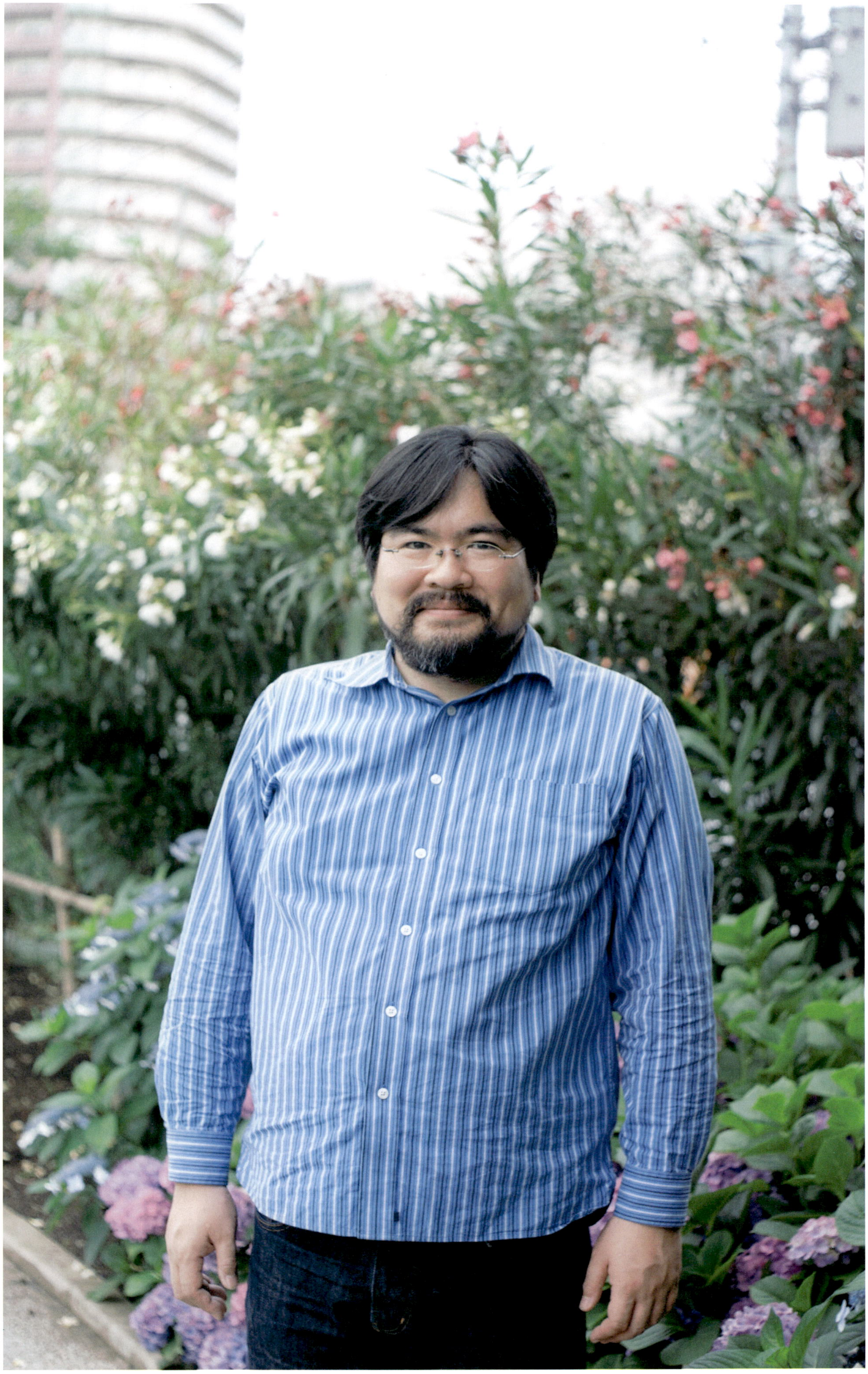

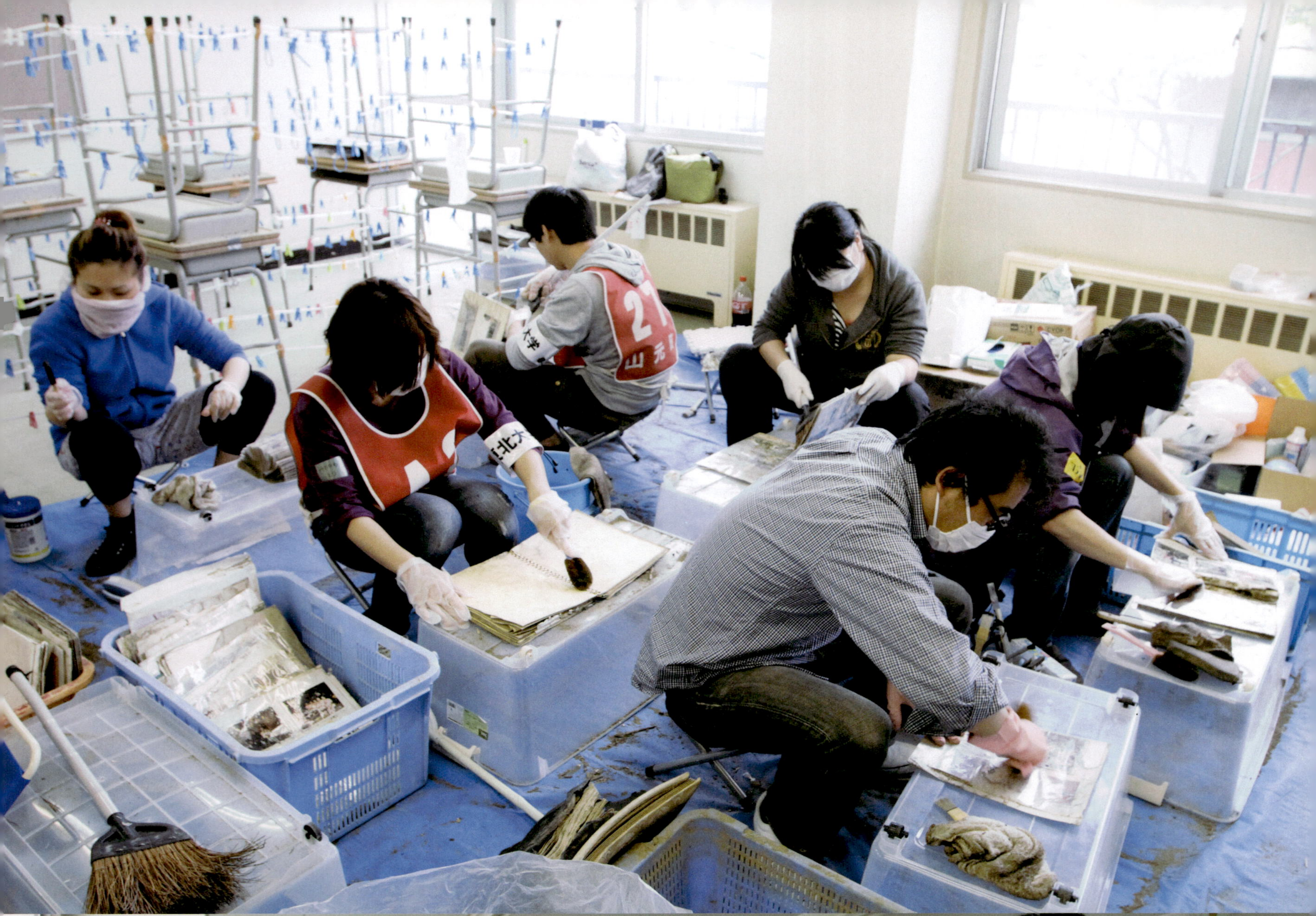

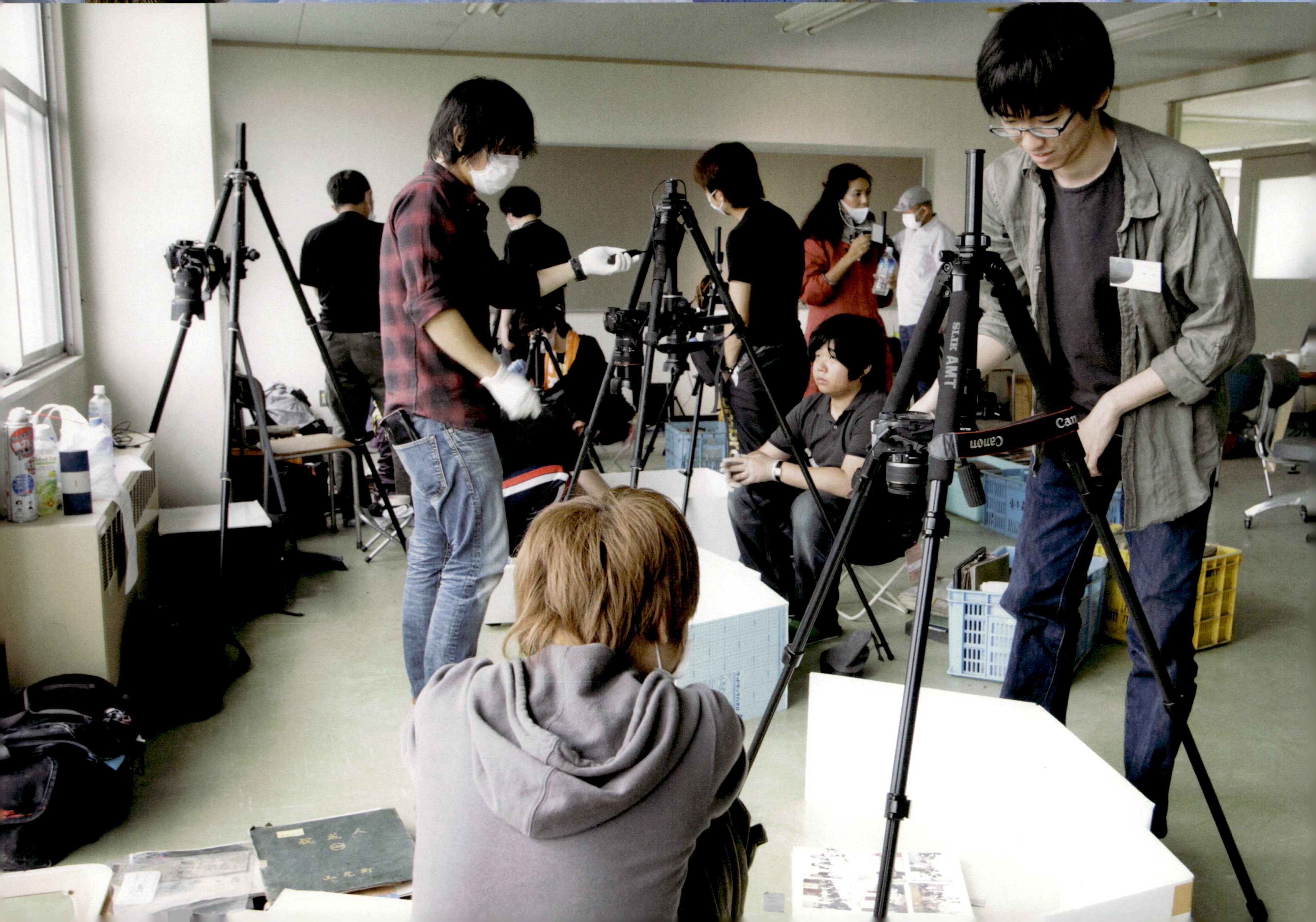
SLIK AMT
Canon

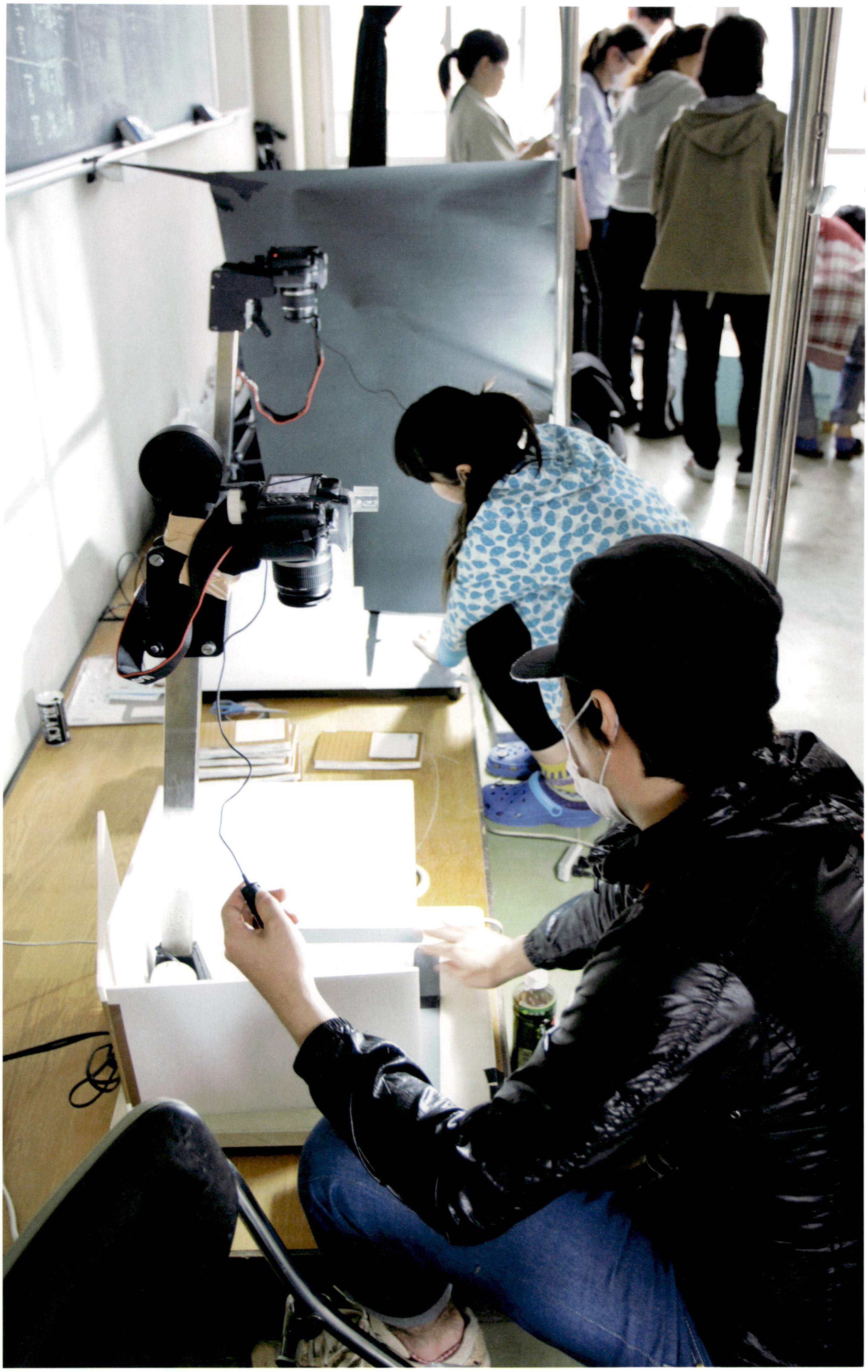

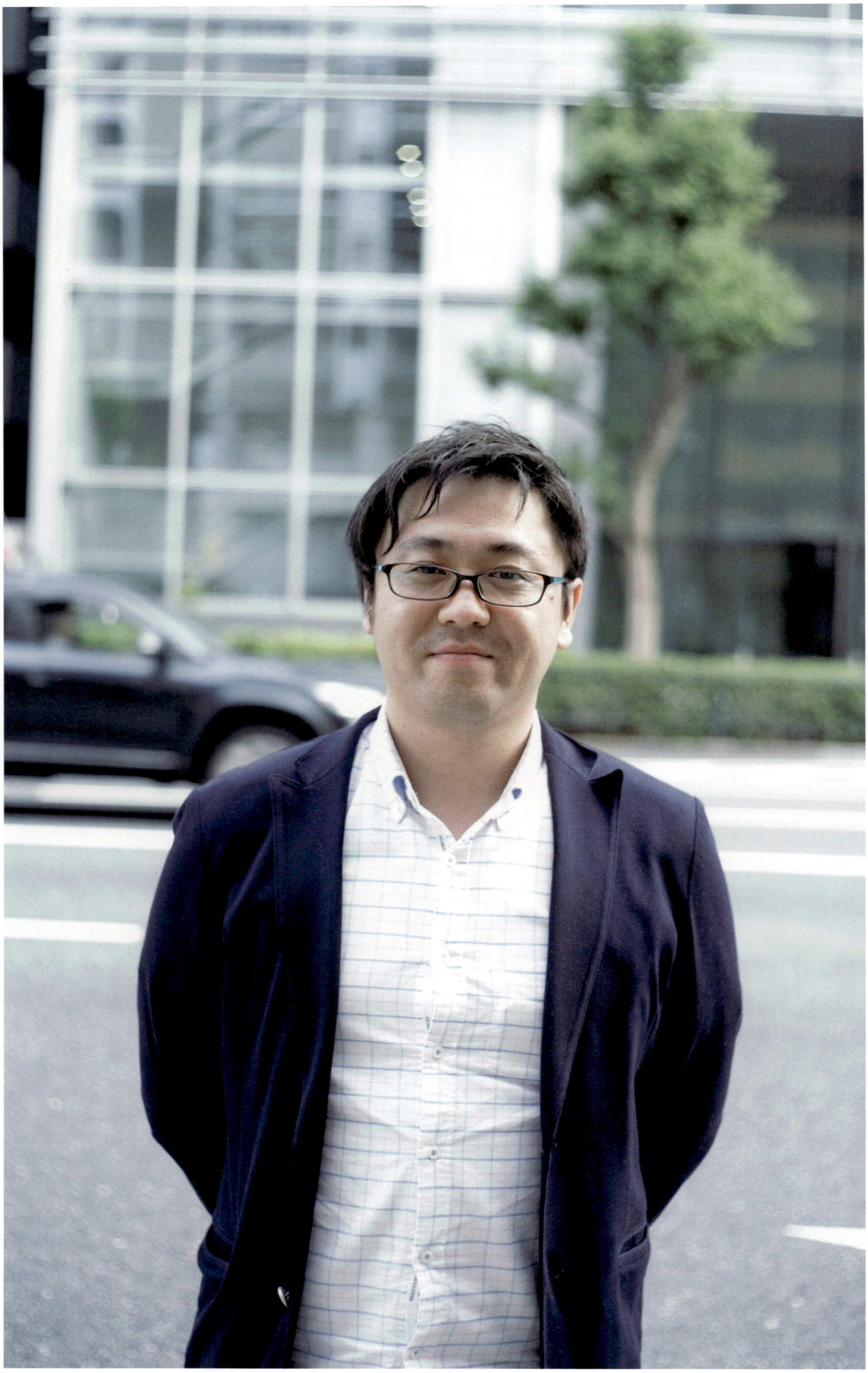

新藤さん

ボランティア募集を始める少し前、どのようにプロジェクトを進めるかという話し合いが行われたとき、やたら体が大きく髭面で声が高いマイケル・ムーアに似た人がいた。もずやというweb制作の会社をやっている新藤さんは、具体的に人が参加しやすい募集のノウハウをもっていた。Webは大きな入り口になりうるが、それは出口も大きいということであり、シンプルに意味が伝わらないと人はすぐに出て行ってしまう。プロジェクトのキーパーソンは何人もいたけれど、参加の入り口を整備する新藤さんがいなければプロジェクトはこんなにうまくいかなかっただろうと思う。

Shindo-san

Before we put out ads for volunteers, we had a discussion on how to effectively gather them. At the meeting, there was a man who resembled Michael Moore: he was huge, bearded, and had high-tone voice. The man, Shindo-san, was the owner of a web design & development company called Mozuya and knew about effective web recruitment. The internet allowed us to instantly get in contact with so many people, but at the same time if people weren't able to quickly find out what we were doing, they could easily lose interest and simply disappear. We had several key people on the project, but without Shindo-san who helped with improving and maintaining the "entrance" for the prospective volunteers, we couldn't have continued to operate so successfully.

星さん

ある日、作業をしているとつなぎの作業服を着た人がいちごを差し入れに来てくれた。山元町はいちごの有名な産地とのことだった。ぼくはしばらくいちごを持ってきてくれた星さんのことを農家の人だと思っていたのだけど、本当は山元町に住んでいる旅行業の人で思い出サルベージを立ち上げたひとりだと知った。それから、ぼくらは仲良く

なりいろんなことを話し合った。やがて一緒にLOST & FOUND PROJECTを立ち上げ、写真と一緒にいくつかの場所を旅することになった。ぼくらはすぐにボランティアと被災者という関係ではなく、友達になった。

Hoshi-san

One day while we were working, a man wearing overalls called Hoshi-san came to the workshop and gave us strawberries. He told me that Yamamoto-cho was well-known for its strawberries. I thought he was a farmer at first, but in fact he was a local travel agent and one of the founders of "Memory Salvage". We quickly became close and shared many ideas and thoughts. Later, we launched the "Lost & Found Project" and traveled together to numerous places to exhibit the photographs. Our relationship was not that of volunteer and earthquake victim, we were friends.

2011.5.22　72日目

作業が順調に進むなかで、ダメージが酷く誰の写真か判別がつかないだろうと思われる写真が出てきた。それは少しずつ、しかし着実に増えていった。これらの写真をどうすべきかという話し合いが何度もあった。このままでは処分されてしまう運命にあるのではないかとみんな心配していたのだ。どうすればいいかはわからないけれど、処分されてしまうのは悲しいというのが話し合ったみんなの気持ちだった。ぼくはそのときとくに考えがあったわけじゃなかったけれど、「なんとかするからとりあえず捨てずにおこう」と言って、その写真を入れるための箱を作った。その箱には「もうダメBOX」と名付けた。そして判断基準は現場で手を動かしている人が決めればいいんじゃないか、ということになった。これは暫定的な対応で、その時点で処分される可能性を保留しただけだった。やがてそれらの写真がLOST & FOUND PROJECTを生み、いろんな場所を旅していくことになる。

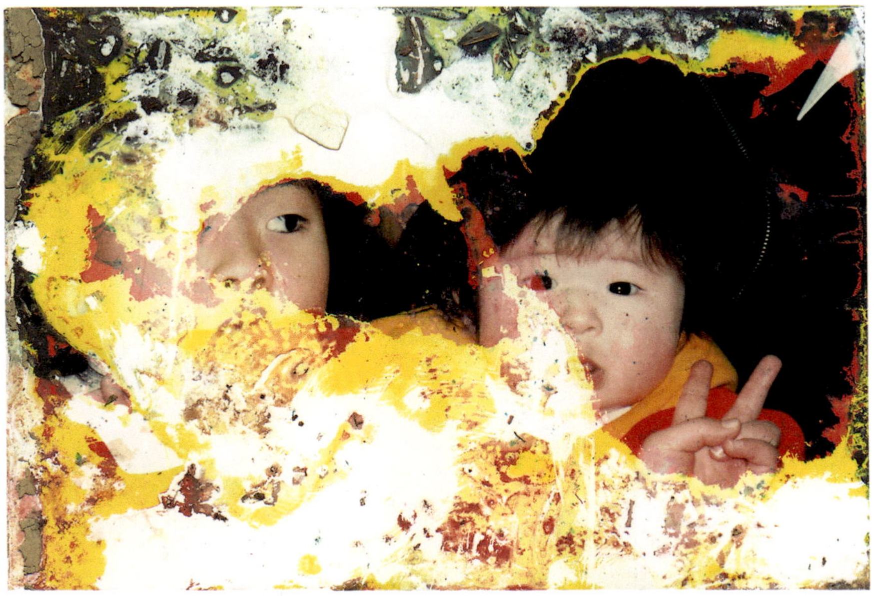

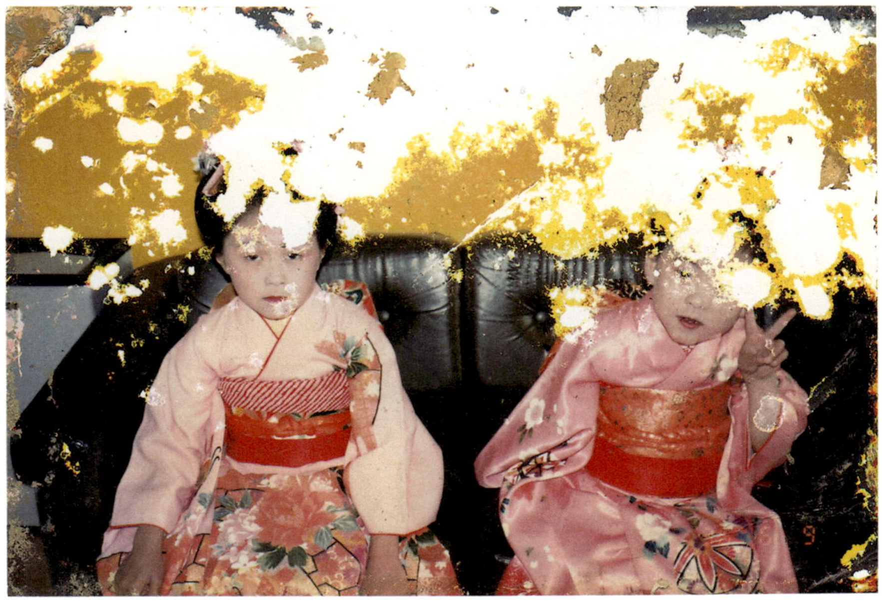

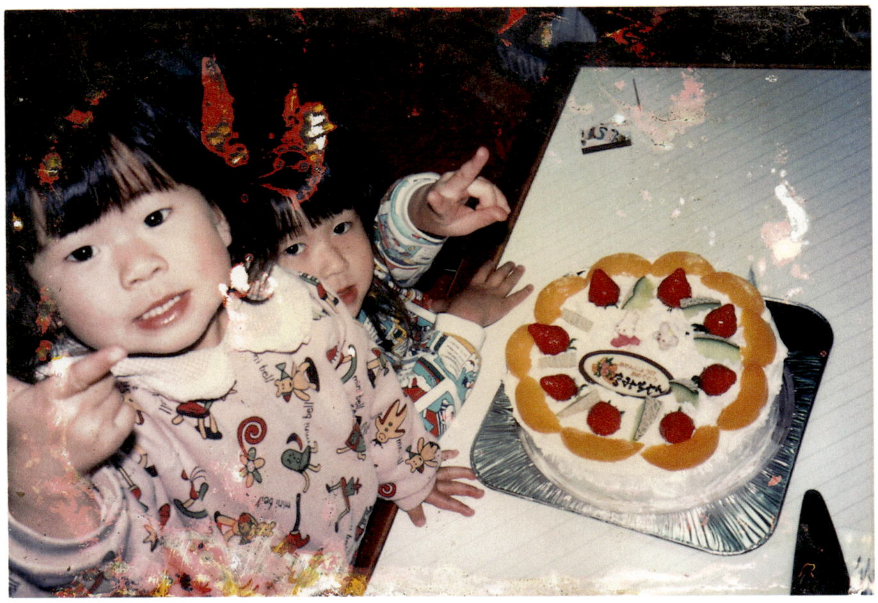

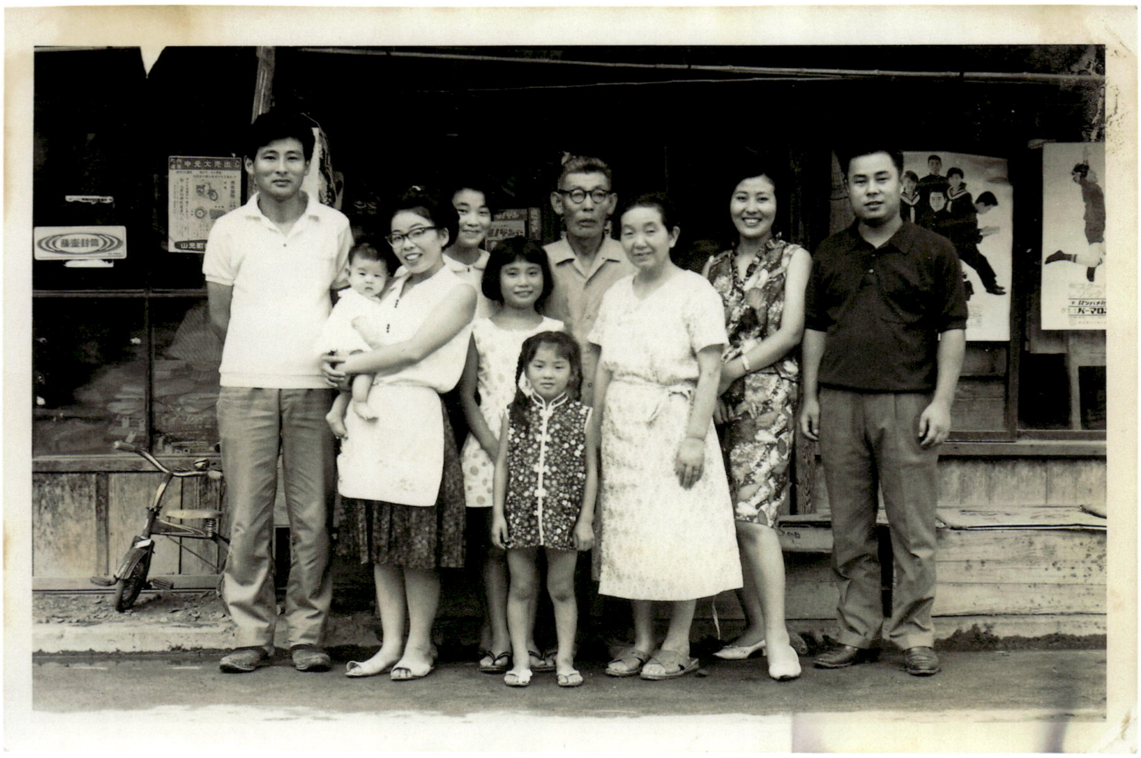

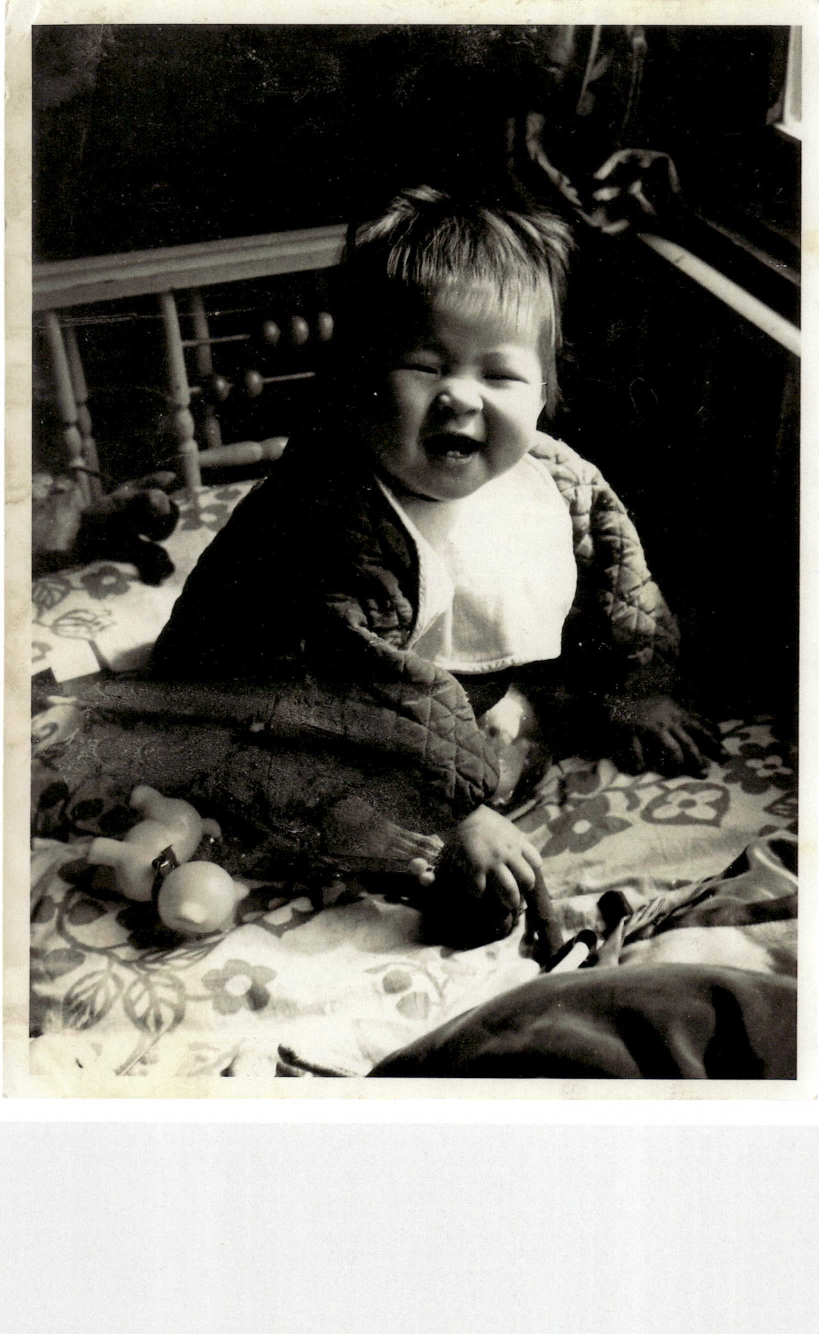

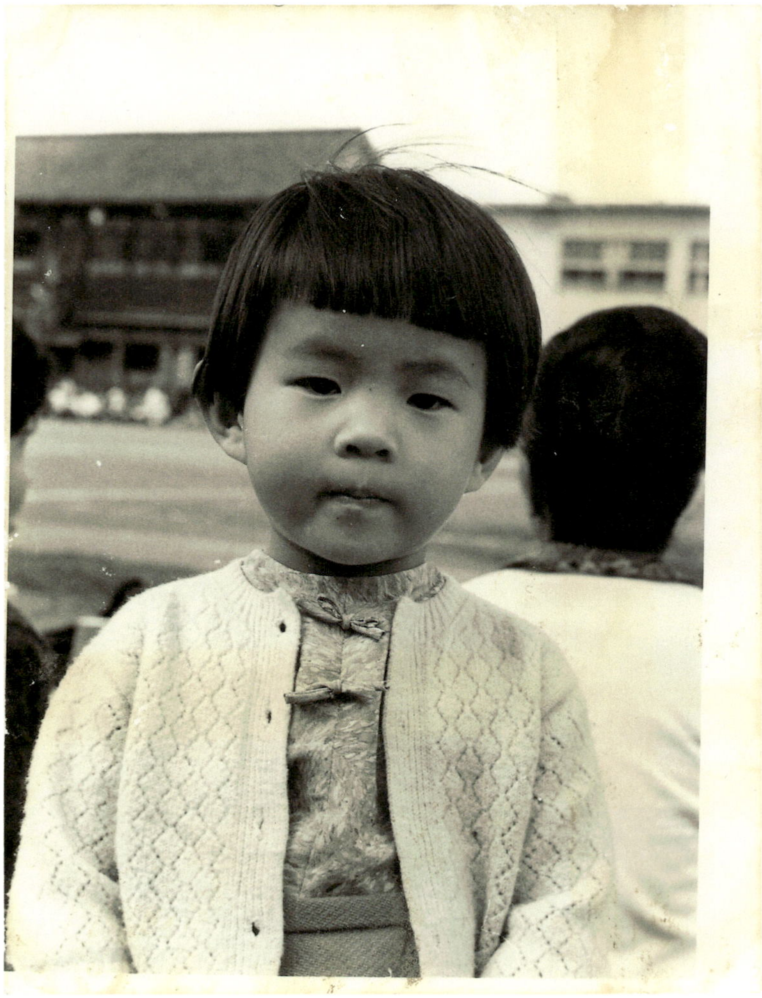

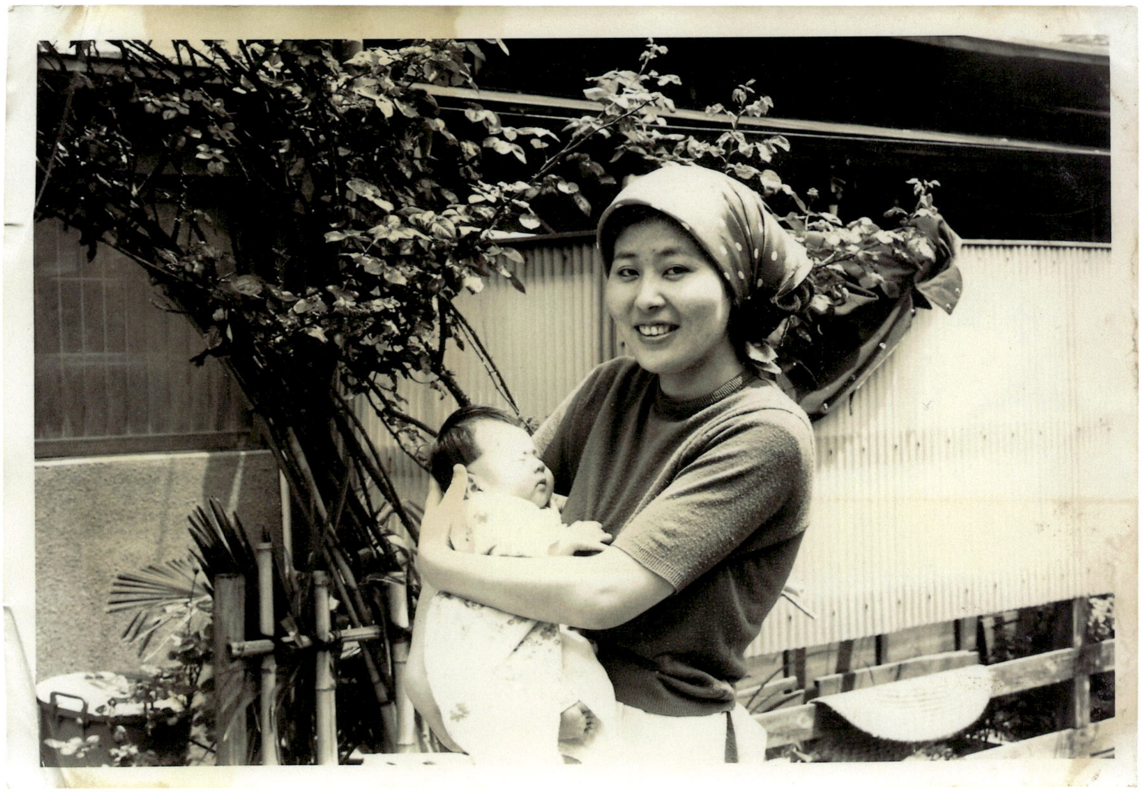

島田さんの話　2013.7.27

ここで、島田さゆりさんに話を聞きにいった時のことを書いておきたいと思う。彼女は山元町で商店を営んでいた写真が趣味の人で、震災後自分で探したり思い出サルベージの活動場所に探しにきたりして、２０００枚以上の写真が手元に戻った人でもある。この本を書く上で、写真が返ってきた人の言葉はとても重要だと思っていたので、会いに行っていくつか質問をさせてもらった。

――あなたがこの震災で失ったものはなんですか？
家や車や家財道具など全部です。全部津波が流していきました。

――多くのものを一度に失ってしまった時の気持ちというのは、いっ

たいどういうものだったんですか？
これは現実ではないんじゃないかという思いがあって、何度も家のあった場所を見に行きました。なんとか家族を支えないといけないと気を張っていたので、現実を噛み砕いて受け入れる余裕はありませんでした。その後、家族はここから車で一時間ほどの仙台にある親戚の家に避難させました。私は自分にできることをやろうと思い、山元町の避難所で炊き出しを作っていました。

——その後、現実をどのように受け入れていったのですか？
一週間ほどすると、避難所にもある程度支援が届くようになり、これで私の役目も一段落だなと思いました。そして、仙台の親戚の家にいる家族に会いに行って顔を見た時、自分が帰る場所である家は、山元町ではなくここなの？という思いが湧いてきて、それが現実を受け入れざるをえない瞬間でした。

——写真が初めて戻った時のことを教えてください。
とにかく嬉しいの一言です。久しぶりに心から笑った瞬間でした。それまでも笑うことはあったのですが、様々な人にお世話になっていたこともあり、自分の心を抑えていたんだと思います。あの頃は毎日が大変で７キロほどやせました。今はそこから５キロ戻りましたが（笑）

——写真というものへの考え方は変わりましたか？
根本は変わらないけれど、写真が好きな気持ちが強くなりました。震災の後のゴールデンウィークに、東京に住む娘が津波に流され泥だらけになったアルバムを洗うのを手伝いにきてくれました。一枚一枚写真を洗いながら思い出にふれることで、写真を撮って思い出を残しておくことの大事さを再確認しました。今はそれまでの写真に加えて新たに思い出を撮り始め、新しいアルバムを作っています。そして、写

真の残し方についても考えるようになりました。手元に置いておきたいと思うようになったんです。プリントだと膨大な量になるので、SDカードに入れて持っておきたいと思っています。

——写真を保存するならクラウドなどインターネット上でもいいんじゃないですか？
それはそうなんですが、手元にあると安心するんです。頭ではクラウドが安全だというのは理解できるんですが、気持ちの問題なんです。

——そうなんですね、ありがとうございました。

島田さんはもともと写真を撮るのが大好きで、家族の思い出を残すのが趣味だった。震災前、４８枚入りのアルバムが２５０冊以上あったんだそうだ。ぼくは島田さんと話をさせてもらうまで、写真を残したいのならクラウド３ヶ所くらいに置いておけば確実だし、それが一番いいんじゃないかと考えていたのだけど、SDカードを手元に置いておきたいという気持ちを聞いて、改めて写真というのはただの物とは違うんだなということを知った。撮る人、そして撮られる人の思いを注入されて、物から一歩人間に近い存在になるんじゃないだろうか。

The Story of Shimada-san　2013.7.27

I would like to write about a conversation I had with Sayuri Shimada, a hobby photographer and manager of a general store in Yamamoto-cho. After the earthquake and tsunami, she started to look for her lost photographs. Sometimes she visited the Memory Salvage workshop to see if we had any of her photographs. In the end, she managed to retrieve more than 2000 photographs. To properly document our project, I thought it was really important to publish the voice of someone who had actually had their photographs returned to them, and so I went to ask her some questions.

——What did you lose in the earthquake?

I lost everything - my car, house and all the furniture. Everything was swept away by the tsunami.

——What feeling did you have when you realized that you had lost everything at once?
At first, it felt like it wasn't really happening; I visited the vacant space where my house once stood over and over again. I didn't have time to accept all the facts, and I had family to take care of. I was desperate. I later sent my family to a friend's place in Sendai, about an hour away by car. I stayed in Yamamoto-cho to help organise soup kitchens at a temporary shelter. I wanted to do anything I could.

——How did you come to accept reality?
After a week, our shelter began to receive support from outside. At that time I felt that I had done my share of the work. I went to Sendai to see my family and I couldn't help but feel, "Is where I will return to from now on, not Yamamoto-cho?" From then on I began to accept reality. I had to.

——Can you tell me about the first time your photographs were returned to you?
I was overwhelmed with joy, and smiled from the bottom of my heart for the first time in so long. Of course there had been moments when I laughed, but that had been when I realized that I had been suppressing my feelings whilst being supported by so many people. Back then, life was tough. I lost 7kg, but have since gained back 5kg (Laughs).

——Did your attitude towards photography change?
The passion I had for photography hasn't changed, but I love photography now more than ever. During the first Golden Week holiday after the earthquake, my daughter, who was living in Tokyo, came back to help me clean the albums that had been swept away by the tsunami and were still covered in dirt. As we cleaned the photographs one by one, we shared the memories they presented. That was when I realized the importance of photography; it could keep our memories together. In addition to the photographs that were retrieved, I've now started to take more pictures and create new albums. I also have started to consider new ways of storing the images. I really want to keep them by my side all the time, but because that's physically impossible with prints, I am thinking of storing the data on SD cards.

——Wouldn't it better to save the images using cloud storage online?
That's true, but I feel more secure having them with me. Logically, I understand that cloud storage is safer, but I guess it's more about how I feel.

——Thank you very much for your time.

Before the earthquake, she owned more than 250 albums, each containing 48 photographs. Before speaking with Shimada-san I thought that the best and safest way to store the images would be on multiple cloud accounts. After hearing that she wanted to store the images on SD cards and keep them with her, I realized that photography transcends its physical existence and by revealing the feeling of both the photographer and the subject it becomes more human - not just a printed image.

2011.5.22 Day 72

As the cleaning went on, there were considerable numbers of photographs that were badly damaged and it was impossible to recover their original images. We had a lot of discussions about what to do with them, knowing that if we didn't find a solution then they may have to be discarded, which would have been a great pity. While I didn't have any ideas at the time, I said that I would work something out and that we had to keep them. For the time being, I made a box for the photos and named it the "Hopeless Box", with the volunteers determining which photos would be put into the box. It was only a temporary solution to keep them intact, and eventually, the photographs were presented in the "Lost & Found Project" exhibition, and traveled to places all over the world.

2011.6.22 103日目

写真の洗浄とデータ化がある程度進んだところで、写真を返すための場所が作られた。アルバムは全てナンバリングされ、箱に入れられてずらりと並んでいた。バラバラで見つかった写真は、一枚ずつナンバリングされてファイルに入れた。全ては町の中で見つかった場所ごとにエリア分けされて並んでいた。ほとんどのアルバムは台紙がしっかりしていて元々それなりの重さがある、そのうえそれらは津波の水を吸ってさらに重くなっていた。部屋中に並べられた箱の中から一冊ずつアルバムを取り出し確認して、自分のものではなかったら元に戻す、という作業を延々と続けるのはお年寄りにはかなりしんどいようだった。すぐに見つかればいいけれど、なかなか見つからないと心が折れる。そこでまずはアルバムのデータからインデックスを作ることになった。アルバムの表紙の写真と、アルバムの中の写真から本人が自分のものだとわかりやすそうな写真を3枚ピックアップして一枚の紙にプリントした。これをファイリングすることで、ページをめくるだけで一冊ずつアルバムを確認することができるようになった。

2011.6.22 Day 103

As the process of cleaning and digitalizing the photos began to go smoothly and the reproduced photographs started to accumulate, we created a space for returning them to the owners. All the clean photographs were put back into the original albums, and the space filled quickly with rows of boxes containing the albums. The photographs that we found individually were numbered and filed together, and were sorted based on the areas where they had been found. Most of the albums had hard covers and were quite heavy, and had become bulkier after absorbing water during the tsunami. People had to go through the heavy albums, and to repeat taking each one out and then putting it back until they found their own. The task was exhausting especially for the elderly. It was no problem if they found their album right away, but if they couldn't, it became endless and burdening. To solve this problem, we created an index from our database - we printed a cover sheet using three images that people would recognize, and then put the sheets into index files.

2011.6.26 117日目

ぼくはデータ化部隊をまとめる立場にあったので、あまり返却作業は手伝えなかったけれど、返却に立ち会ったときいまでも強くおぼえているできごとがあった。インデックスのファイルが並ぶ部屋に、ひとりのおじいさんがいた。一緒にファイルを見ていると、そのおじいさんの若い頃の写真が見つかった。「おー、これおれだ」「本当ですか、よかったですねえ。ずいぶん男前じゃないですか〜」なんてことを話しながらファイルをめくっていると、若い親子の写真が出てきた。子供は5才くらいだった。「ああ、これ孫の友達だ」「おお！見つかりましたか、よかったですね」「でも、一家みんな流されて死んじゃったんだよ」ぼくは「そうなんですか」としか言えなかった。いまでも何と言えばよかったのかわからない。写真を見つけるということは生きた過去を取り戻すことでもあるけれど、死んでしまって戻らない人がいるということを突きつけてしまうことでもあった。

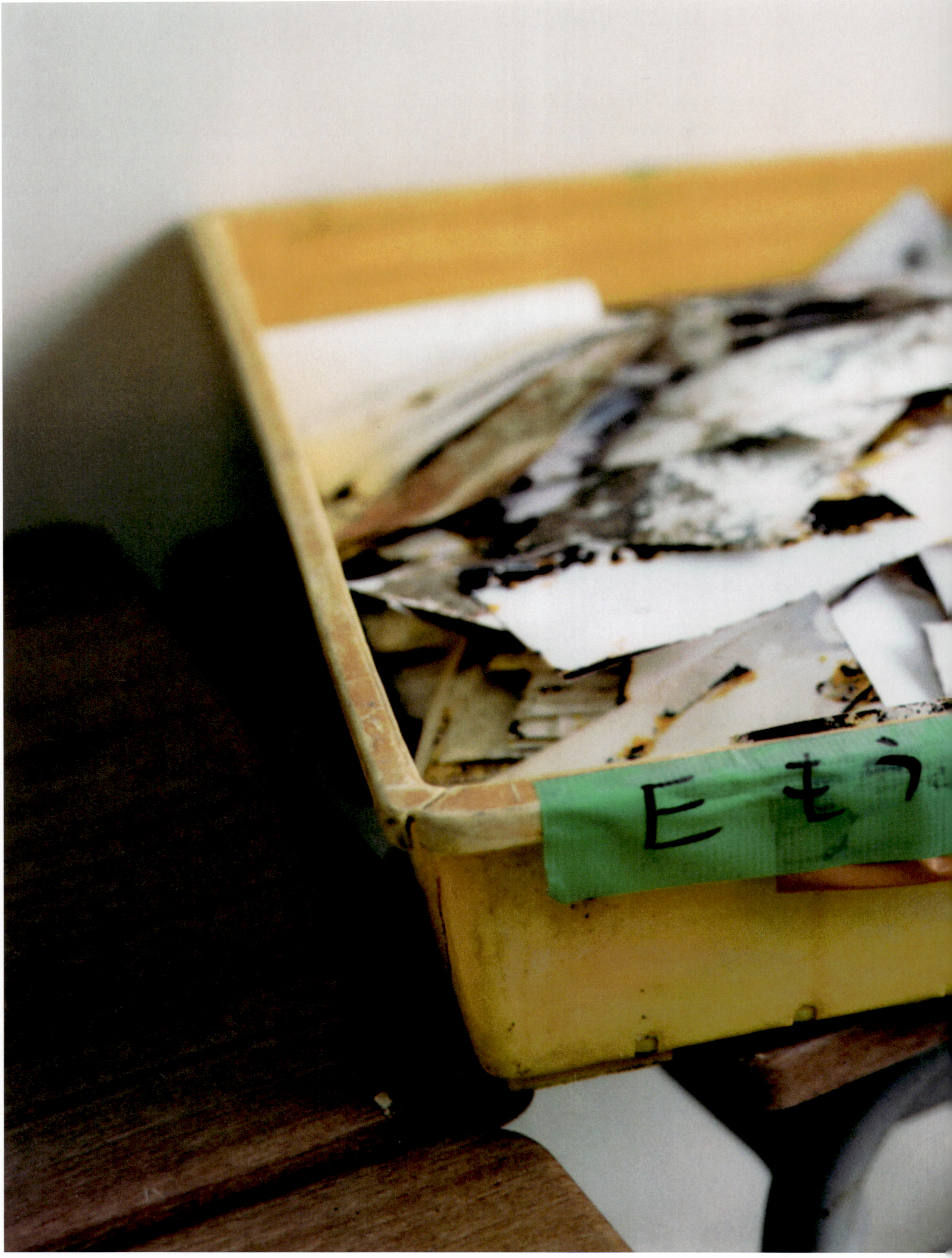
E もう

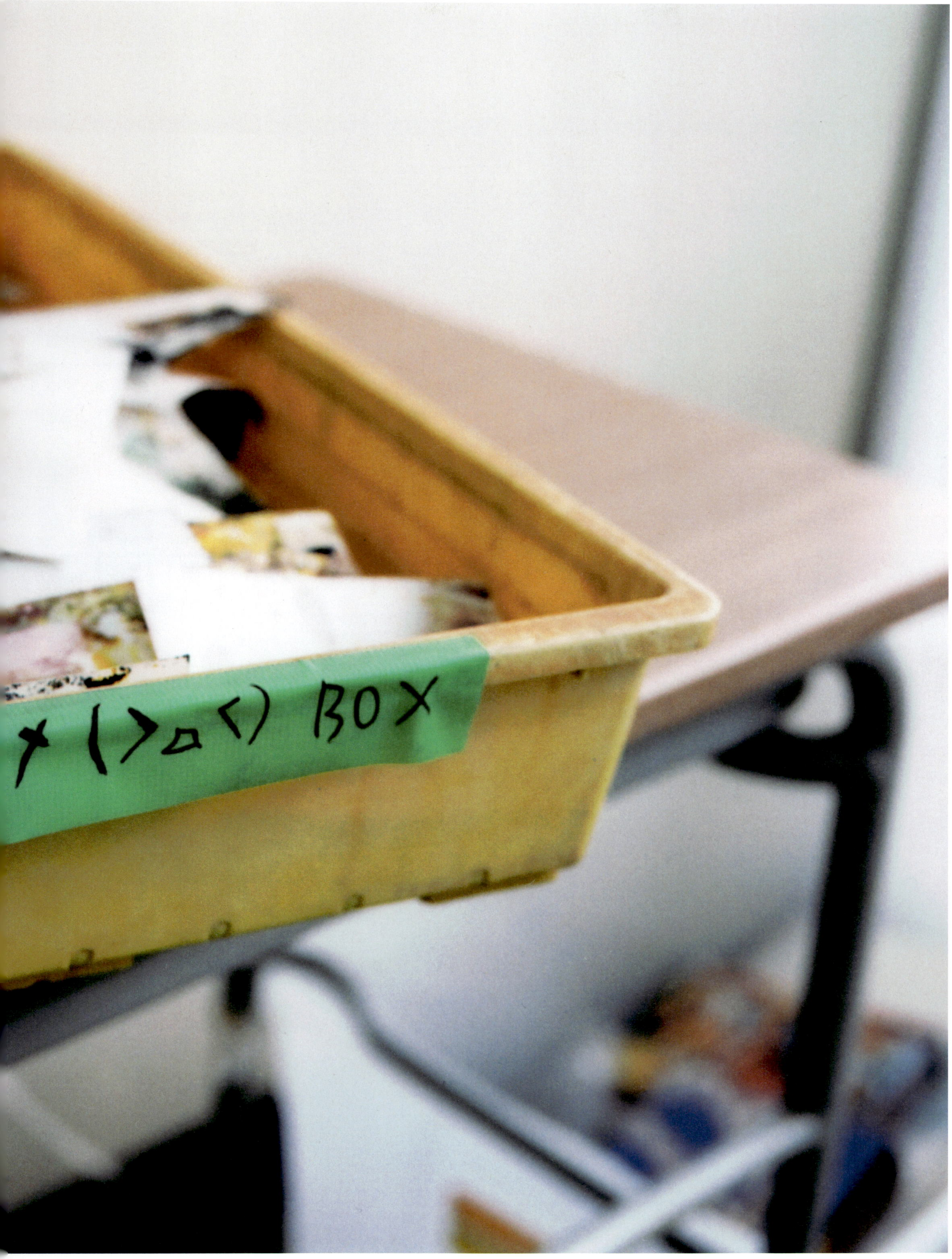
BOX

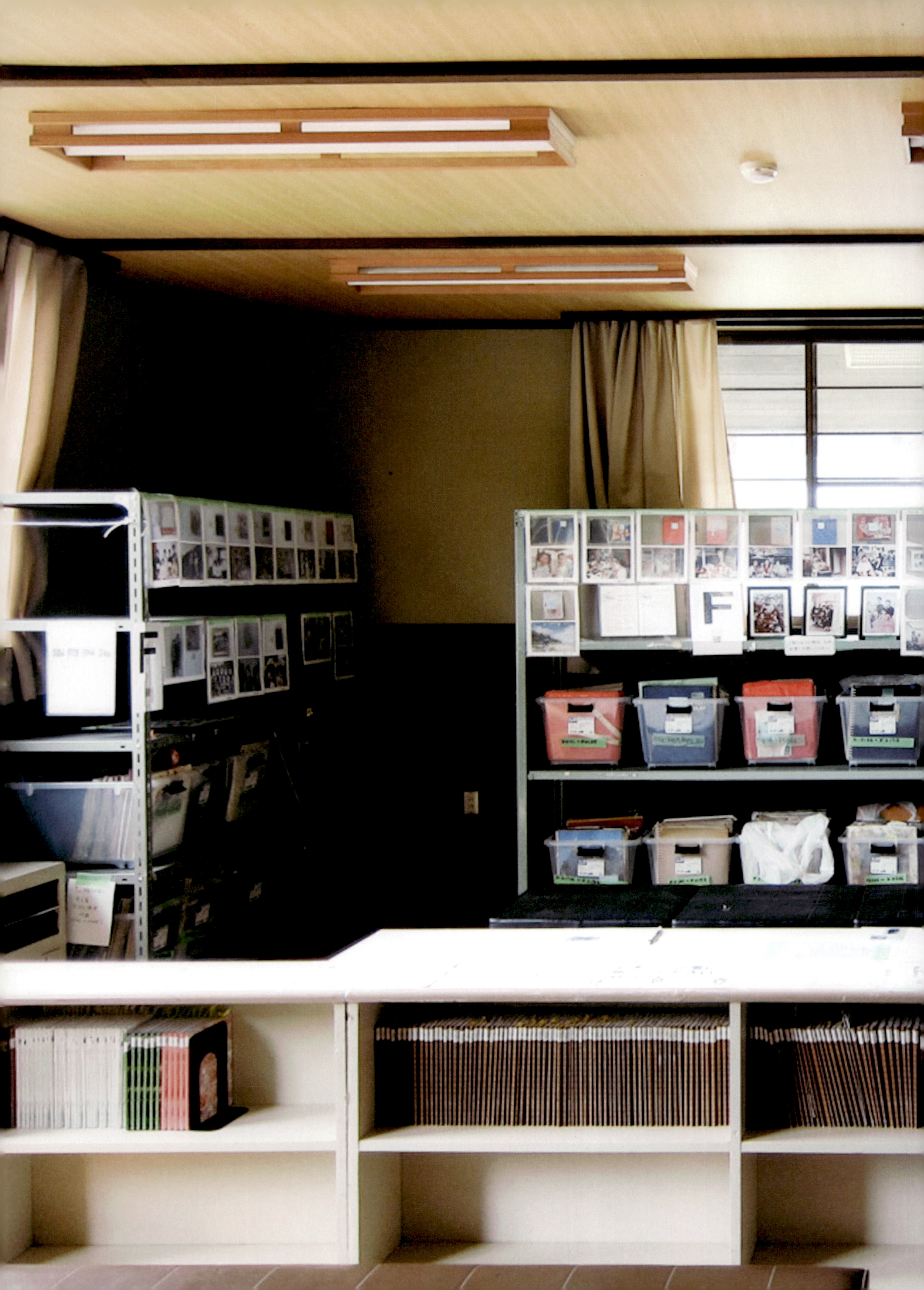
F

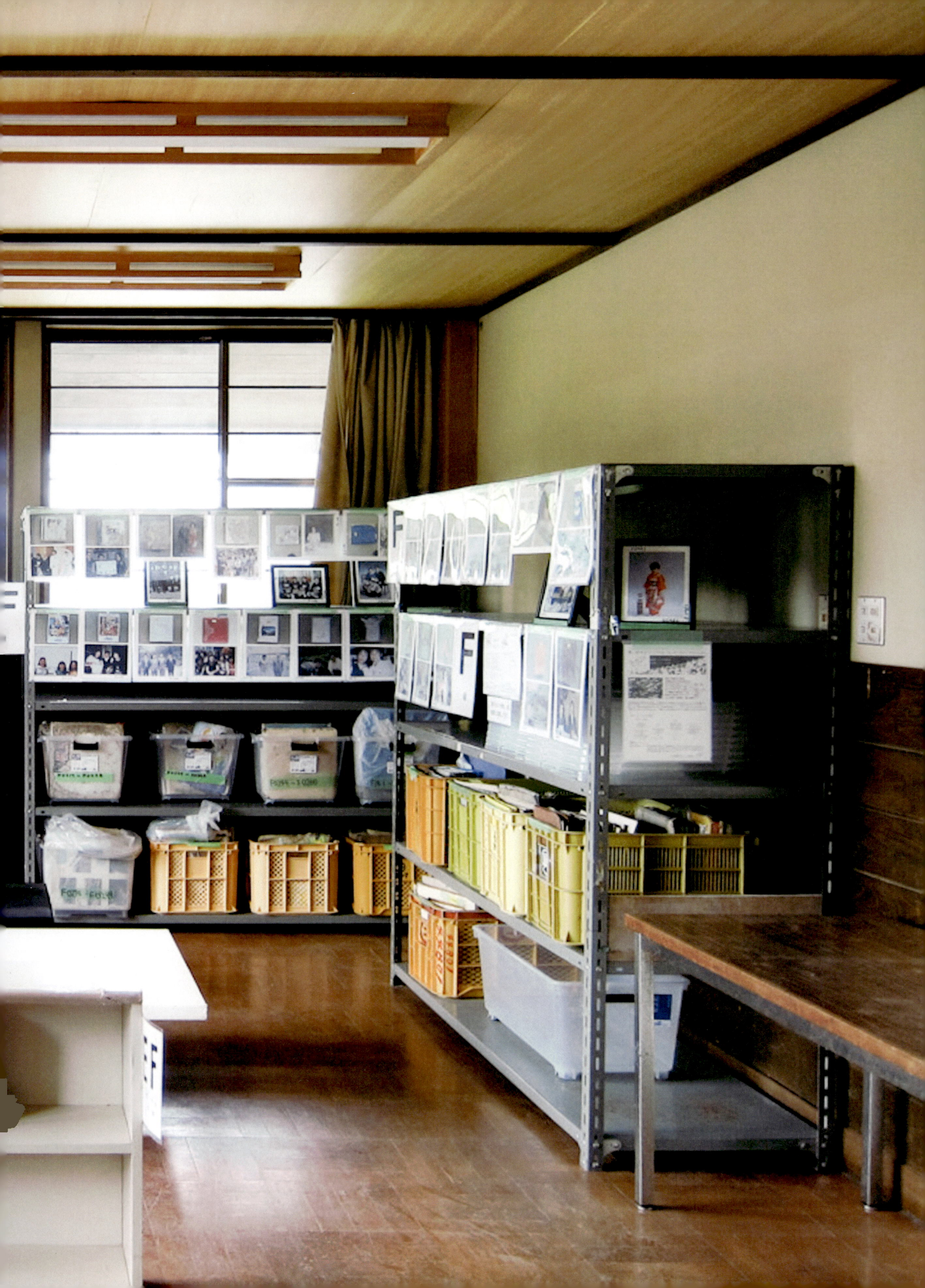
F
F

2011. 6. 26 Day 117

As I was in charge of the digitalizing team, I wasn't able to help with returning the photographs, but I still remember vividly what I once experienced at the returning place. In the room where the index files were placed, an elderly man was going through the photographs. I took a look at them with him for a while and he happened to find a photograph of his, when he was younger. "Wow, this is me." "Really? That's amazing - you look very handsome." We chatted as he continued flipping through the file and found a photograph of a young couple and their child, a boy who looked around five years old. "That boy is my grandson's friend." "Great! You found another one you know, that is great." "They died when they were taken by the tsunami." I could only say "Right" to that, and I still don't know how to respond. I had believed that for these people, photographs offered proof of their past lives, but there was more to it, as they were at times confronted by the fact that what was lost is really gone.

2011.7.17 128日目

プロジェクトのスタートから３ヶ月ほど毎週末みんなで代わる代わる作業して、ほとんどの写真の洗浄とデータ化は完了した。概算で、写真は７５万枚あった。初めて目にしたとき、絶対に無理だろうと思っていたこともみんなで力を合わせることで達成してしまった。人間やればできる。

2011. 7. 17 Day 128

Three months have passed since the start of the project. We worked in shifts every weekend to continue the process and have completed almost all the cleaning and digitalizing – a total of approximately 750,000 photographs. We thought it would be absolutely impossible to finish, but together we achieved it – we really can do anything.

2011.7.24 135日目

複写された膨大なデータは、ニフティの協力によりデータベース化され、地域ごとに分けられパソコンで閲覧できるようになった。また、

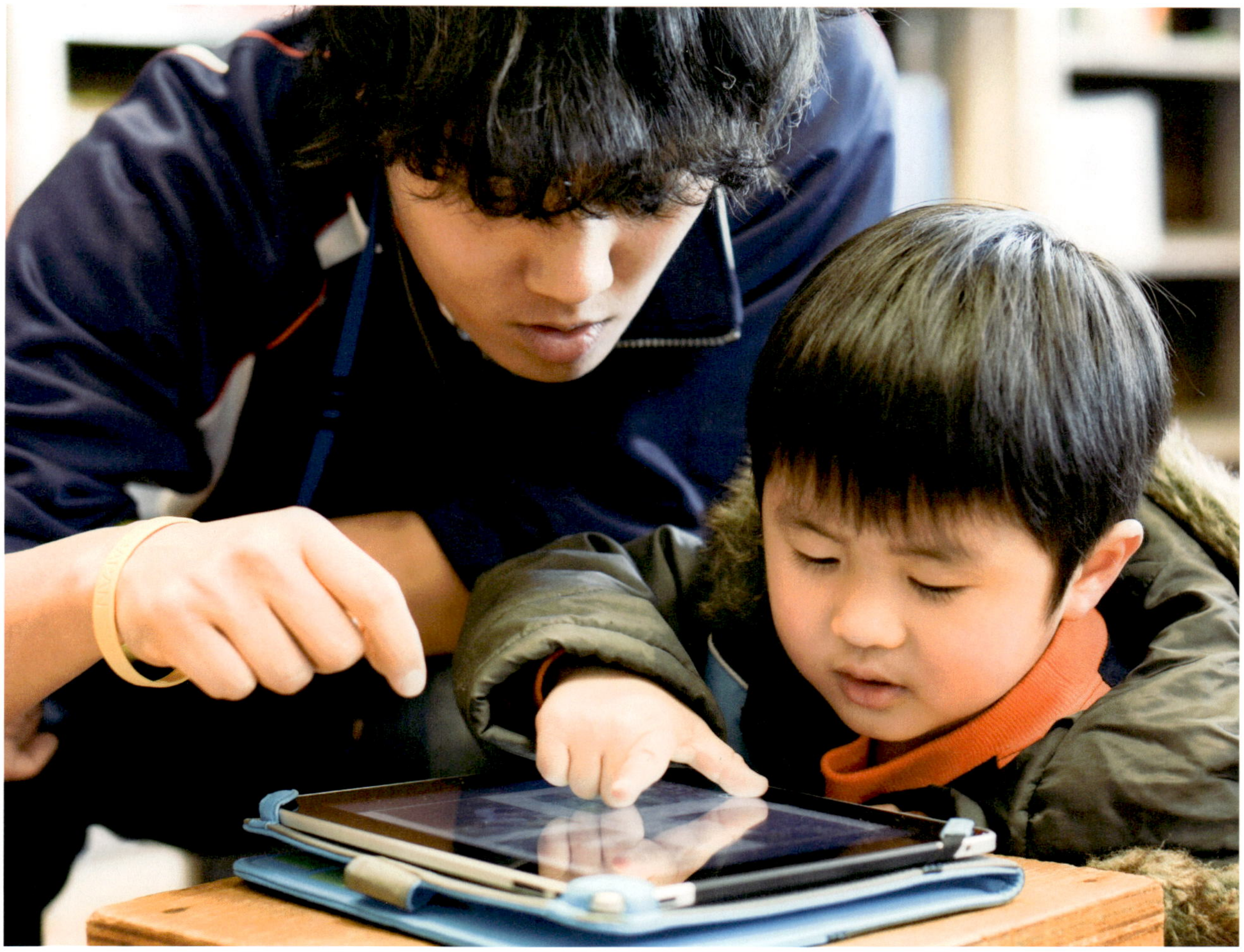

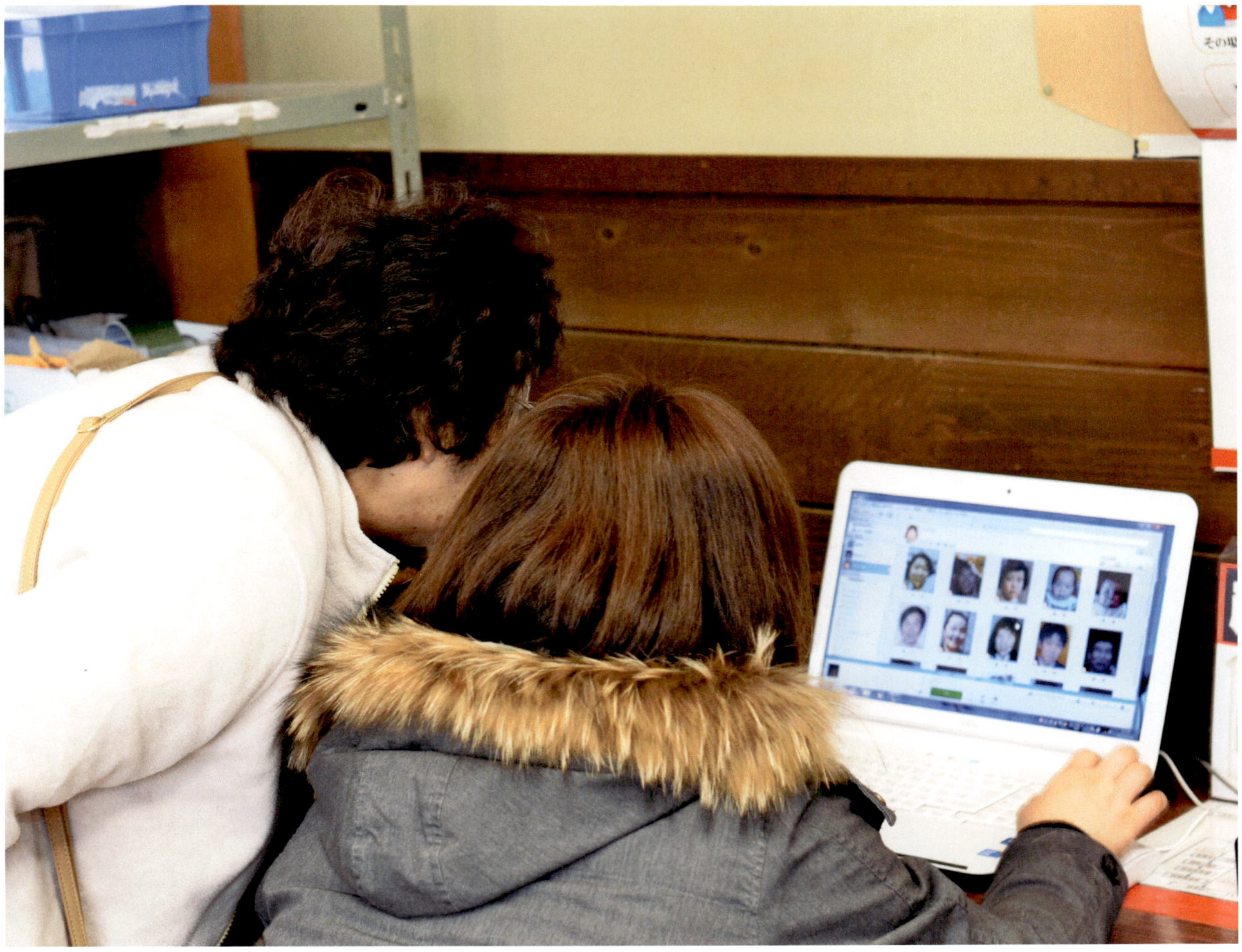

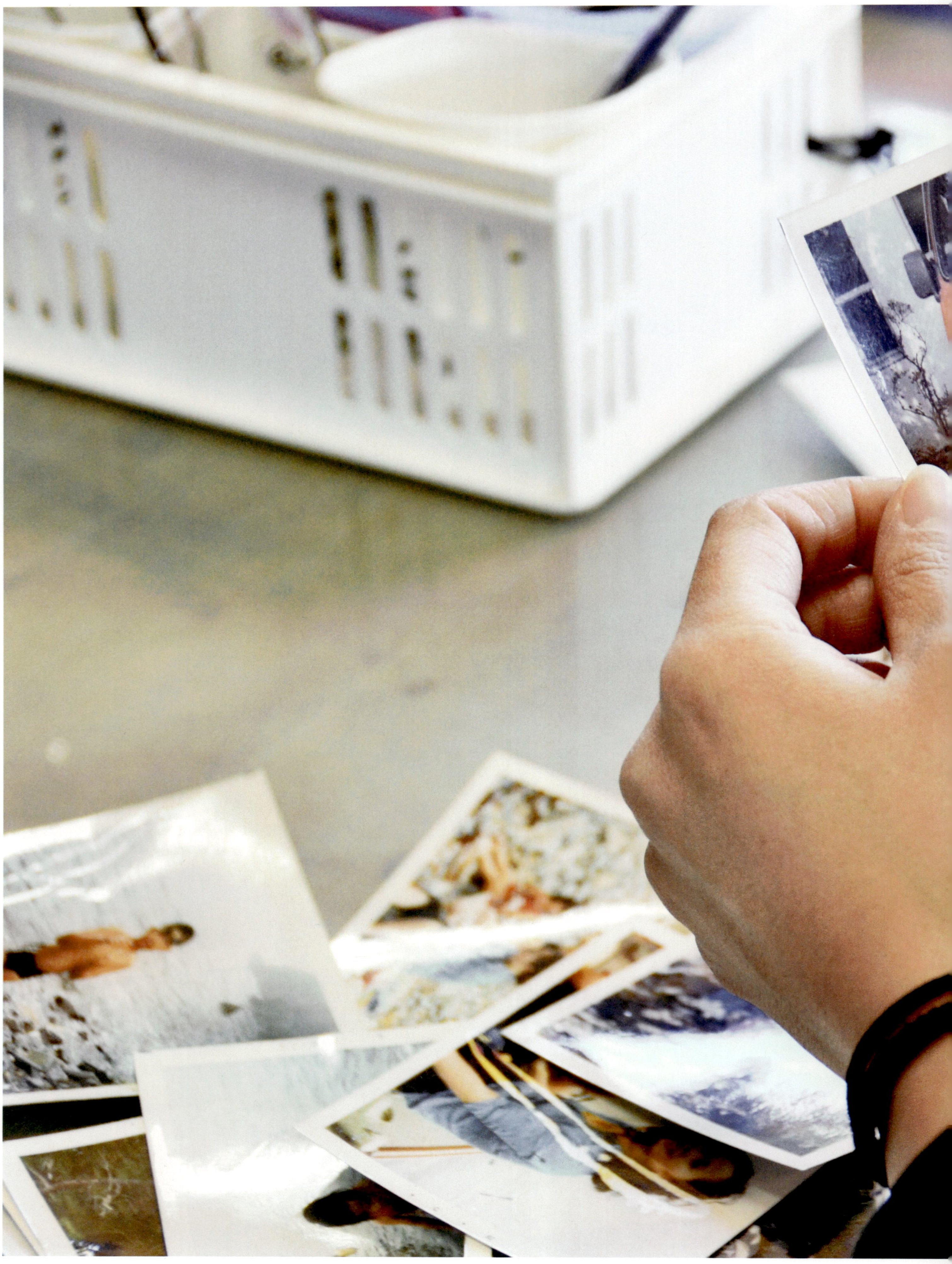

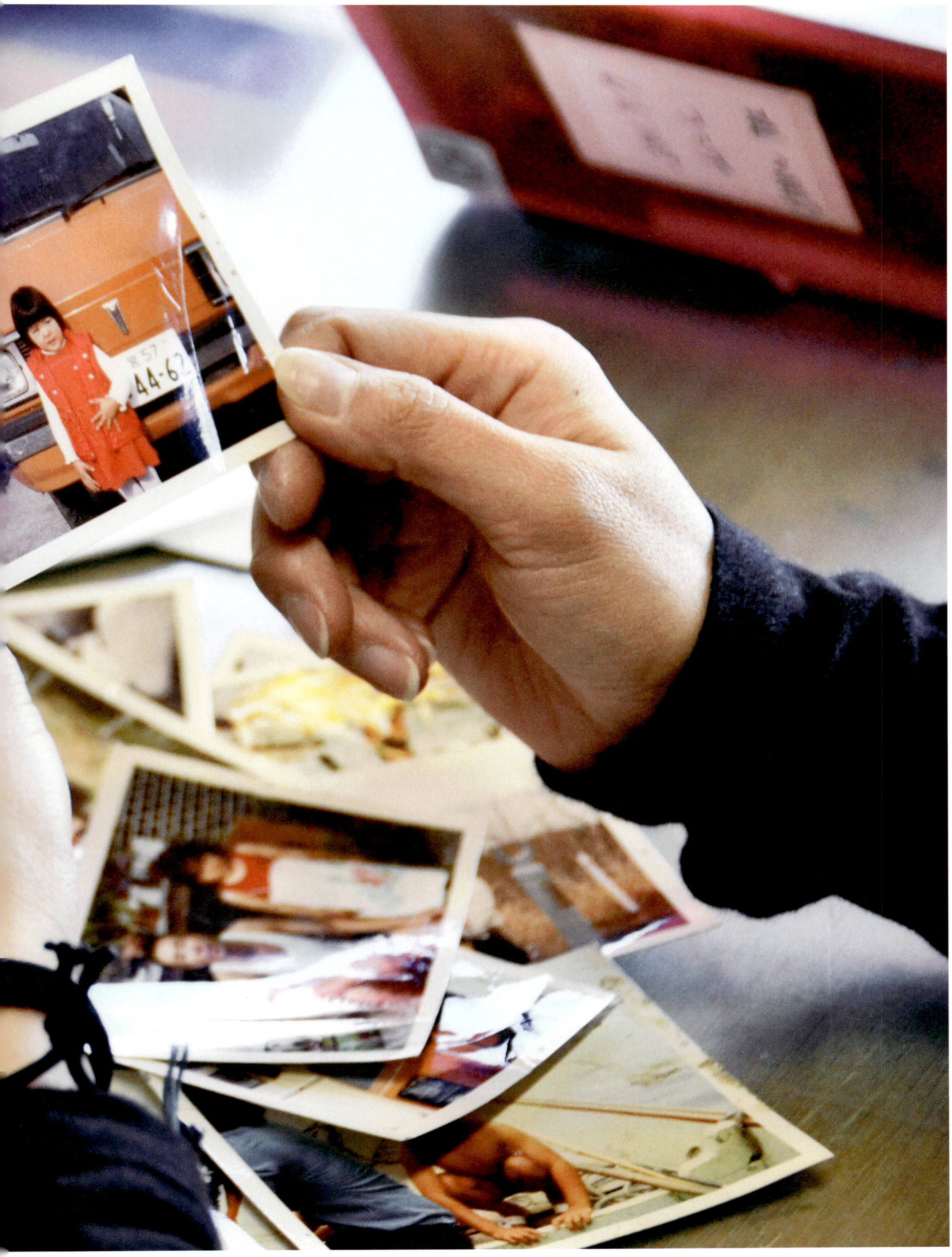
44-62

写真の洗浄マニュアル
Photo cleaning manual

1. 道具を準備します。

洗面器など水を入れられる大きめの容器。なければ浴槽でも大丈夫です。水、ハケまたは筆（ない場合は、指でも泥はおとせます）、ハサミ、ふきん。必要に応じて、マスクや手袋も用意しましょう。普通の水道水が適しています。できれば洗浄用とすすぎ用の２槽の水を用意できるとベストです。

1. Prepare the cleaning kit

Water, brushes (you can use your fingers too), scissors and towels. Large containers, such as washbowls, to put water in (bathtubs also work). If required, wear a mask and/or gloves. Ideally, prepare separate containers for cleaning and rinsing. Regular tap water is suitable.

2. アルバムから写真をはずします。

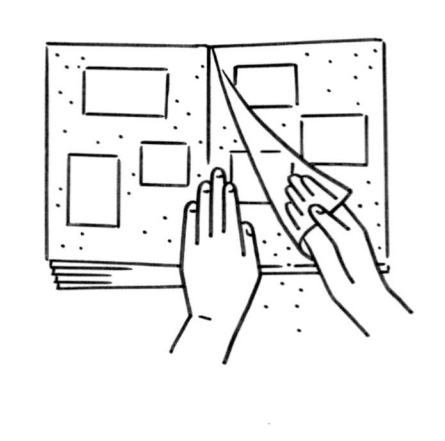

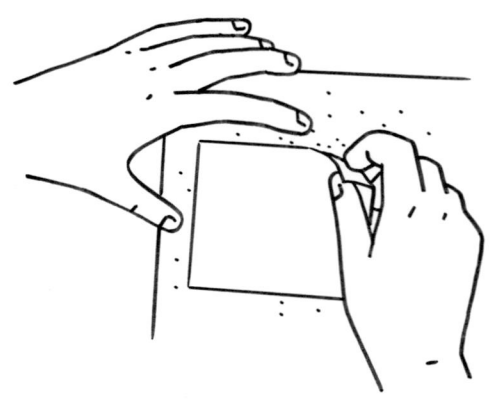

台紙からはがせる写真ははがします。だめならハサミで台紙ごと切り取ってください。アルバムのビニールがついたままの写真は、ゆっくりビニールからはがせるか試してみてください。（それでもはがれないときは、はがさずにビニールの表面の泥を落として、デジタルカメラでページを真上から撮影します）分解したページを乾燥させます。

2. Remove photographs from the album

Remove the photographs from their pages. If the photographs have been stuck to the pages and can't be removed, simply cut the photographs out. If the photographs are stuck between a transparent plastic sheet and adhesive paper, try to slowly peel away the plastic. (If you are unable to remove the sheet, leave it in place, remove any dirt from its surface, and photograph the images from directly above) Separate each page from the album and let it dry.

3. 写真を「洗える写真」と「洗えない写真」に分けます。

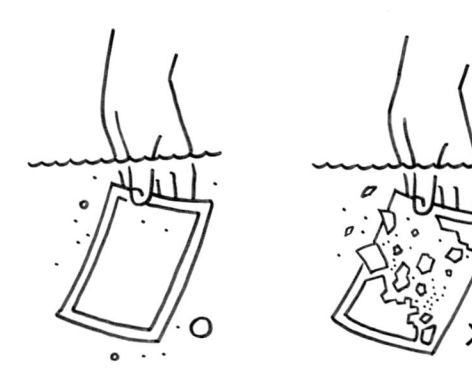

写真を慎重に水につけてみて、表面の画像がすぐにとけてしまったり、表面がはがれてしまったりするものは洗えません。複数の写真がくっついているものも、水にしばらくつけてゆっくりとはがせるか試してみてください。

3. Separate photographs into cleanable and uncleanable

Gently immerse the photograph in the water. If the image begins to decompose or the surface starts to peel away, the photograph cannot be cleaned. If several photographs are stuck together, try to gently separate them in the water.

---

4. 写真の洗浄に入ります。

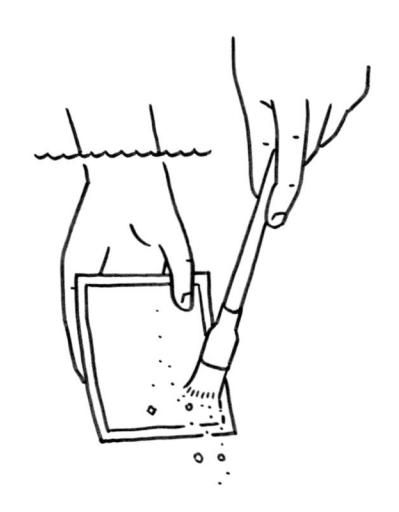

写真を1枚ずつ、30秒から1分間水につけてから、そのまま水の中で、ハケか指でやさしくゆっくりと写真の隅から泥を落としていきます。一枚一枚とても慎重に洗ってください。表面がぬるぬるする写真は画像がくずれやすいので、なるべく触らないようにして泥だけ落とすように特にやさしく扱ってください。洗い終わったらすぐに水から出してふきんの上に並べてください。洗っているうちに水が汚れたら、その都度新しい水と入れ替えてください。

4. Cleaning the photographs

Immerse each photograph in the water for 30 to 60 seconds. Using a brush or your fingers, gently remove any surface dirt, working from one edge of the photograph to the other. Carefully clean the photographs one by one. If the surface feels slimy, the photograph has begun to decompose. Try not to touch the surface, and using your utmost care, remove as much dirt as possible. Once the photograph has been cleaned, remove it from the water and let it dry on a towel. Change the water constantly as it will quickly become dirty.

---

5. 洗浄した写真を日影で乾くまで干します。

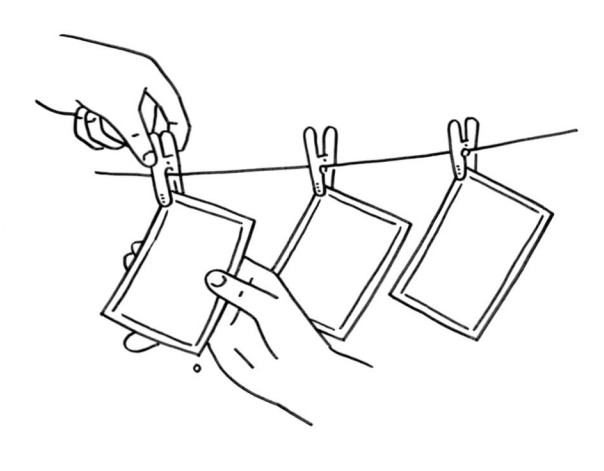

洗濯バサミではさんで乾かせばせまいスペースでも乾燥することができます。また、寝かせた網戸に写真をならべて乾かしてもいいです。

5. Dry the photographs in a shaded area

If space is limited, use a string and pegs to hang up the photographs. Screen doors placed horizontally can also be used for drying the photographs.

その後東北大学院生の保良くんの努力により別のデータベースも作成され、グーグルのピカサというフリーソフトの顔認識システムを活用することで、探しにきた人の顔と似た顔の写真を膨大なデータの中から探せるようになっていった。このようにして約３年間で３０万枚ほどの写真が持ち主に返っていった。返却作業は２０１４年になっても溝口くんを中心に継続されている。

2011. 7. 24　Day 135

The vast amount of digitalized files were put into a database and organized based on the area that they were found with the support from the internet company Nifty, meaning that people could now browse them from their computers. Also, thanks to Hora-kun, a graduate student at Tohoku University, another database was created using Google's free software PICASA which allowed people to search more effectively using its facial recognition software. Over the past three years we have been able to return about 300,000 photographs to their owners, and this is still continuing in 2014, led by Mizoguchi-kun.

LOST & FOUND PROJECT

「もうダメBOX」の中にたまった写真をどうするのか、決断をしなくてはいけないときが迫っていた。どうにかするとは言ったものの、他の作業が忙しくて全く手をつけていなかった。現場からはあの写真どうするんだ、傷みも激しいしもう処分した方がいいんじゃないかとの意見も強くなっていた。これまで写真に関わってきて、また星さんをはじめプロジェクトの仲間と話し合ってきて、この写真の実物を現地まで来られない人に見てもらうことには意味があるだろうとは考えていた。山元町に通うようになるまで、ぼくが知っていた情報はテレビや新聞やインターネットによるものだった。そこでは人の死が丁寧に目につかないものにされていた。地震が起きてすぐの頃、太平洋側の多くの町が津波の被害にあったなかで、死者の数が被害の大きさを

伝えるものさしとして使われていた。死は数字に変換されて扱われた。やがてそれは短時間の放送にうまくまとめられた悲劇や、希望の話になっていく。終わったこと、区切りのついたものとして扱われる。誰も死と向き合わせようとしない、誰も「お前もそのうち死ぬんだぞ」とは言わない。山元町が死の雰囲気に満ちていたわけではない、むしろ穏やかで静かな場所だった。でもぼくらは誰かの写真と向き合い続けた。そこには泥まみれになった誰かの人生が確かにあった、赤ん坊の写真を見ればみんなが、生きているといいなと思い、また同時に死んでいる可能性に悲しくもなった。そこには誰かの楽しかったときの記憶があった、今はぼろぼろになってここにある。この写真を前にすると、そんな誰かの存在を、その身に起きたことを想像しないわけにはいかない。センセーショナルなものとしてではなく、静かに誰かの死を思うことはとても大事なことのように思えた。

LOST & FOUND PROJECT

We had to determine what to do with the accumulated photographs in "Hopeless Box". Although I said I would figure something out, I was too busy with other tasks and so the staff started to ask me about the box. The photographs were heavily damaged, and more and more people thought that it would be best to just discard them. I had been spending a lot of time with the photographs, and after a conversation with Hoshi-san and the other members, we began to think it would be meaningful to show the actual photographs to more people, including those who couldn't visit the town to see them. Before I started to visit Yamamoto-cho, the only information I acquired came from television, newspapers and the internet who carefully excluded images of the deceased. After the earthquake, when many towns were hit by the tsunami, the number of the deceased became some sort of a measure to convey the degree of the damage: the death was translated into number, and that was how the media dealt with the catastrophe. It would soon be made into well-packaged tragedy or story of hope. By then, it would be over; it would be the thing of the past. Nobody was trying to deliver the death right in front of people's eyes. Nobody said to people, "You may die soon too." It wasn't that Yamamoto-cho was filled with despair; the town was rather calm and quiet, but it was there that we continually were faced with someone's photographs, and it was there that we saw someone's life covered in mud. Seeing a photograph of a baby, we all hoped that the baby was still alive, yet simultaneously we were saddened by the possibility of the baby's passing. The photographs contained memories of happy lives. They were with us, even though they were seriously damaged. Being in front of the pictures, we couldn't help but imagine the lives of the photographed, and what had possibly happened to them. It was nothing sensational, but to think of someone's death, very quietly, had become important procedure for us.

返すもの

たとえ写真を見せることにどんなに意味があったとしても、それだけではフェアじゃないと考えていた。写真を町の外に出すということは、見せ物にすることでもあり、どんなに他の場所で理解されたところで山元町に返すものが何もないんじゃ意味がないと思っていた。簡単に思いつくのは寄付金だった。しかし町を元に戻すには莫大なお金が必要で、ぼくらに集められるような額じゃ話にならないということは明白だった。山元町に観光客を呼べばいいんじゃないかとも考えたが、そのとき山元町には宿泊施設もなく観光資源と呼べそうなものもなかった。いろんなことを話し合ったけれど、名案は出てこなかった。このままでは写真は処分されてしまう、でもそれもしかたのないことかもしれないと思い始めていた。

Something to Return

Although it was meaningful to show the photographs to more people, we couldn't seem to justify ourselves. Taking the photographs out of the town meant exploiting them. No matter how much attention they would get, we still had to think of something to return to Yamamoto-cho. The easiest option was to call for donations at every exhibition we hosted, but restoring the town needed a lot of money, far more than we could collect. Maybe we could have the exhibition in Yamamoto-cho to attract tourists, but back then there was no accommodation in town and the resources for tourists were scarce. We discussed it for a long time but couldn't find a solution, yet if we continued doing nothing, the photographs would be discarded. Gradually, many of us started to think that was the only option remaining.

仮設住宅

家を流されてしまった人たちが住む、仮設住宅というものがある。それはプレハブでできた集合住宅で、山元町にも8ヶ所ある。それぞれに自治会という町内会のようなものがあり、自治会長さんがいる。本来なら住人から自治会費を集め、回覧板のプリント代や作業したときに出すお茶やお菓子などこまごまとした出費に充てられるわけだが、同じ被災者から自治会費をとるのは心苦しいと言って自腹で負担している自治会長が多かった。小さな出費も長い期間になると、少しずつ負担になっているとのことだった。これならぼくらに集められる寄付金でも、役に立つかもしれないと思った。

Temporary Housing

There were temporary housing units for people whose houses were destroyed by the tsunami. The prefabricated houses were built in eight areas of Yamamoto-cho, with each of them forming a self-governing neighborhood group to help the residents. The leaders of some of the groups needed to collect a small community fee for printing community letters, or providing tea and snacks for the workers. But the leaders felt guilty about collecting money from those who had suffered, and covered the expense themselves. Although the amount was small, it became an ongoing burden and we thought that one way we could help would be to collect money for them.

決断

写真を見せる意味はあるだろう、集めたお金を持っていく場所もある。けれど写真を持ち出すことが本当にいいことなんだろうか、寄付金がちゃんと集まらなかったらどうしよう。そんなことをずっと悶々と考えていた。そんなとき星さんが言ってくれたことがある。「やってみなきゃうまくいくかなんてわからないじゃないか、ダメだったら一緒

に謝りにいってやるよ」これでやっと小心者のぼくにも決心がついた。どのように進めるのか計画を立て、町役場に行った。自分たちがやろうとしていること、集めた寄付金の届け先、もしも問題が起きたときの責任は自分がとります、ということを話し合いLOST & FOUND PROJECTがスタートすることになった。ネットや印刷物を通してではなく直接写真を見てもらうために、展示という方法をメインに見せていくことにした。

The Decision

We knew that it was meaningful to present the photographs, and we knew where to send our donation money, but what if we couldn't raise enough money for the temporary housing communities? What if it was ethically wrong to show the photos publicly? We kept thinking about the questions until one day Hoshi-san said to me: "You will never know how it goes because you haven't even started. If it goes wrong, I'll go and apologize with you." That turned my timidness into a firm resolution, and we soon laid out the solid plan and visited the town hall. We told the officials what we were trying to do, how to use our donation money, and that we would be responsible for any of the damages the project may possibly cause, and that was how the "Lost & Found Project" began. We chose to show the photos in an exhibition format because we wanted people to see them face-to-face, not through printed matter or the internet.

ポスター

どのように寄付金を集めるかも考えていった。日本のぼくらの世代は普段募金をする習慣もあまりないし、もししようと思ってもいくら入れればいいのかあまりよくわからない。そこで、ポスターを作って販売し、売上から印刷費などのコストを引いた７０％が寄付になるように設定した。ポスターは３種類作成し、それぞれにこのプロジェクトのこと、山元町の紹介、思い出サルベージの説明の情報を記載した。

Posters

I also had to consider how to raise funds for the exhibition. In addition to Japanese people being unfamiliar with fundraising activities, we had no idea how much money would be required. As a start, we made posters, with 70% of the sales going into our fund, and the remainder being used to cover printing costs. Three different posters were produced, with each one including an introduction and explanation of Lost & Found, Yamamoto-cho, and Memory Salvage.

希望

思い出サルベージに関わった経験から、全てを想定し計算通りに物事を進めていくことは不可能だし意味がないと考えるようになっていった。ぼくの予想では全ての写真がデータ化できるなんてことはあり得ないはずだった。しかしそれは外れた。思いもよらないことはつねに起きる。良いことも悪いことも。展示は伝えたいことをしっかり形にする、そしてそれを見た人がどんな行動をするかは任せようと思った。ポスターを買う人もいる、募金をする人もいる、山元町に行く人だっているかもしれない、きっとみんな少しずつ何かをするんじゃないかと思った。それはぼくには見ることができなくても、どこかでいろんなものが繋がり、ぼくじゃない誰かが何かを形作るかもしれない。そうなればいいなぁと思っていた。

Hope

After the experience of being involved in the Memory Salvage project, I had started to believe that planning for what came next was both impossible and meaningless. At first, I didn't think it would be possible to scan all the photographs we had, but I was proven wrong. Things always take unexpected turns; sometimes, good things happen; other times, bad things do. I decided that my mission was to present the exhibition as comprehensively as possible, and it was up to each visitor as to what they felt and how they reacted. Perhaps they would buy a poster, donate some money, or even visit Yamamoto-cho but regardless of how big or

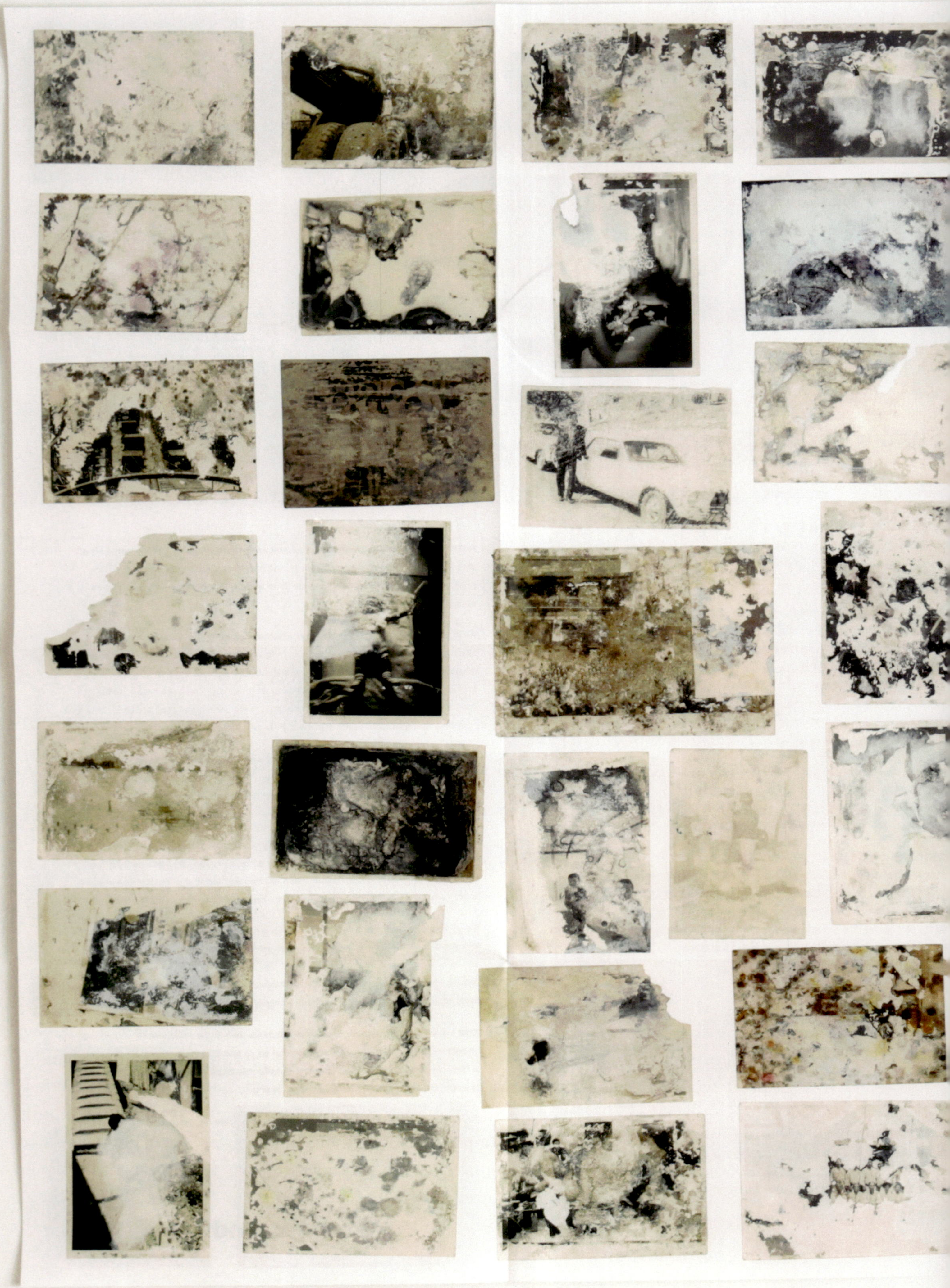

LOST & FOUND PROJECT

Family Photos Swept by 3.11 East Japan Tsunami

Contact
LOST & FOUND PROJECT Executive Committee
E-mail: info@lostandfound311.jp

With the cooperation of:
Yamamoto-cho town office
The Japan Society for Socio-Information Studies
AKAAKA ART PUBLISHING Inc.
Photo Gallery International
trimdesign
NPO Yuriforimiyagi
Mozuya Inc.
Yamanote Photo

2011年3月11日まで、ここにある写真たちは全て誰かの家にありました。

地震とそれに伴う津波は、家を、そしてその中にある多くのものを流していきました。
海辺の町は、一面ガレキだらけになったそうです。そこには車も服も冷蔵庫も、
写真やアルバムもそして人も、全部ごちゃ混ぜに泥だらけになって、
静かに横たわっていました。

それから少しして、生存者の捜索が終わりガレキの撤去が始まると、
自衛隊や消防署員や警察官や、町にいるいろんな人がその中から写真を拾いあげ、
別の場所に集めておくようになりました。
それは誰に頼まれたわけでもなく、
はっきりとした目的意識があったわけでもありませんでした。
ほとんど何もなくなってしまった場所で、戻るものが何もない場所で、
それでも何かを戻せたらと思ったのではないでしょうか。
集められた写真は体育館いっぱいになっていきました。

地震から2ヶ月近くが過ぎた頃、集められた写真たちを持ち主の手に戻そうという
「思い出サルベージ」プロジェクトが本格的に始まりました。
東京をはじめ日本の各地からボランティアが集まり、
集められた写真は少しずつ洗浄され、データ化されていきました。

写真の状態は様々でした。
比較的きれいなものから、バクテリアによる浸食が進み表面の像が
ほとんど溶けてしまったものまで。そしてここにある写真の多くは、
損傷が激しく持ち主の判別が難しいと判断されたものと、
運よく持ち主が見つかったものから貸してもらったものです。
3月11日までは、誰の家の引き出しにもあるような家族の、
仲間との思い出の写真だったはずです。

ぼくらは写真を撮ります。何枚かは大事にされ、
その他はあまり顧みられずに置いておかれます。
ぼくらは楽しい時、何かいいことがあった時、
誰かに見せたいものと出会った時写真を撮ります。

ここにある写真も同じでした。
一枚一枚その想いに大小はあれど、誰かが残しておきたいと思った場面でした。

この写真たちを前に何を思うべきなのか、答えは出ません。
見つかった写真を喜ぶべきか、もう持ち主の手に戻らない写真を悲しむべきなのか、
それともいなくなってしまった人たちのことか。
何か答えを出そうとするたびに、足りないものが出てくるような気がします。

それでも見つめることからしか何も見えてこないのだと思います

Until the day of March 11th 2011, all the photos we have here today were in people's homes.

After the earthquake hit, a massive tsunami swept away houses, and everything that was inside them. Coastal towns were buried in rubble. Cars, clothes, refrigerators, photo albums: everything was swallowed up and turned to waste as people stood speechless.

As the search for survivors ended and attention turned to the clean up mission, Self-Defense forces, firemen, and policemen who were in Tohoku to help survivors began to pick up photos they found in the mud, and to store them in an elementary school gymnasium. They were not asked to do it, nor did they have a clear sense of their objective. Perhaps they were just desperate to find something in of the rubble that could be saved. Over time, the gymnasium began to fill up with salvaged photographs.

Two months after the earthquake hit, a group called the "Memory Salvage Project" began to sort out the photos and prepare them for return to their owners.
The images were cleaned and digitized by volunteers who came from Tokyo and other parts of Japan.

The images varied in condition, from relatively clean to damaged beyond recognition. Some of the photographs you see here were so badly eroded by bacteria that they could not be cleaned, and therefore could not be returned. But each of these images, kept in a drawers or cabinet, was someone's treasured memory until that fateful day.

We all take photographs. A few special ones are cherished, and the rest forgotten. We take pictures when we are having fun, when we want immortalize a moment shared with another person. The photographs you see here were also taken under those circumstances. The depth of emotion might vary from snap to snap, but each one captures a point in time that somebody wanted to keep.

What are we supposed to feel and think when we look at these pictures?
Should we be happy that they were found at all, or sad that they will never be returned to their owners? Or should we simply mourn for the dead? The more I struggle to find answers, the more missing pieces I seem to find.

But without looking at the pictures, I don't think we'll see anything at all.

www.lostandfound311.jp

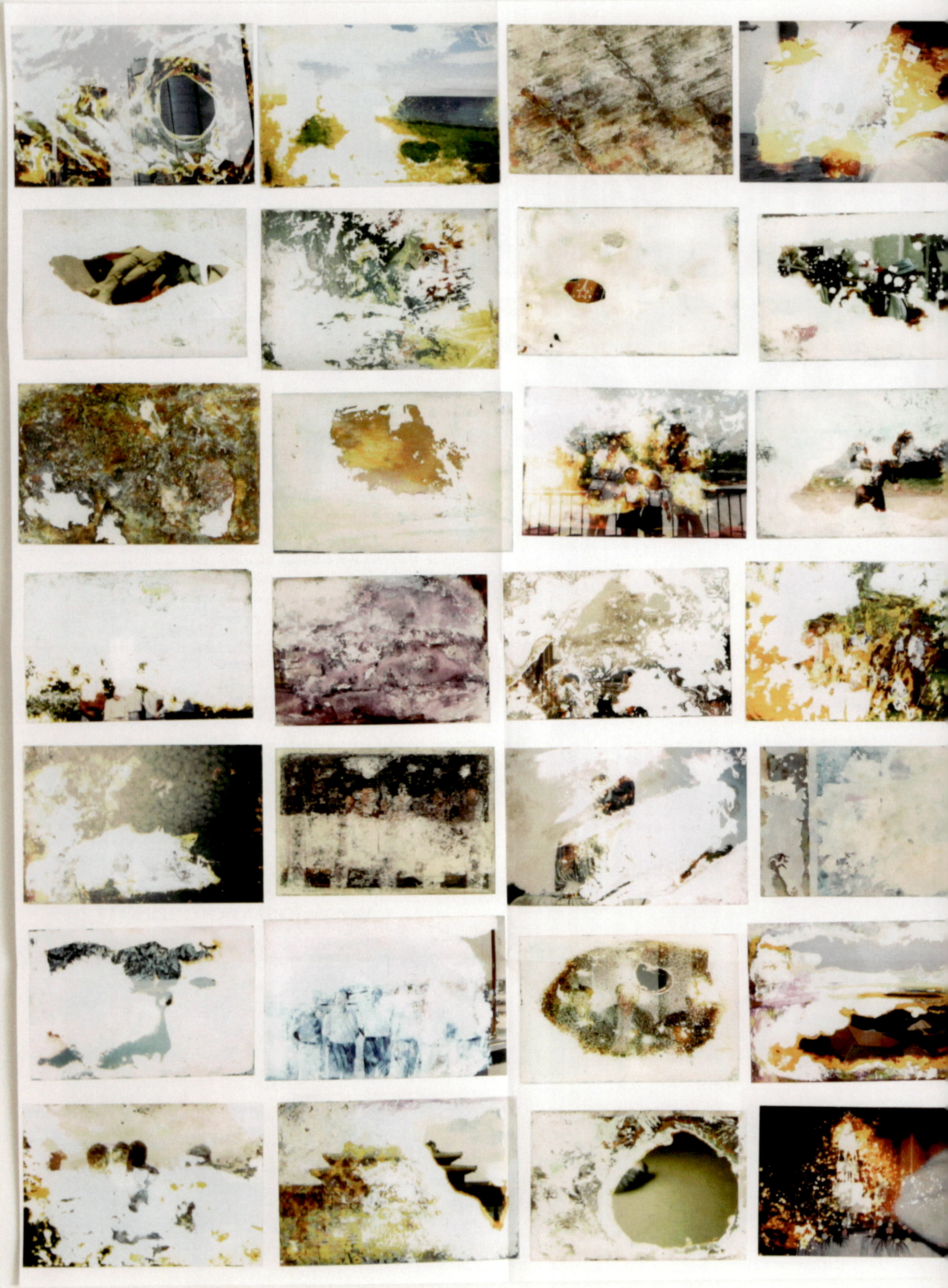

About "The Project Salvage Memory"

www.omoidesalvage.jp

Contact
LOST & FOUND PROJECT Executive Committee
E-mail: info@lostandfound311.jp

「思い出サルベージアルバム」は、被災した写真を持ち主の手に返すために、
日本社会情報学会の若手研究者達が始めたプロジェクトです。
関わる人全てがボランティアで参加しています。

津波で傷ついた何十万枚という写真の泥を掃き、洗い、カメラで複写することで
データ化し、写真の持ち主に返そうとしています。
初めは大学関係者が中心で進めていたプロジェクトも、ツイッターやブログを通じて
カメラマンや写真の専門職、そして企業など様々な分野の人々が参加し、
全国からボランティアが集まる大規模な活動へと広がってゆきました。

[作業工程]
① 泥はきと洗浄
② ナンバリング
③ カメラで複写してデータ化
④ インデックスファイルや検索システムを使って持ち主探し

今までに500人以上のボランティアが関わり、三ヶ月かけて作成されたデータを
活用してアルバム約1100冊バラ写真約19200枚が持ち主の手へと返っていきました。

2011年11月の現在、データ化した写真を元に、
より多くの持ち主を探す活動を続けています。

"The Project Salvage Memory" was started by a team of young researchers from The Japan Society for Socio-Information Studies, who felt the need to return the photographs which were swept by the tsunami to their owners.
Everyone who is involved in this project is a volunteer.

We are trying to return a few hundred thousands of photographs which were damaged by the tsunami by sweeping the dirt off, rinsing with water and reproducing them in the digital format.

The people who were working in the early stage of the project were professors, college students and volunteers, but as the project became known through twitter and blogs, many people who specialize in photography, professional photographers, and private companies from various fields started to join the project.

The cleaning process involves the following steps.
1) Sweeping dirt off and rinsing photographs with water
2) Numbering
3) Reproduce the photographs in the digital format
4) Find their owners by using index files and the search system

More than 500 people volunteered for this project, and 680 photo albums and 12,000 photographs have been returned to their owners by using the data which took 3 months to build.

As of November 2011, we are continuing to look for owners of the digitized photographs.

www.lostandfound311.jp

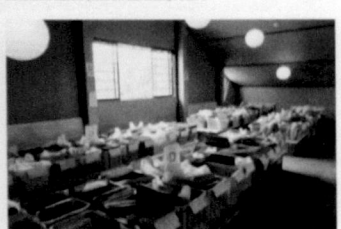

small their actions were, they would each react to the exhibition in their own way. I may not have witnessed all of the reactions, but I sincerely hoped that as a result of the exhibition, things would start to flow, and maybe someday, someone else would start something because of what I had done.

展示1
2012.1.11−2.11
AKAAKA
東京、日本

最初の展示は、東京にある赤々舎という出版社に併設されたギャラリーを借りて開催した。赤々舎はぼくが２０１０年に写真集を出版した会社であり、展示の相談をするとすぐに無料で場所を提供してくれることになった。展示の方法は、壁一面に写真を貼り付けることにした。こうすることで多くの人生がかつてそこにあったことを伝えられるのではないかと考えた。そして壁に近づけば、一枚一枚誰かが残したいと思った記憶があることを見てとれる。見に来た人が写真と向かい合い、自分の頭と心でそれぞれに感じてもらえればいいなと考えていた。被害の大きさではなく、静かな悲しみの深さを感じられるものにしなくてはならないと思っていた。それと同時にどうすれば多くの人が来てくれるのか、できるかぎりのことをやらなければと考えていた。展示が始まってすぐはあまり人が来なくて、これは大丈夫かなぁと思っていたけど、インターネットや雑誌や新聞に展示のことを掲載してもらってからは、一気に多くの人が来てくれるようになった。会期中の出来事で記憶に残っていることがある。それは展示を通じて写真の本来の持ち主と出会えたことだ。ある日、新聞に掲載された写真を見て、これは自分の家にあった写真だと気づいた人が家族で会場に来てくれた。「すごい偶然ですね、ぜひ写真を持っていってください」と言うと、「写真はおじさんに焼き増ししてもらったから大丈夫、これはこ

About
"The Project
Salvage Memory"
LOST&
FOUND
PROJECT
www.lostandfound311.jp
March.11 2011–
Yamamoto-cho
Miyagi, Japan
www.lostandfound311.jp
LOST&
FOUND
PROJECT
Family Photos Swept by 3.11 East Japan Tsunami

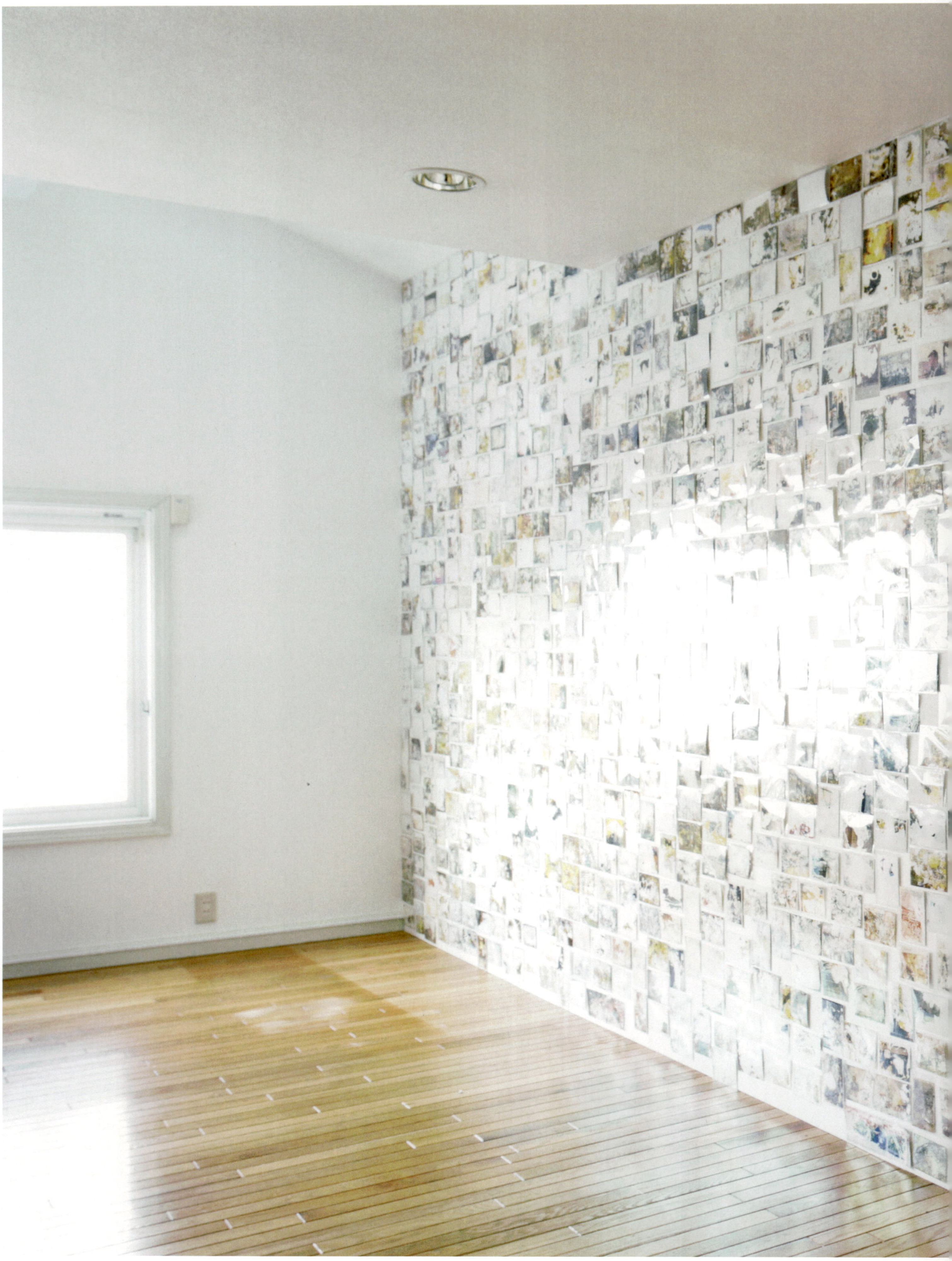

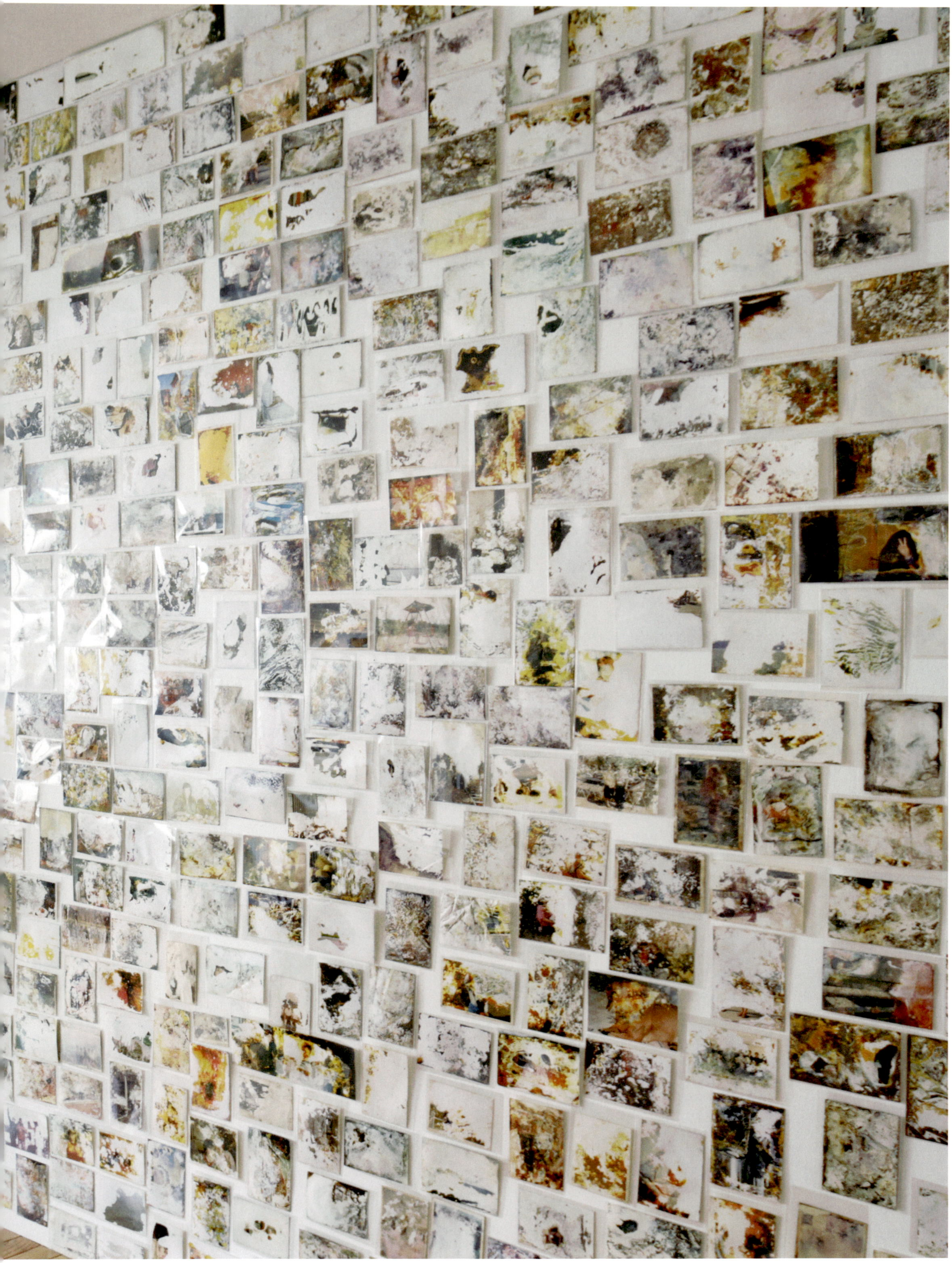

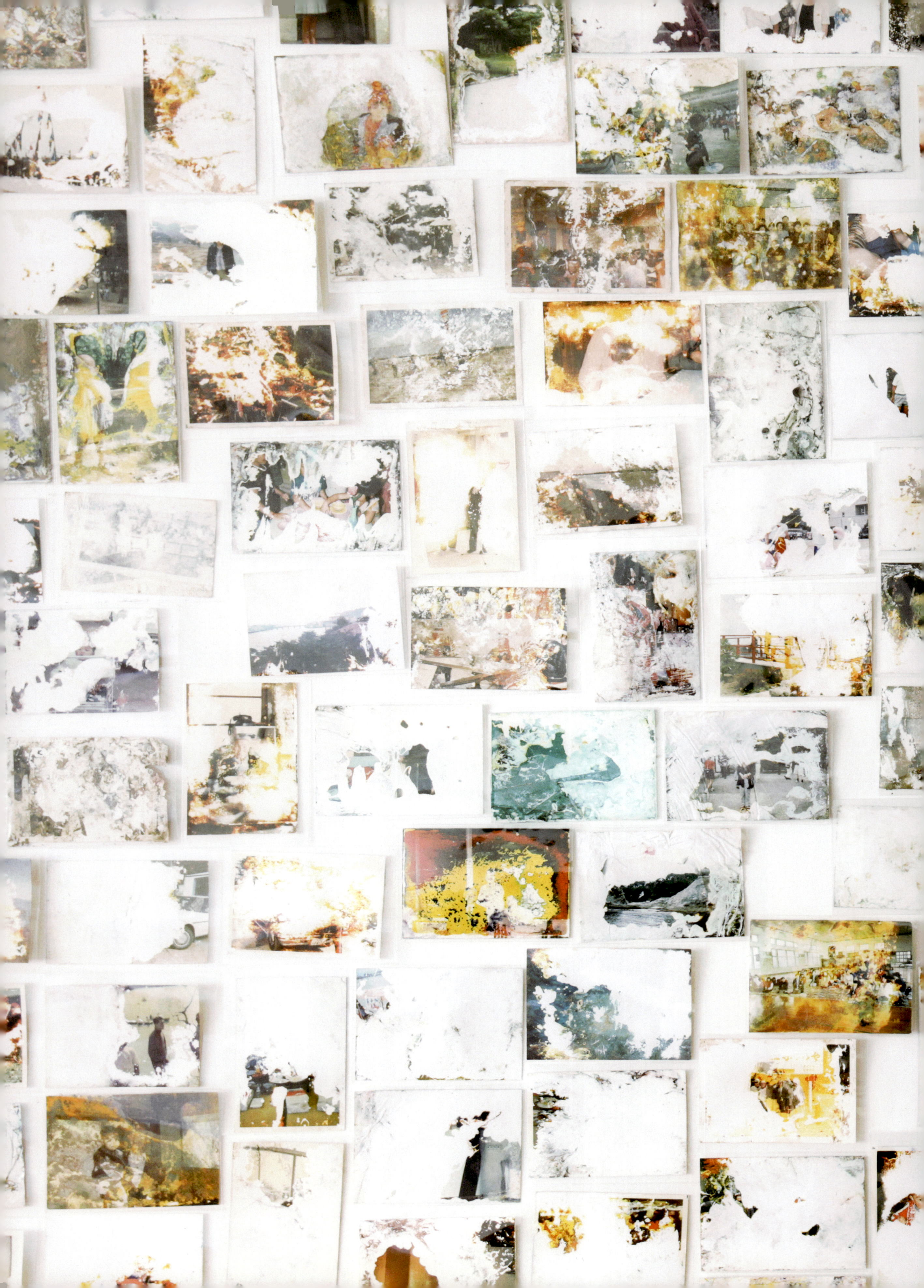

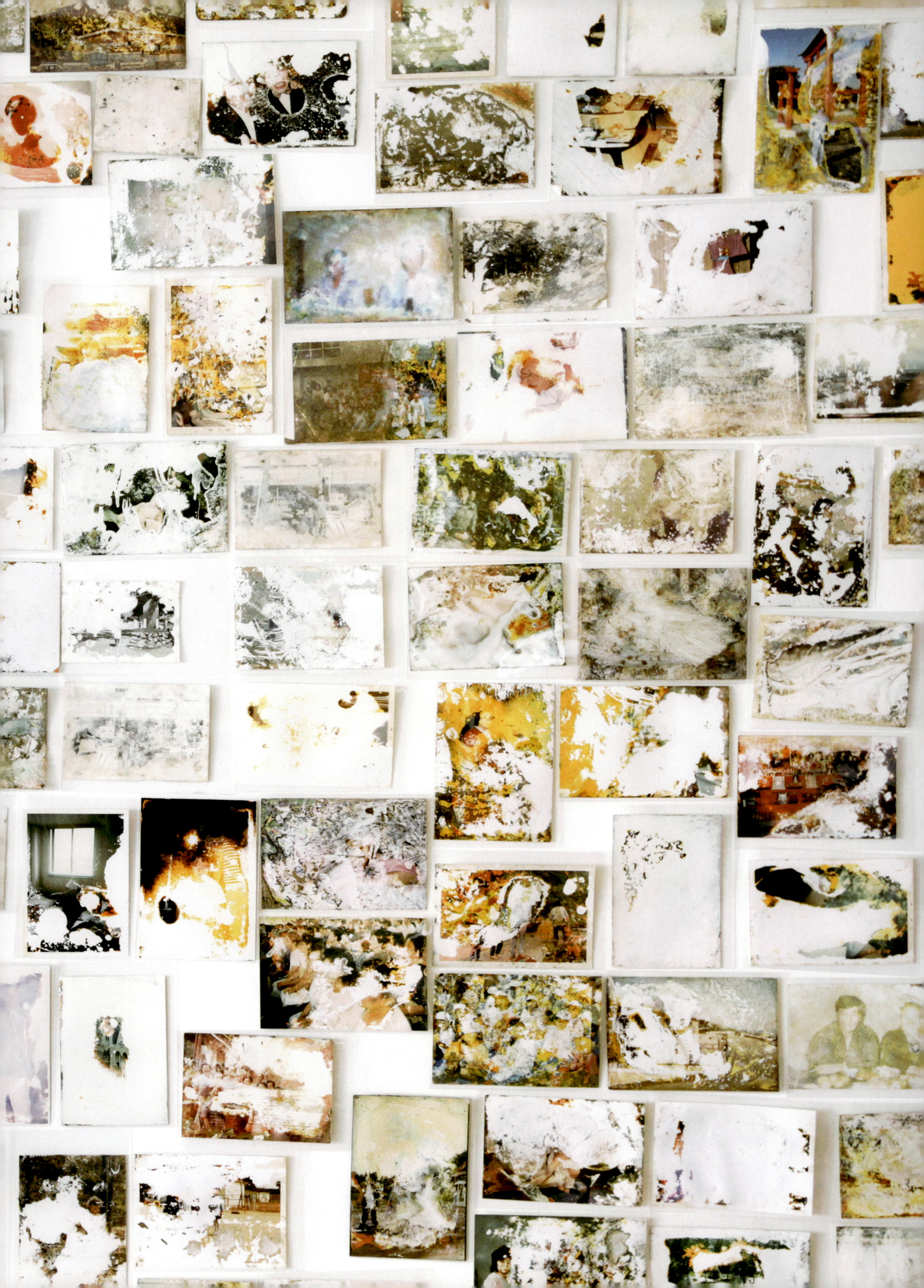

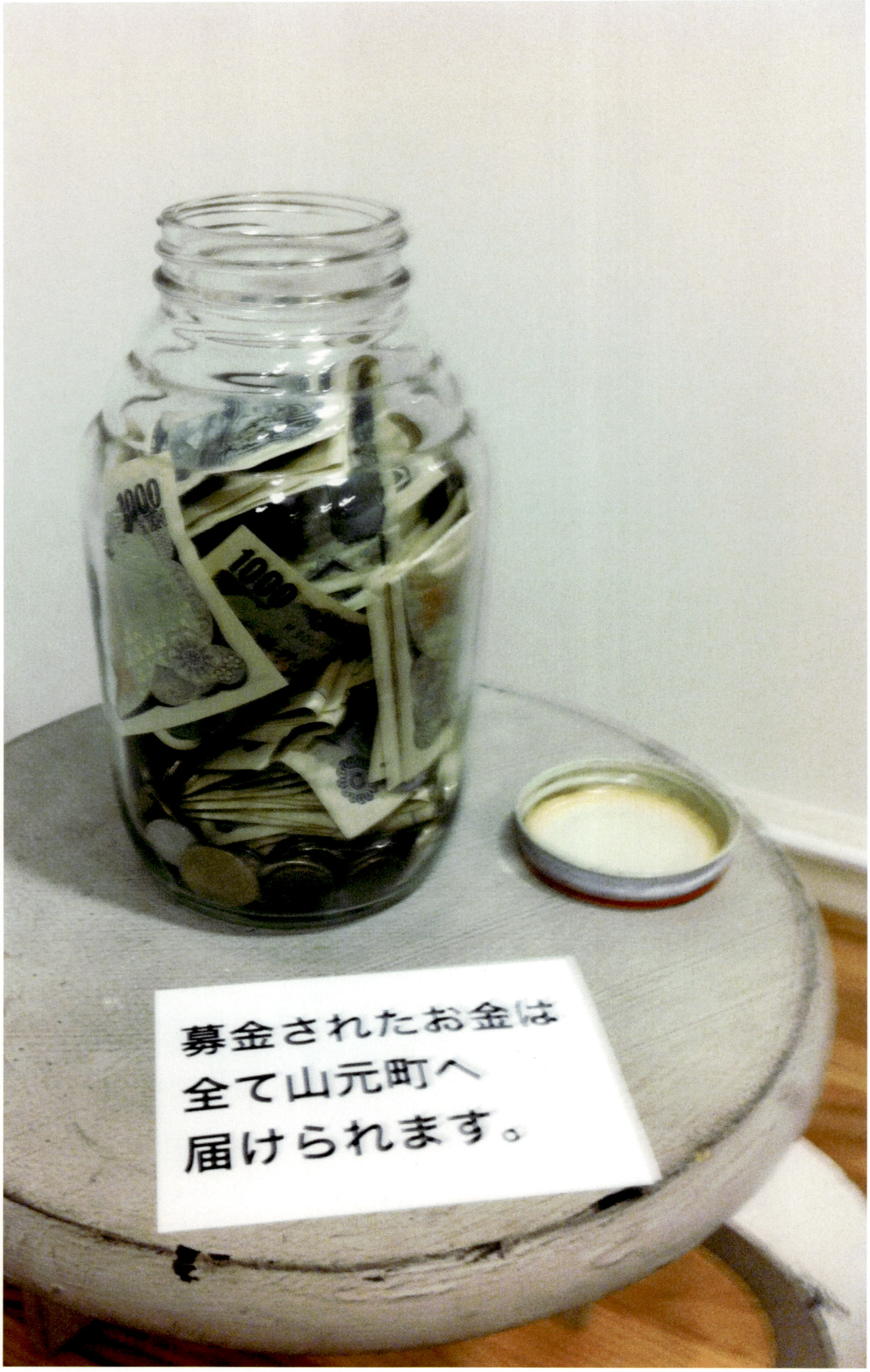
募金されたお金は
全て山元町へ
届けられます。

のまま展示で使って」と言ってくれた。そして別の日にもうひとり写真を見つけた人がいた。その人はポスターに使わせてもらった写真に写っている人だった。その写真の実物は展示していなかったので、ぼくは毎日家に帰ると大量の写真を一枚ずつ確認していき、1万枚くらい見たところで発見して本人に手渡すことができた。やっぱりダメージが酷くても処分してしまう判断をしなくてよかったと思った。そして何よりも写真の持ち主の人たちにこのプロジェクトを応援してもらえてよかった。どんなに意味があると確信していても、写真の本来の持ち主が嫌がるような形でプロジェクトを続けることはできない。

The first exhibition
2012 1.11-2.11
AKAAKA,
Tokyo, Japan

The first exhibition was held at the gallery of AKAAKA, a Tokyo-based publisher. In 2010, AKAAKA published my photography book and when I approached them about the exhibition they immediately offered their space. We covered the walls with photographs in order to convey the immense number of people that once lived in the area. Once visitors got close to the wall, they could see that each photo contained memories that the photographer had wanted to keep forever. I hoped that the visitors would feel something personal as they viewed the photographs. Rather than devastation, I wanted the exhibition to present a deep and silent sense of sorrow. We had to figure out how to attract people to the exhibition. I became worried when only a few people came to the show after it opened, but as magazines, newspapers and blogs began to write articles about the exhibition, more and more people started to visit. There were several memorable moments when I met the owners of photographs featured in the exhibition. One day, after reading a newspaper article about the show, a woman realized that they had printed an image that once belonged to her. She visited the exhibition with her family, and upon meeting her I said, "What an amazing coincidence, please take the photograph with you", but she replied by saying that we could keep it, as her uncle had already reprinted the photograph. A few days later, another woman showed up and discovered an image that had once belonged to her. She was in the photograph that we had used for the poster and as we weren't exhibiting the photograph at the venue, every day when I got home I would search through the remaining photographs one by one. After looking through about 10,000 images, I finally found the photograph and was able to return it to her. I was really glad that I didn't discard any photographs, even the ones that had been severely damaged. I was even happier to know that the owners of the photographs supported the project. As much as we knew that the project was meaningful, we couldn't have continued if the owners had been opposed to what we were doing.

外国に行ってみよう

東京での展示の準備と同時に、海外での展示も計画していった。海外でやってみようと思ったのは、まず第一にこれだけ誰もが写真を撮って残す現代において、このプロジェクトが伝えるメッセージには国境も言葉も関係ないと考えたことと、できるかぎり多くの人に関心をもってもらい少しずつ応援を集める方がお金だけを集めるよりもいいことだと思ったからだった。海外での展示を模索していた２０１１年の１１月、パリに行く用事があると言うと、友達が何人かの人に会いに行くようにと紹介してくれた。そのうちのひとりが大学で哲学を教えるフランス人のセルーアさんだった。初めて行く言葉の通じないパリで、８００枚の写真をリュックに入れてガイドブックを片手に動き回り、オペラ座の前で子供に１０ユーロだまし取られたりしながら、一人ずつ会いに行ってアドバイスをもらった。セルーアさんにはパリでどこか展示をできる場所がないか探してもらうことになった。日本に帰ってから少し経ち、セルーアさんから「今度香港に行くんだけどムネマサも来ないか？」とメールが来た。これもいい機会かと思い、香港に行って展示に関する話をしたのだけれど、何度も「もっとクリアにしなさい。あなたは何がやりたいの？」と言われた。ぼくは「今ある情報は全部伝えているし、海外でできることとできないことの判断をするための経験がないんだから、何がやりたいか言いづらいよ」なんてことを答えたのだが「あなたはアーティストでしょ、もっと自分のやりたいことをハッキリと持ちなさい」ということだった。結果的にパリでの展示は実現しなかったものの、このときのやりとりはとて

も勉強になった。日本では物事を進める場合、できないことを並べた上で実現可能なことを探していくのだけど、どうやら海外ではできるできない以前に、まずは自分が強く実現したいことを打ち出す必要があるんだと学んだ。いくつかの国に行った感想としては、海外では「おれは好きにやる、おまえも好きにやれ」であるが、日本では「おれは我慢する、おまえも我慢しろ」だという気がする。どちらがいいとか悪いとかでなくそういうもんなんだなぁとは思っているのだが、今でも自分のことを強く主張するのは苦手だなと感じる。とにかく、セルーアさんのおかげで、海外でのコミュニケーションは手順が違うということを学ばせてもらった。香港のマーケットでぶらぶらと買い物しながら散歩しているときに、セルーアさんが「アーユーアングリー？」と言った。急に何を言い出すんだと混乱していたら、セルーアさんがお腹をさするジェスチャーをした。「おー、ハングリーね！イエスイエス、アイムハングリーだよ！」フランス人は英語でも「H」を発音しないことを知った。こんな感じで通訳をしてくれる人がいないときは、全然話せない英語と最大限のジェスチャーでコミュニケーションをした。一年間いろんな国に行き、英語はあまり上達しなかったけど、ボディランゲージ能力だけはだいぶ向上した。

Going Abroad

Whilst preparing for the Tokyo exhibition, we started to plan a number of exhibitions outside of Japan. We considered that in an era where everyone takes photographs, the project's message could touch people regardless of their nationality or language. We also thought that it would be more effective to hold exhibitions in many places in order to raise interest in the project, as well as seeking donations. In November 2011, whilst looking for opportunities to take the show abroad, I had a chance to visit Paris, where a friend introduced me to a few people they knew. It was my first visit to the city and I couldn't speak any French, but with a guidebook in hand and 800 photographs in my backpack, I set out on a journey to visit each person. One of the people I met was Seloua Luste Boulbina, a French lady who was teaching philosophy at a college in Paris. After speaking with her, she promised to find a place in Paris where we could hold an exhibition. Not long after I returned to Tokyo, I received an email from Seloua that said, "I am going to Hong Kong, do you want to meet me there to discuss some possibilities?" I thought it would be a good opportunity, so I flew to Hong Kong to meet her and talk about the exhibition. She kept telling me that I needed to make the exhibition outline and statement clearer so that people could immediately understand what I wanted to do. In response, I said to her, "I've told you everything about the project, and I don't have experience exhibiting abroad, so it's difficult to know what to expect." She replied, "You are the artist, you should be more confident about what you do." The Paris exhibition was not realized, but the series of discussions I had with Seloua gave me the chance to consider the exhibition more thoroughly. In Japan, we often start by identifying the impossibilities, but in other parts of the world it might well be the opposite: they start by insisting on what they want to do, regardless of whether it can be realized. As I took the exhibition to many different countries, I found that while in Japan people tend to think "Everyone is patiently enduring the harsh situation, so should I" but abroad, it was more like, "People are doing as they like, so will I." It's not that one is better than the other, but nonetheless I am still a bit hesitant about expressing my opinions. Thanks to Seloua, I realized that outside Japan people communicate in entirely different ways. One day, whilst window-shopping at a market in Hong Kong, Seloua suddenly asked if I was angry. I was confused as it was totally unexpected. As she pointed to her stomach I realized that she had asked if I was hungry. "Oh, hungry! Yes, yes, I'm hungry!" Apart from my lack of distinguishing English vowels, I realized that French people don't pronounce the "H" sound. When we were alone without an interpreter, I communicated using my hopeless English and as many gestures as I could think of. I traveled to many countries over the course of the year and despite my English never really progressing, my body language skills improved significantly.

海外からの声 01　セルーア
Voice 01 Seloua

1.
プロジェクトを手伝うことになった理由は？
Why did you decide to help the Lost & Found project?

福島※で起きた災禍に心を痛めていたころ、Lost & Foundプロジェクトについて知ったの。TVでは、暮らしの全てを失った人々が写し出されていて、彼らは冷静で、カメラに向かって涙をみせることもなかった。世界中の人々が、日本で起きたことを悲しんでいたわ。日

本の人々に深く同情して、何か出来ないかと考えていたその時、日本人と結婚し東京に住む親友からムネマサを手伝ってくれないか、と打診されたの。ムネマサは毎年開催されているパリフォトのため、ちょうどパリを訪れていたから、早速彼に会ってLost & Foundについて聞いて、日本から彼が持ってきた写真と、Lost & Foundの活動を記録した映像を観せてもらった。それで私は、人々が地震後、瓦礫に埋もれた写真を集める活動をしていたことを知ったの。

※ 海外の報道では津波被害のあったエリアをまとめてFukushimaと表記されることがあった。

when i discovered lost and found project, i was touched by the catastrophic accident of fukushima. i watched people on the tv news who have lost everything in their life. they were stoic and hardly ever cried. i remember the emotion all around the world. i felt great sympathy and solidarity toward japanese people. a close friend of mine who lived a long time in tokyo and who is married with a japanese asked me what i can do for munemasa. munemasa went to paris for paris photo, an annual photo fair. he explained to me the lost and found project and showed me photos he brought with him from japan. then, i watched a video on the lost and found project and became aware of the huge work japanese people did to collect photos among the ruins of this disaster.

2.
初めてLost & Foundの写真を見た時、どのように思いましたか？
What did you think at first when you see the Lost & Found photo?

写真は、箱に入れられて丁寧に保管され、さらにそれぞれ小さな透明のプラスチックに入れられていた。たとえ、何が写っているの判らなくなってしまったものでも。その行為に強く心を打たれたわ。少しずつ、Lost & Foundの意義を理解する事もできた。被災地に住む人々は家を失い、生活と思い出までも失ったの。日本は世界で最もカメラ文化が発展した国の一つで、多くの人が沢山の写真を抱えていたはず。もしかしたら、写真の存在は他のどの国よりも重要なものだったのかも知れない。ときどき箱から取り出される、イメージの消えた写真たちには、いつも目を奪われた。色の模様が残るだけで、何も判別出来なかったけど、これらの写真たちも、ほかの写真と同じくらい大切なものであったはず。誰がそれらを取捨選択できると言うの？

photos were arranged in a box. each of the photos were filed in small transparent folders, even if there was nothing left to look at. i was strongly impressed. step by step i understood the lost and found project. people on fukushima's area have lost their houses, their lives and their memorabilia. even more : everyone knows that the japanese people traditionally take pictures everywhere they go and on every occasion. in this sense, photos are probably more important than elsewhere. i then understood the significance of the lost and found project. in the same time, i was affected by all "the photos without images". colors remained but nothing else. in the same time, these photos were as precious as the others. and who has any right to select photos?

3.
ムネマサとの思い出を教えて下さい。
Could you tell me your memory with Munemasa?

ムネマサのことは大好きよ。寛大で、冷静で、押し付けがましくもない立派な人間だと思う。彼は、全身全霊をこのプロジェクトに捧げ、効率よくプロジェクトを進めていたわ。また彼は、優れた写真家でもあるの。初めて会ったとき、写真集を買って、彼の写真がすぐに好きになった。特に、彼のディティールへ向ける視線に強く惹かれたの。例えば床の上、ウェディングドレスの側にケーキのくずが散らばっている風景。そんな些細なものごとから、素晴らしいイメージを引き出す力をムネマサはもっているわ。

i love munemasa. hés a good person. he's generous and reserved. he's never pushy. He gave his talent to the project wholeheartedly. he was also extremely efficient. i think that munemasa is a good photographer. the first time i met him i bought his photo book and appreciate a lot his photos, especially one of them which shows his sense of detail. on this photo, i observed a cakecrumb on the floor next to a bride dress... i believe that munemasa is able to create or organize great things through minute objects.

ラッコさん

海外での展示を企画するにあたって一番の問題は、ぼくが全く英語を

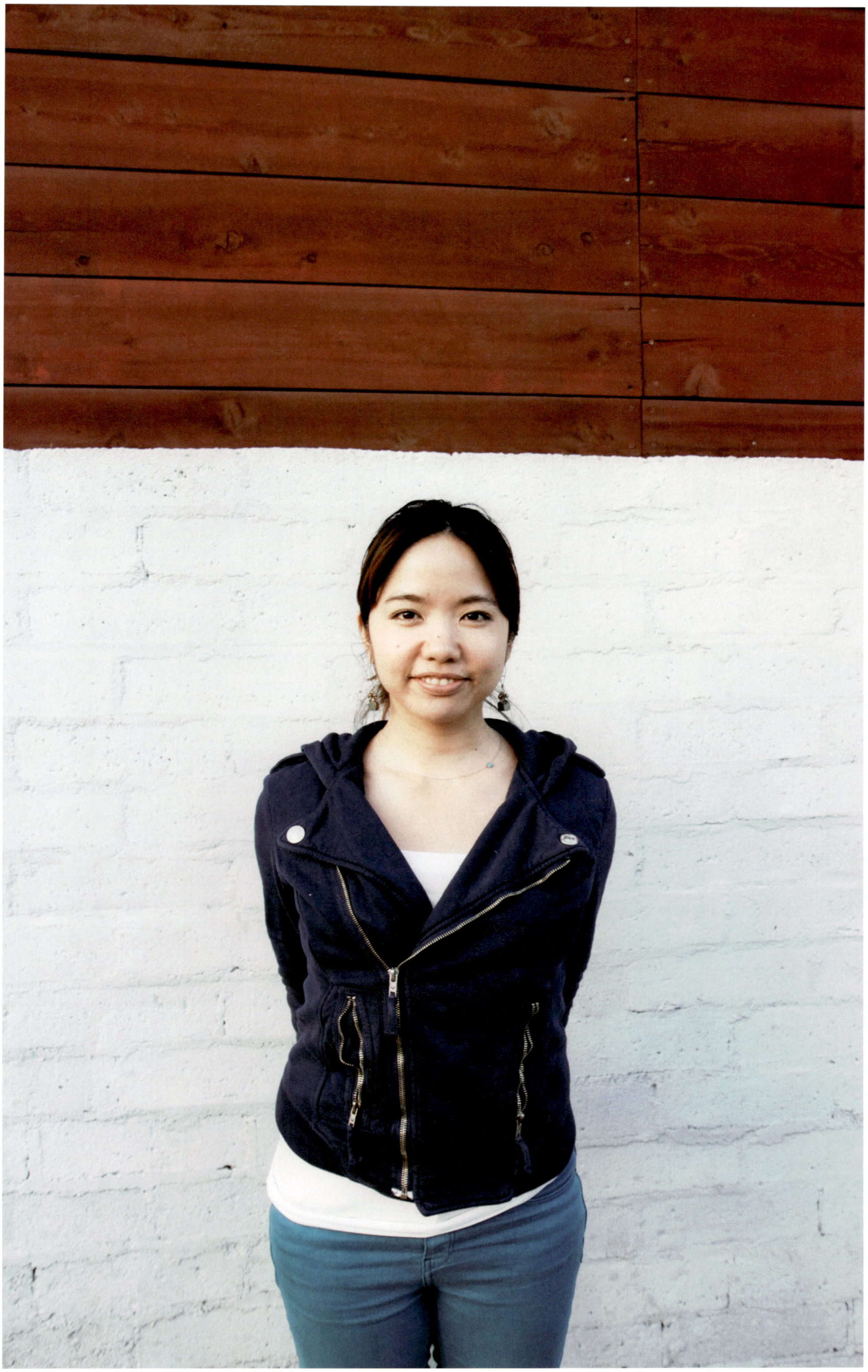

話せず海外の知り合いも皆無であることだった。そこで「思い出サルベージ」に参加していて、かつてロサンゼルスに住んでいて英語も話せる清水桜子さんをプロジェクトを始めるときにスカウトした。あだ名はラッコさんで、笑顔のキュートなヤングガールだ。ロサンゼルスに着いてから知ったのだけど、東京やニューヨークぐらいの町を想像していたら遥かに大きな場所だった。言葉も話せず車の運転もできないぼくは、通訳してもらい、運転してもらい、友達を紹介してもらって泊めてもらい、ニューヨークではラッコさんの実家にもお世話になった。まさに保護者だった。いつか恩返しをせねばと思っている。そしてぼくはアメリカについて最初の夜に行ったレストランに、財布もパスポートも入れたままのバッグを忘れた。そんなわけで初めて教えてもらった英語は「I left my bag」だった。

Lacco

The biggest and the most obvious problem when planning exhibitions abroad was that I had no English skills, or any friends overseas. Therefore, I found a young lady working on the Memory Salvage Project, Sakurako Shimizu, who helped me with organizing the exhibitions. She had previously lived in Los Angeles and spoke fluent English, as well as having the loveliest smile. Everyone called her Lacco. After arriving in LA, I immediately realized that the city was nothing like Tokyo or New York: it was enormous. Without any English or driving skills, I was beyond hope. Lacco was my interpreter and drove me around the city, introducing me to many of her friends, one of whom offered me a room to stay in. When I went to New York, Lacco even arranged for me to stay at her parents' house - she was like my guardian. On my first night in America I left my bag, with my wallet and passport inside, at the restaurant where we had eaten dinner. Accordingly, the first English sentence I learnt from her was "I left my bag." I feel deeply indebted to her.

展示2
2012.3.8-25
ヒロシワタナベスタジオ
ロサンゼルス、アメリカ合衆国

海外での展示場所を探し始めたときに、ラッコさんが知り合いのつながりでロサンゼルス在住の写真家の渡邊博史さんを紹介してくれた。写真展のために来日していた渡邊さんに会いに行くと、広いスタジオがあるから運営を自分たちでやるなら好きに使っていいですよと言ってくれた。これで1ヶ月のロサンゼルス滞在が決まった。会期中に震災での経験を伝えるトークイベントを企画し、山元町の星さんにもアメリカに来てもらった。展示をしたスタジオは夜になると赤外線の無人センサーを入れていたのだけど、この頃毎晩のようにセンサーが反応して警備会社の人がやってくるということがあった。夜のスタジオには誰もいなかったけれど、アラームは鳴り続けた。星さんと、もしかしたら夜になるとお化けが歩き回ってるのかもねー、なんてことを話していた。山元町では夜になると海辺に多くの人影が歩き回っているという噂が広まっているらしかった。こうやってみんなで海外旅行に来れたんだから怒りはしないでしょ、まぁでも急に海外につれてこられてビックリしてるだろうなあ、というような話をした。この会期中にラッコさんの知り合いで、ニューヨーク在住のジャーナリストのジェイクさんの主催した大震災の追悼イベントに参加することになった。また、ジェイクさんのつながりで、NEWYORKERのwebサイトでプロジェクトのことを紹介してもらってから、海外での展示の認知度が上がったように思う。

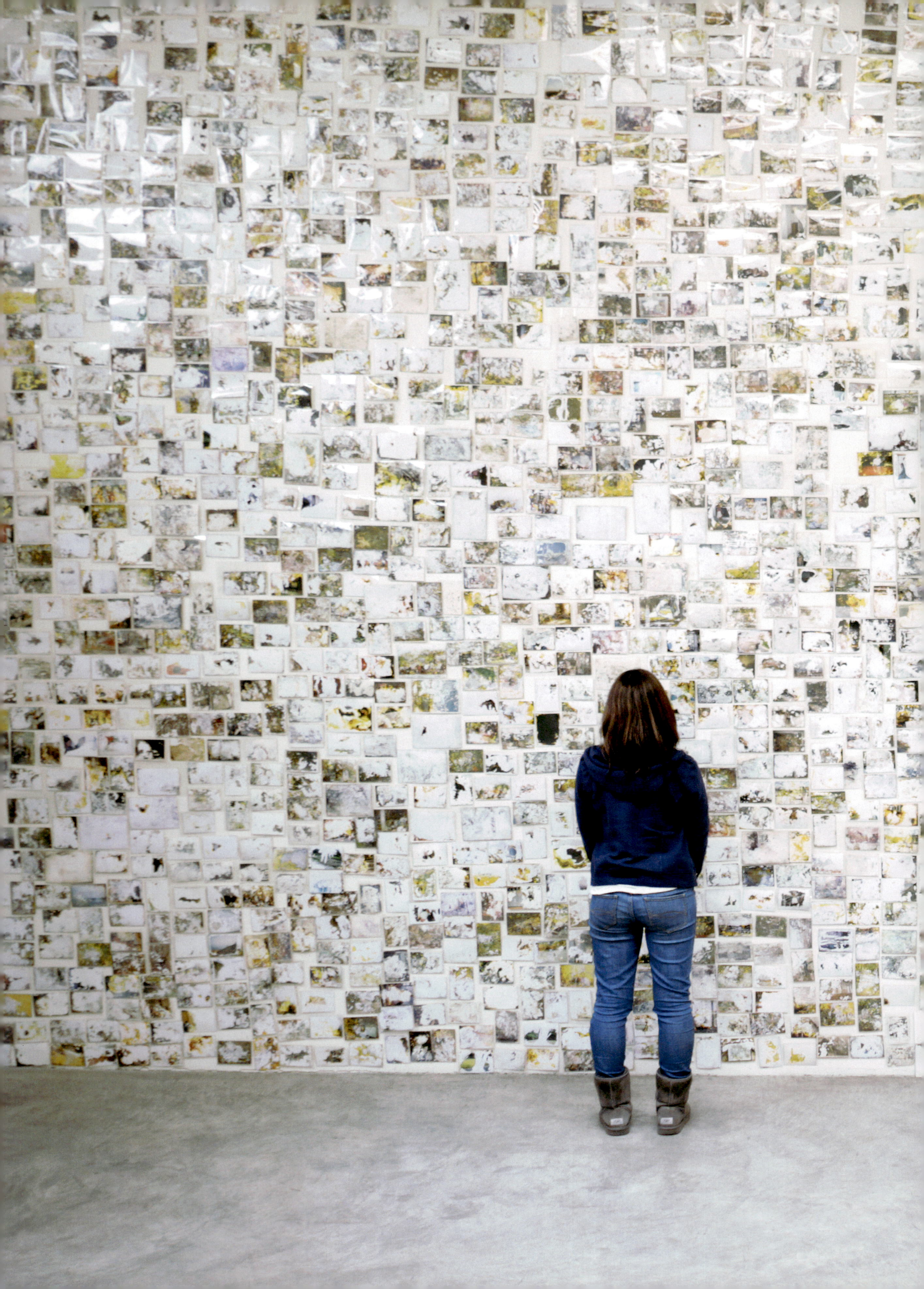

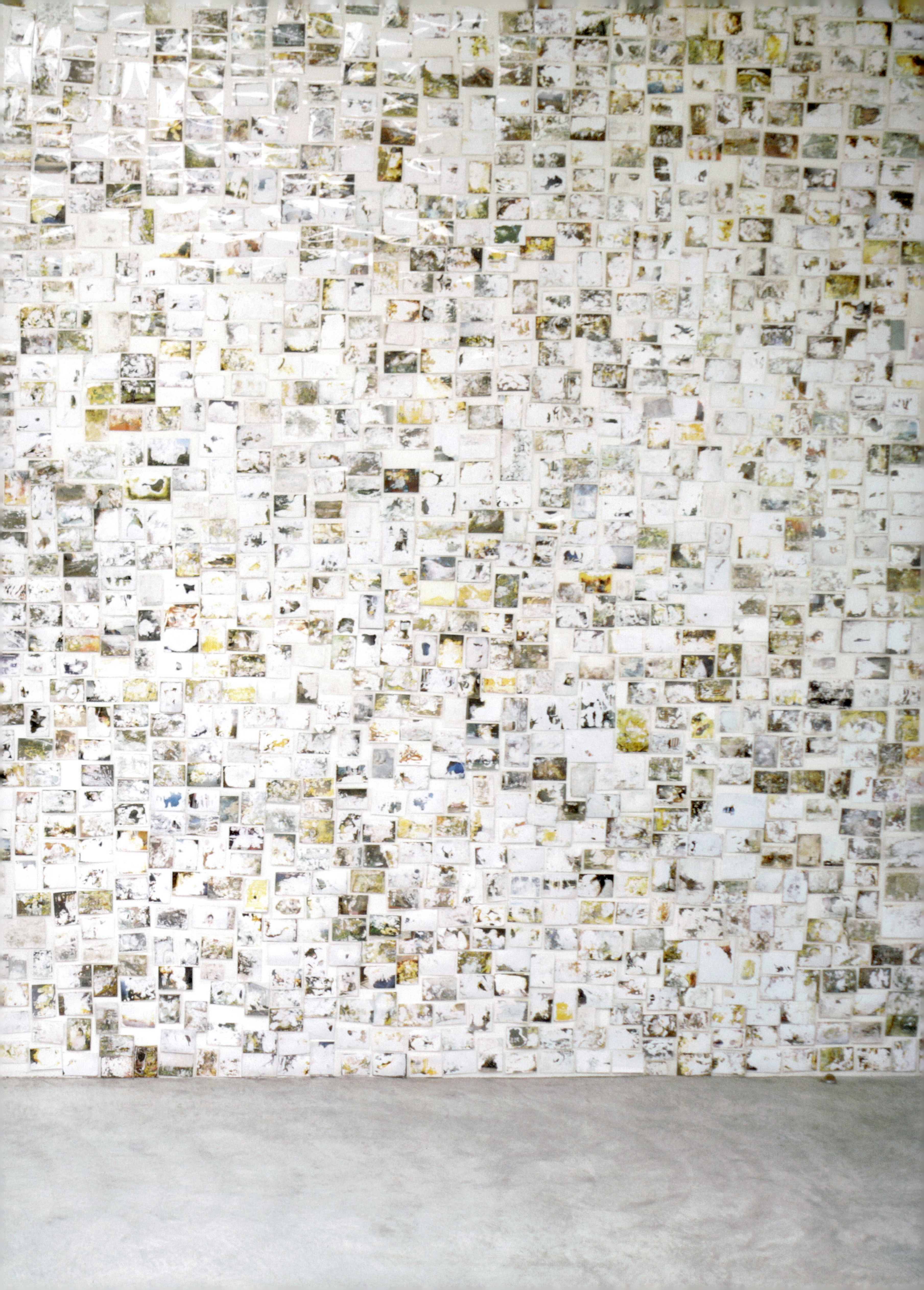

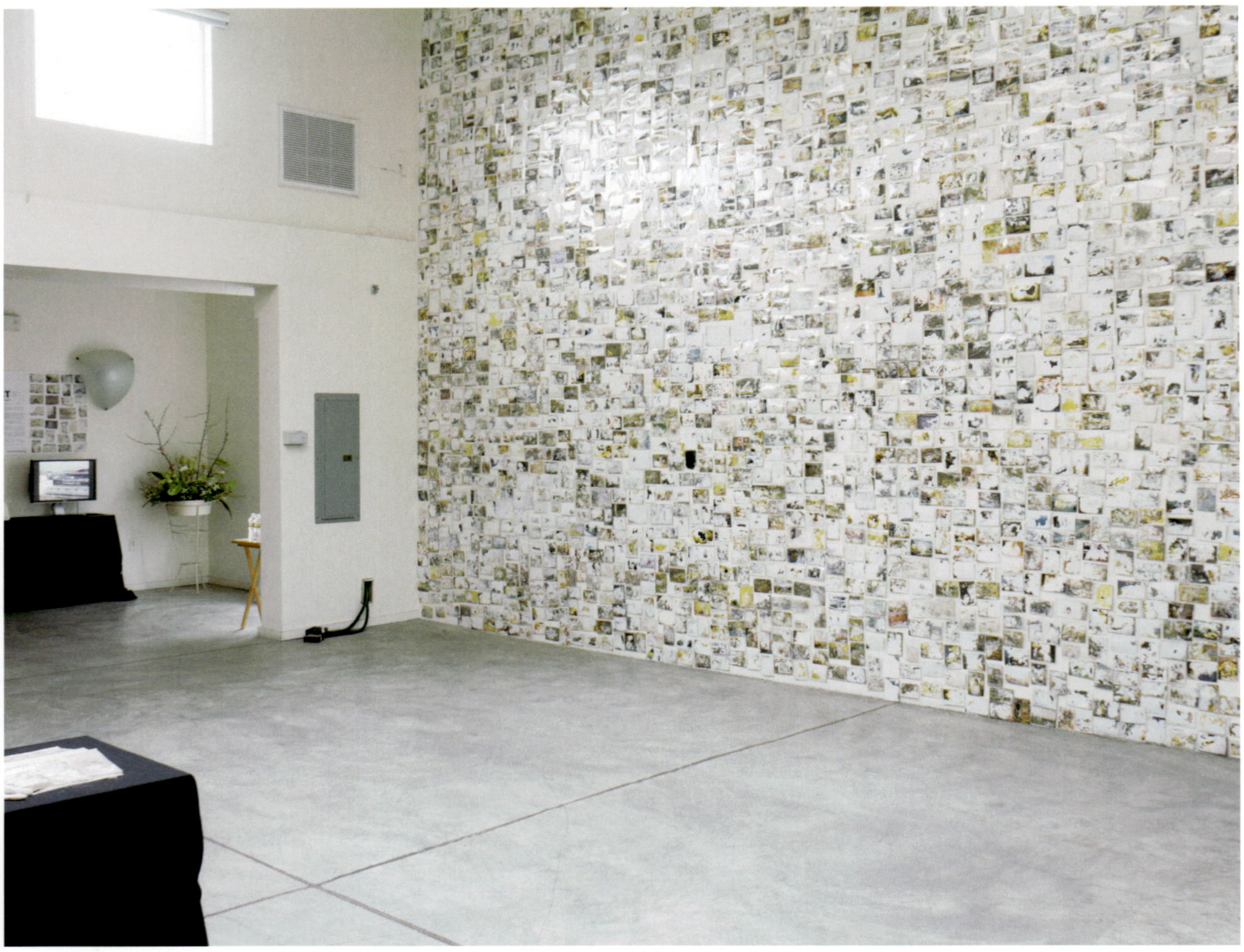

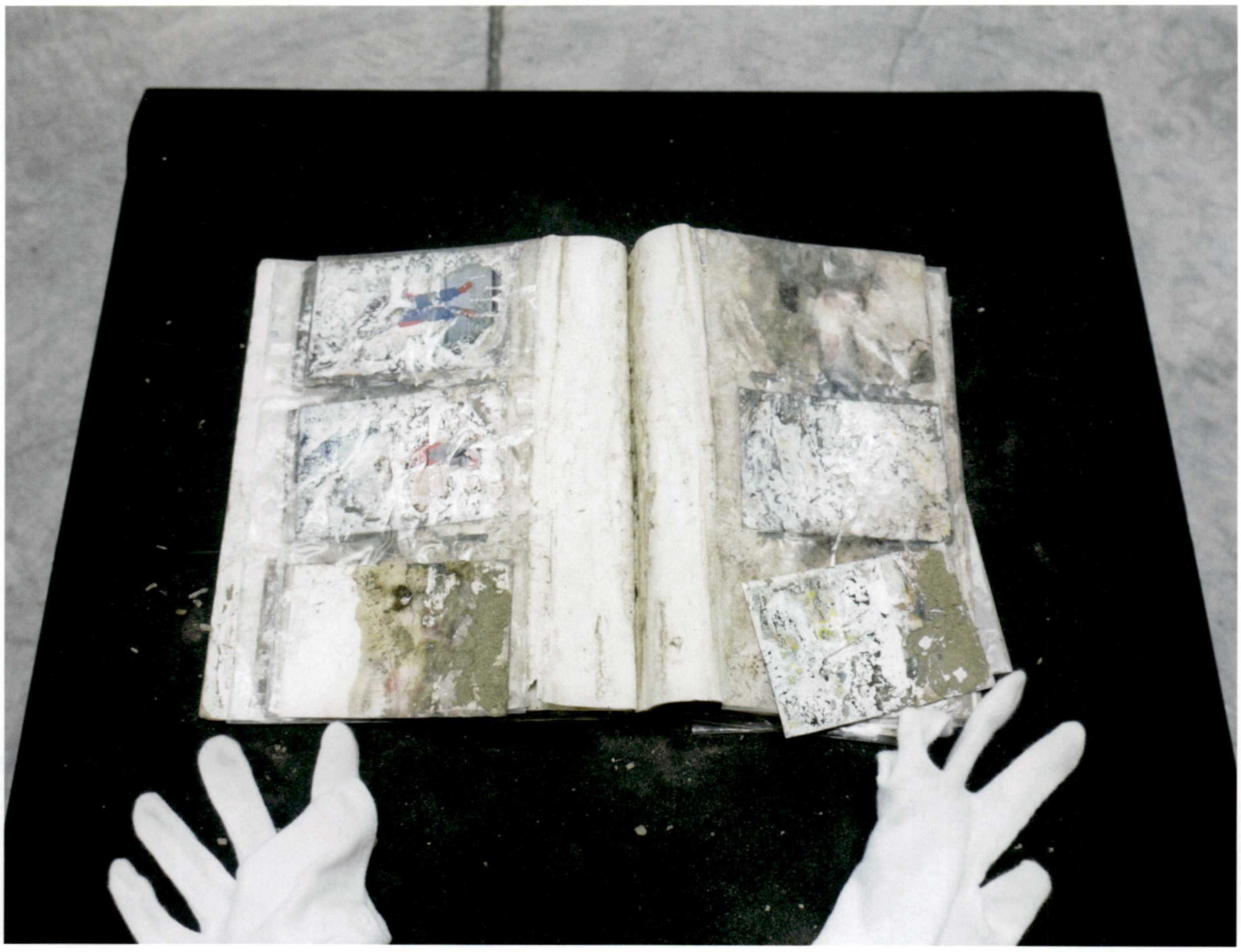

The Second exhibition
2012 3. 8-25
Hiroshi Watanabe Studio,
Los Angeles, USA

Not long after we started looking for a venue, Lacco introduced me to Hiroshi Watanabe, a photographer living in LA. When Hiroshi came to Tokyo for a show, I arranged to meet with him to explain about the exhibition. He told me that he had a big studio in LA, so provided that we could organize the exhibition ourselves, we could use the space as we liked. We later decided to visit LA for a month. During the exhibition we arranged a talk about our experiences during and after the earthquake and so I invited Hoshi-san from Yamamoto-cho to come to LA to join us. At night, the studio's security system was activated and almost every night of our stay, the alarm would go off. Not long after a security patrol would come by to investigate. The alarm continued to go off, even though no one was in the studio. Hoshi-san and I thought that maybe the ghosts were visiting us. According to him, there was a rumor that many ghostly figures were being seen walking on the beach in Yamamoto-cho. "Well," he said, "we brought the ghosts with us, they should be happy to travel abroad for free, but maybe they are a bit surprised to suddenly find themselves in LA." During my stay in America, I visited New York to participate in the one-year memorial event for the earthquake organized by Jake Price, a journalist based in New York. Jake worked on an article on the exhibition for the New Yorker Magazine's website, which increased interest in the exhibition.

展示3
2012.4.2-27
アパチャー・ファウンデーション
ニューヨーク、アメリカ合衆国

アパチャーでの展示は、日本で写真集の編集や写真家とのコラボイベントを数多く手がけるアイヴァンさんの紹介で実現することになった。日本とアメリカは写真サイズの規格が違うから、アメリカの家庭でよく見かけるようにフォトフレームに入れて展示をした方がもっと伝わりやすいのではないか、との意見をもらったので、ロサンゼルスのリサイクルショップをいくつもまわってフォトフレームを買い集めた。あるお店でそこにあったフォトフレームをほぼ全部レジに持っていく

と、店員のおじいさんに「こんなに何に使うんだ？」と聞かれた。こういうプロジェクトのために日本から来てるんだと説明すると、「お前らいいことやってるな！全部１ドルにしてやるよ」と言って安くしてくれた。日本だとレジの人が勝手に値段を変えるなんてことはあり得ないので、アメリカっておもしろい国だなあと思った。ちなみにそのとき、隣にいたおばあさんは「私なら全部タダにしてあげるのに、こいつ、せこいのよ」なんて冗談を言っていた。ニューヨークでの滞在中は、ラッコさんの実家に泊めてもらった。窓際にはフォトフレームに入った家族の記念写真が並べてあって、清水家の歴史を眺めることができた。日本の家ではそういうふうに写真を並べているのを見たことがなかったけれど、これがアメリカンな家庭か、こういうのもいいもんだなあと思った。日本で部屋に飾られている写真といえば遺影くらいだろう。

The Third exhibition
2012 4.2-27
Aperture Foundation,
New York, USA

The exhibition at Aperture was made possible with the help of Ivan Vartanian, a Tokyo-based editor of numerous photography books and the organizer of various photography-related events. He told us that the standard sizes of photographs differ in the United States and that it would be nice to exhibit the photographs in the same frames that are often found hanging in Amercian living rooms. I visited thrift shops throughout LA to buy all kinds of photo frames. At one shop, I took all the photo frames I could find to the cashier, where the elderly owner asked me what I planned to do with them. I explained the project to him and told him that I had come all the way from Japan for the exhibition. He replied by saying, "You guys are doing a great thing! OK, I will sell you these frames for a dollar each." That was one moment when I realized how amusing Americans could be; it would have been impossible to get such a big discount in Japan. At the time, an old lady jokingly said to us, "If I were him, I would give you all of them for free, but he's too greedy." In New York I stayed at Lacco's parents' house. They had many framed family pictures by the window, from which I could trace the history of the Shimizu family. In Japan, it is uncommon to have that many photographs in

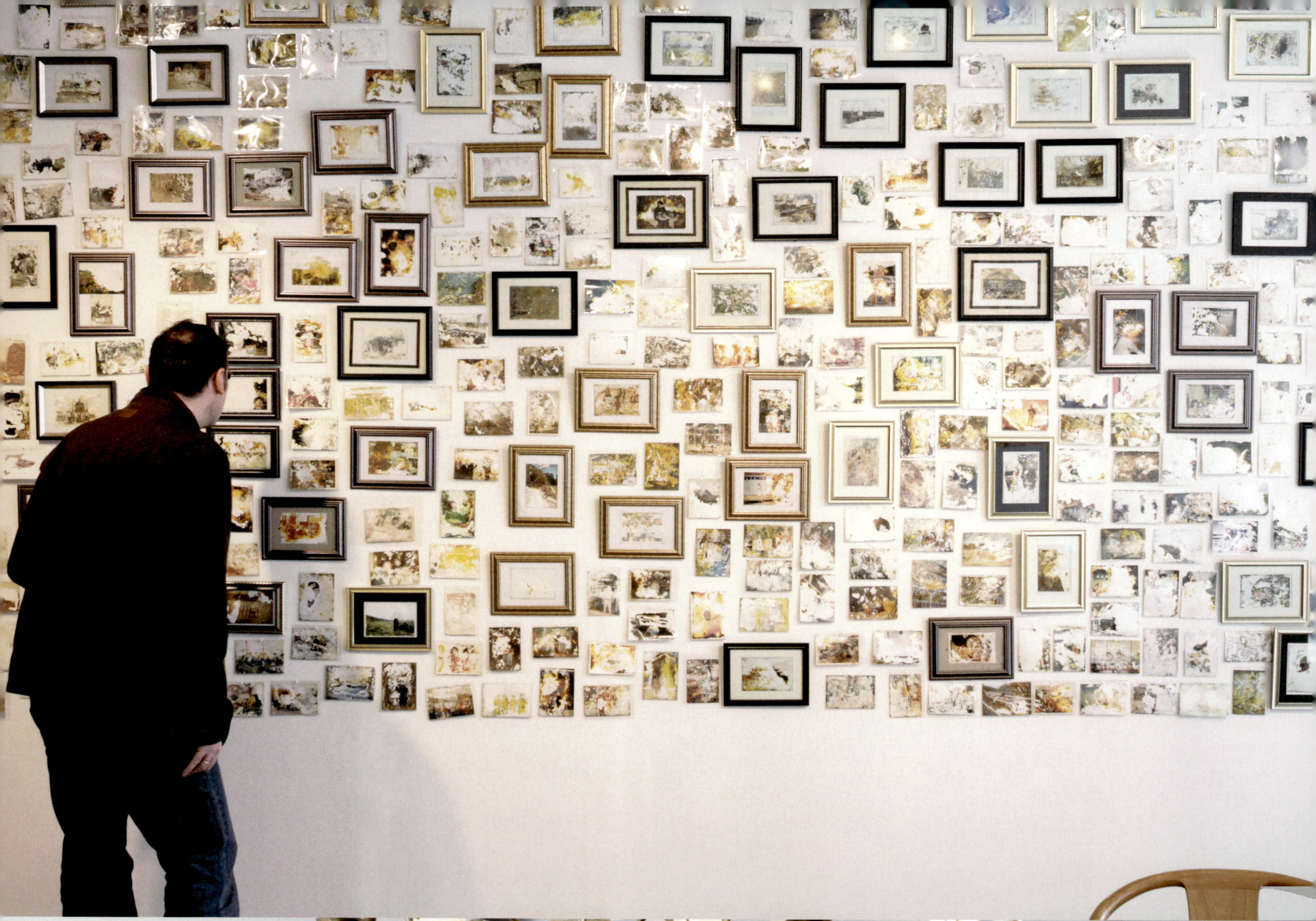

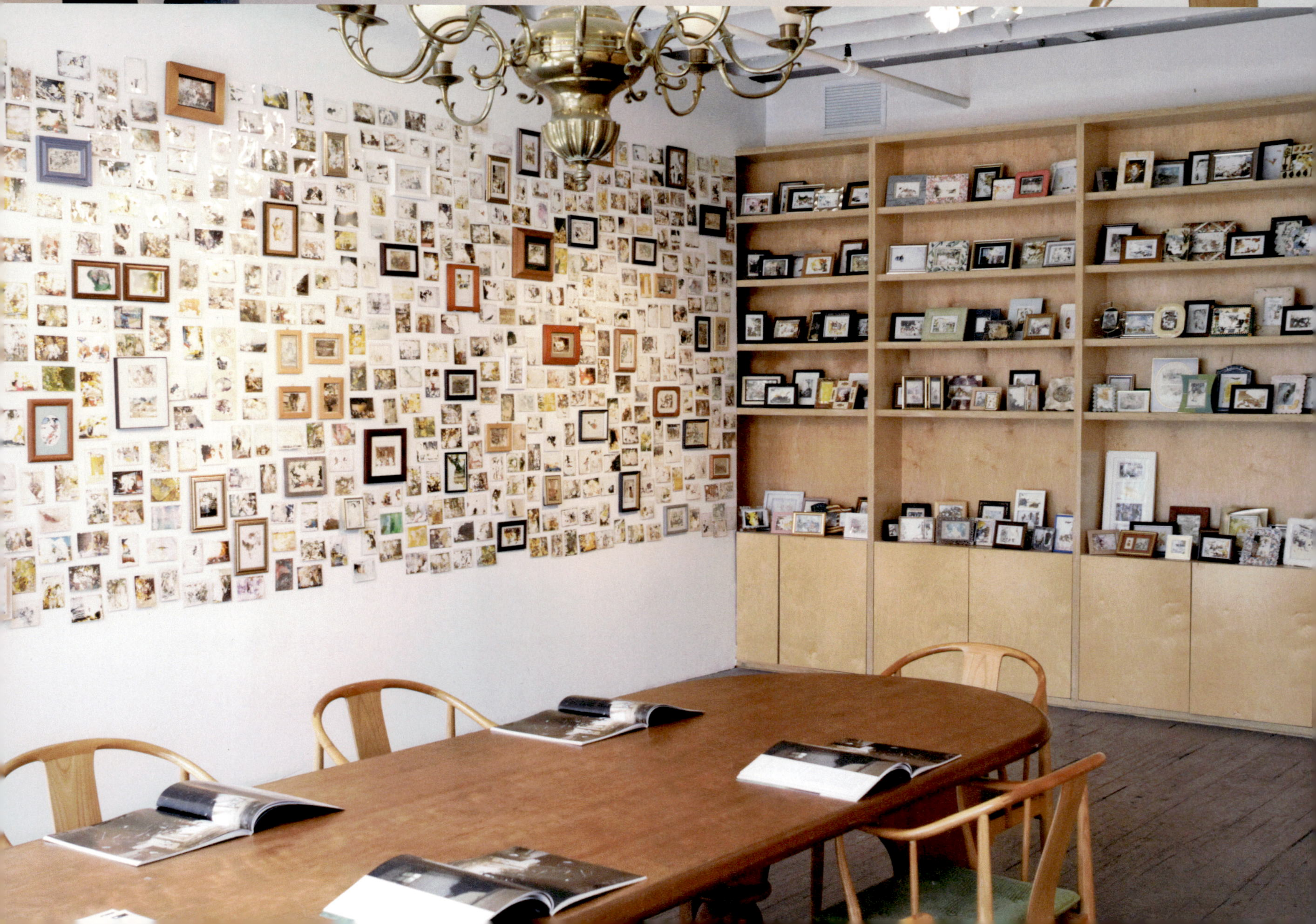

the living room and so I was astonished to see how differently the Americans dealt with private photographs. It was something that I found particularly heartwarming, as the only photographs I could remember seeing in Japanese rooms were solemn black and white portraits of deceased family members.

展示4
2012.6.5-7.1
現代写真センター
メルボルン、オーストラリア

メルボルンでの展示は写真家の旗手浩さんの友達で、キュレーターでありアーティストでもあるクリスチャンさんが企画をしてくれた。旗手さんは一緒に飲みに行ったりする兄ちゃん的存在の先輩写真家で、自費でオーストラリアまで同行し通訳もやってくれた。2週間ほどメルボルンの近くに住むクリスチャンの両親の家に泊めてもらっていたのだけど、クリスチャンはよく酔っぱらってパパと喧嘩をしていた。二人を引き離し、旗手さんはクリスチャンと話し、ぼくはパパの話を聞いていたのだけど、英語のわからないぼくは半分も理解できなかった。「ムネマサ、理解してるか？」「３０％！」「オーケー」というやり取りが滞在中何度かあった。またある日の夜、みんなでワインを飲んでいるとパパが箱を出してきた。開けると中には、家族の写真がたくさん入っていた。クリスチャンの小さい頃の写真や若い頃のパパやママの写真もあって、それを見ながらいろんな話をした。

写真を中心に和気あいあいとした夜だった、なんだかんだで仲のいいステキな家族だった。クリスチャンの反抗期が早く終わることを祈る。

The Fourth exhibition
2012 6.5-7.1
The Centre for Contemporary Photography,
Melbourne, Australia

The exhibition in Melbourne was organized by Kristian Haggblom, a curator and artist, who had been introduced to me by Hiroshi Hatate. Hatate-san was a fellow photographer who always acted as if he was my older brother, and he paid to come to Australia with his own money to assist me as an interpreter. Over the two-week period, I stayed at Kristian's parents' house outside of Melbourne. While I was there, Kristian often got drunk and fought with his father, at which point Hatate-san and I had to pull them apart. Hatate-san would comfort Kristian, and I would listen to what his father had to say, even though I could barely understand. "Munemasa, do you understand what I am saying?" "About 30% of it!" "Okay." Such conversations occurred a number of times whilst I was there. Another night we were drinking wine when Kristian's father brought out a box containing many of their family's photographs. There were photographs of Kristian as a little boy and of his parents as a young couple... we talked about many things as we looked through the photographs. It was an enjoyable night and the photographs worked to smoothen our relationship. They were a very close family and I hoped that Kristian would soon overcome his rebellious phase.

海外からの声02　クリスチャン

Voice 02 Kristian

1.
Lost & Foundプロジェクトを手伝うことになった理由は？
Why did you decide to help the Lost & Found project?

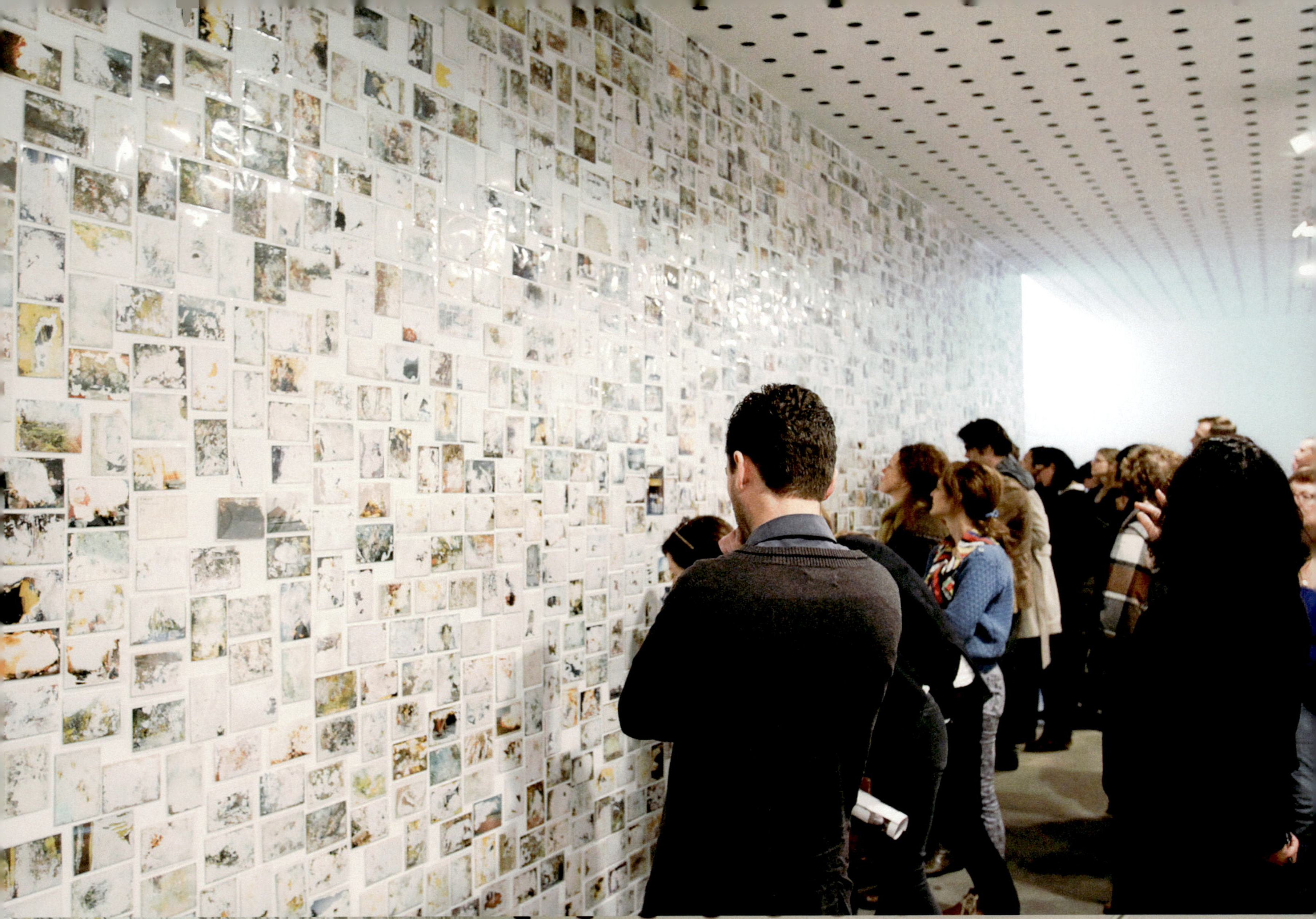

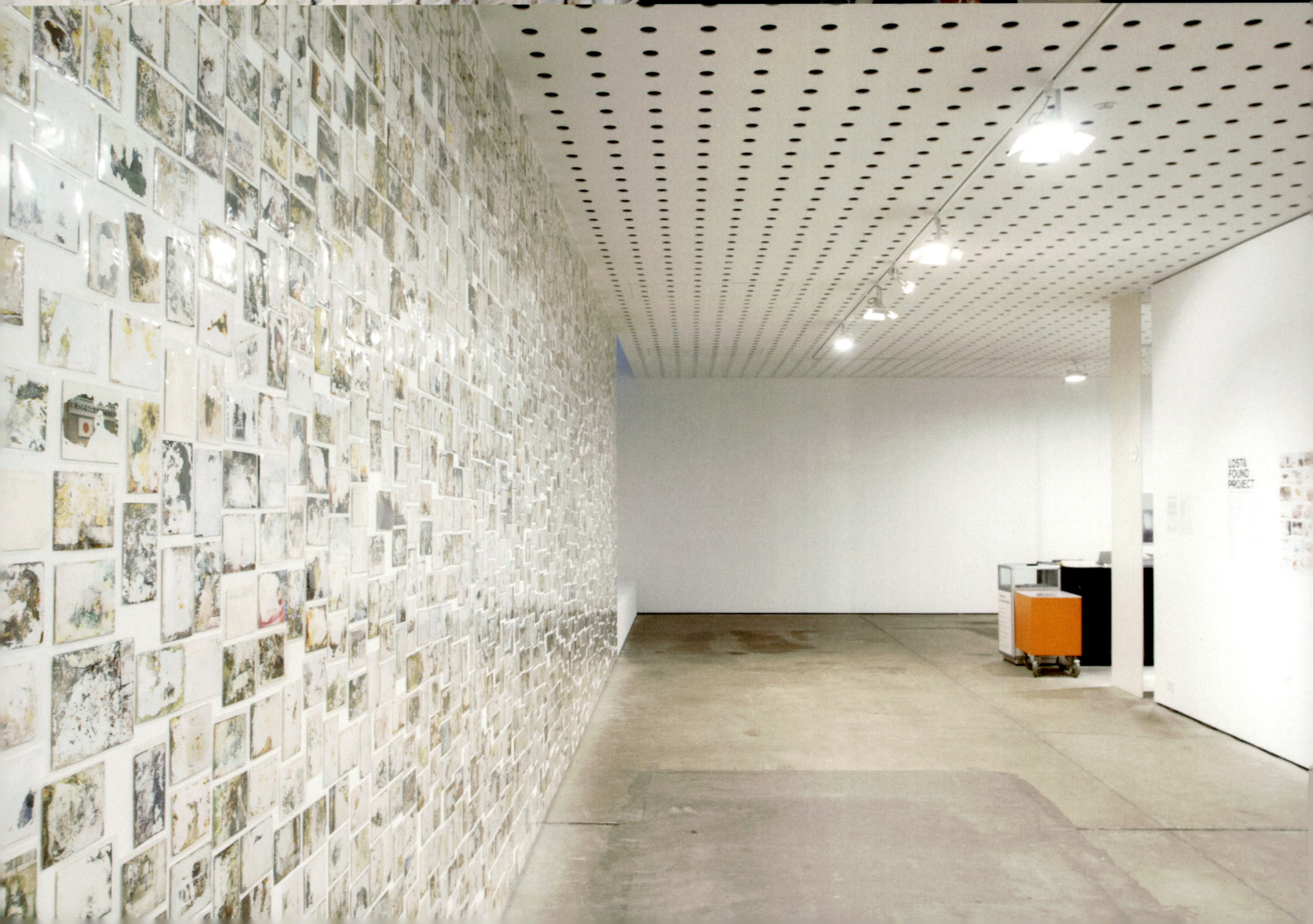
LOST&
FOUND
PROJECT

地震の後、次から次へと現地から送られて来る報道写真に戦慄を覚えた。ちょうど友人の写真家たち(ルイス・ポーターとジョージア・メタクサス)と食事をしていて、テレビに写し出されることが、ただ信じられずにいたよ。僕は日本に7年住んで、妻も日本人だし、娘もコユキっていうんだけど、目にしたことが実際に起きていることだとは思えなかったんだ。現地で起きている現実の恐怖から切り離されていたような気がして、すぐに何か援助をしようと考えた。実際日本に行くこともももちろん考えたけど、オーストラリアでの生活があるので難しかった。だから、このプロジェクトについて知った時は、是が非でも手伝おうと思ったよ。知らせてくれて、感謝してる。また、個人的にも写真の力とその限界についてはずっと考えていたことだから、Lost & Foundは僕にとっても、重要なプロジェクトでもあったんだ。

I was shocked and horrified to see the flow of media images - live - when the accident happened. I was having dinner with some photographer friends of mine (Louis Porter and Georgia Metaxas) and we couldn't believe what was unfolding on television. As you know, I lived in Japan for 7 years and have a Japanese wife and a daughter Koyuki but what I was seeing didn't seem real, I felt disconnected from the horror on the ground. I very quickly knew that I had to assist. At one stage I did plan to go back to Japan and assist but life in Australia kept me here. This seemed like the perfect opportunity - so thank you very much. And to use and question the power of photography is something thats very important to me.

2.

初めてLost & Foundの写真を見た時、どのように思いましたか？
What did you think at first when you see the Lost & Found photo?

正直言って、箱に入れられた上に、それぞれプラスチックに入れられた写真を見た時は、なんて几帳面な人なんだろうと驚いたよ！実際のイメージを見て、津波により欠損したイメージの断片に強く興味をもったんだ。そして、そこに残る顔、特に子供たちの顔に、とても悲しい思いをした。

Honestly, when I first saw the neatly packed boxes with the plastic slips over the photographs in your suitcase, I thought you were very organised! Looking at the actual images I was very intrigued by the damaged details "made" by the incident and also saddened by visible faces, and especially children.

3.
観客の反応は、どのようなものでしたか？
Could you tell me how the audience's response was like?

反応はとても良かったね。人々は強い興味をもって、またプロジェクトを支援したいと申し出てくれる人も多かったし。僕がキュレートしたウォールフラワー・フォトメディア・ギャラリーでの展示では、本当に素晴らしい反応を得ることができて、オープニングのスピーチで涙を流してしまったくらいだ。

The audience response was amazing, people were so intrigued and willing to support the project. There was such a supportive response at the space I curate, Wallflower Photomedia Gallery, that I actually (embarrassingly) cried during the opening speech.

4.
ムネマサとの思い出を教えて下さい。
Could you tell me your memory with Munemasa?

えぇと、ムネマサっておかしな人だよね。でも、とてもまじめで、ひたむきで優しい人間だよ。プロジェクト自体は真剣なものだったけど、オーストラリアに彼が来た時は、旗手 浩（１９９９年に僕が東京で初めて会った写真家が彼だった）と三人で、良い時間を過ごした。ムネさんがこのプロジェクトの達成と海外への巡回展示にかけた努力は、賞賛に値すると思う。

Ahhh Munemasa is a funny man, but also very serious, genuine and giving. It was a sombre project but we also had a great time in Australia with Hiroshi Hatate who is an old friend of mine (actually one of the first photographers I met in Tokyo way back in 1999). Mune-san's efforts in getting this together and touring it extensively should be commended.

展示5
2012.7.2 - 8.31
フォトギャラリーインターナショナル（PGI）
東京、日本

PGIは日本の大御所の写真家が数多く所属する伝統のあるギャラリーで、ニューヨークでの展示を見たディレクターの高橋朗さんに声をかけてもらい展示をすることになった。今までで一番狭い空間で、両面から写真に挟まれることで、見る人が否応なく写真と対峙させられるような展示になった。展示を見た川田喜久治さんから、プロジェクトの写真を複写して作品にしたいとの提案をいただいた。尊敬する大先輩とコラボというとおこがましいが、応援してもらえたことはとても励みになった。運営費にしてくれと少し寄付ももらってしまった。

※東松照明、細江英公などと共にVIVOを結成した日本の重要な写真家。

The Fifth exhibition
2012 7.2 - 8.31
Photo Gallery International,
Tokyo, Japan

PGI is a gallery with a long and illustrious history, having represented many legendary Japanese photographers. After seeing the exhibition in New York, the gallery's director Akira Takahashi approached us and offered the chance to show the project at PGI. At that time, it was the smallest space we had exhibited in, so the visitors were forced to view the walls of photographs up close. Kikuji Kawada* saw the exhibition and proposed a collaborative project in which he would re-photograph the images from the project. I felt daunted about working with a master of photography whom I had always looked up to, but the offer gave me great encouragement, and he even donated some money to the project.
*An important figure in the history of Japanese photography, Kawada was a founding member of the VIVO group with Shomei Tomatsu and Eiko Hosoe.

LOST&
FOUND
PROJECT
Family Photos Swept by 3.11 East Japan Tsunami

展示6
2012.7.28-29
東川町国際写真フェスティバル
北海道、日本

東川町国際写真フェスティバルは、年に一回国内や海外から多くの写真関係者が集まるお祭りで、運営に関わる石毛大介さんの紹介で展示をすることになった。ここでは運営のボランティアとしていろんなところから写真を学ぶ若者がやってきていて、彼らの作品をいろいろと見せてもらいながら、ぼくも自分の作品づくりも頑張ってやらないとこのままボランティアマンになってしまうなあと思った。

The Sixth exhibition
2012 7.28-29
Higashikawa International Photo Festival,
Hokkaido, Japan

Higashikawa International Photo Festival is an annual photo festival that brings together photographers, gallerists, collectors and critics from Japan and abroad. We had the opportunity to present the project, thanks to a member of the committee, Daisuke Ishige. Many young photography students from around the country were working as volunteers, and as I looked through their works, I realized that I had to focus more on my own photo-making or else I may end up as a volunteer myself.

展示7
2012.9.12-10.27
インターセクションフォーザアーツ
サンフランシスコ、アメリカ合衆国

サンフランシスコの展示は、ニューヨークと同じくアイヴァンさんの

紹介でインターセクションフォーザアーツのケビンさんが企画運営をしてくれた。ここではプロジェクトの展示とあわせて、8人の地元のアーティストにこの被災した写真のイメージと情報を提供し、彼らの解釈で作ってもらった作品も展示した。正直なところ、会ったことのない人たちからどんな作品が出てくるのか不安もあったけれど、作品を目にすると真摯に向き合ってくれたことがよくわかって安心した。みんなステキな人たちだった。もっと英語ができればいろいろ話せたのになあと思う。そしてサンフランシスコでは重要ミッションが課せられた。ケビンからオープニングで短いスピーチをしてくれないかと頼まれたのだ。日本語を英語に翻訳してもらって何度も読む練習をしたのだが、本番では英語への苦手意識が炸裂し声も手も震え、散々だった。ビールでごまかせる緊張じゃなかった。

The Seventh exhibition
2012 9.12 - 10.27
Intersection for the Arts,
San Francisco, USA

In addition to the New York exhibition, the show in San Francisco was made possible by Ivan. He introduced me to Kevin B. Chen, who organized the exhibition at Intersection for the Arts. We supplied images and information about the damaged photographs to eight local artists, who in turn created works that were presented alongside photographs from the project. To be honest, having never met the artists I was worried about what would happen, but after viewing their works, I could clearly see their sincerity. Everyone was amazing and I found myself wishing that I could speak English more fluently. In San Francisco I was given an important task: Kevin asked me to give a short speech on opening night. The text was translated and I tried hard to memorize each line and the correct pronunciation of the words, but on the night I grew self-conscious about my poor English skills. My hands and voice started to quiver. It was awful, and even the beers couldn't sooth my nerves.

海外からの声 03　ケビン

Voice 03 Kevin

1.
Lost & Foundプロジェクトを手伝うことになった理由は？
Why did you decide to help the Lost & Found project?

僕たちは、アートを入り口に、広く社会的、文化的、そして政治的問題に取り組むアートスペースを運営している。Lost & Foundプロジェクトについて聞いた時、アメリカの人々に対し、2011年3月11日に日本で起きた地震と津波が引き起こした悲劇についての意識を高める良い機会になると思ったんだ。デジタル化が進む世の中で、写真プリントの効力は、いまだにその強さを失っていない。Lost & Foundと協働することで、災害の大きさについて議論する場を提供し、そしてあの日以来失われ、変化を余儀なくされた幾千もの生活を、きちんと考える機会を設けることができると思ったよ。

As an arts organization that looks at larger social, cultural, and political issues of our time through the lens of art, when we first heard about the Lost & Found project, we felt that it could be a powerful opportunity to raise awareness of the tragedy of the March 11, 2011 earthquake and tsunami in Japan with American audiences. Even as we continue to move into a digital world, the power of a printed photograph continues to resonate universally. We felt that by working with Lost & Found, we could create an accessible platform on which to talk about the immensity of the disaster and also to create a respectful way to honor the thousands of lives that were altered or lost on that day.

2.
初めてLost & Foundの写真を見た時、どのように思いましたか？

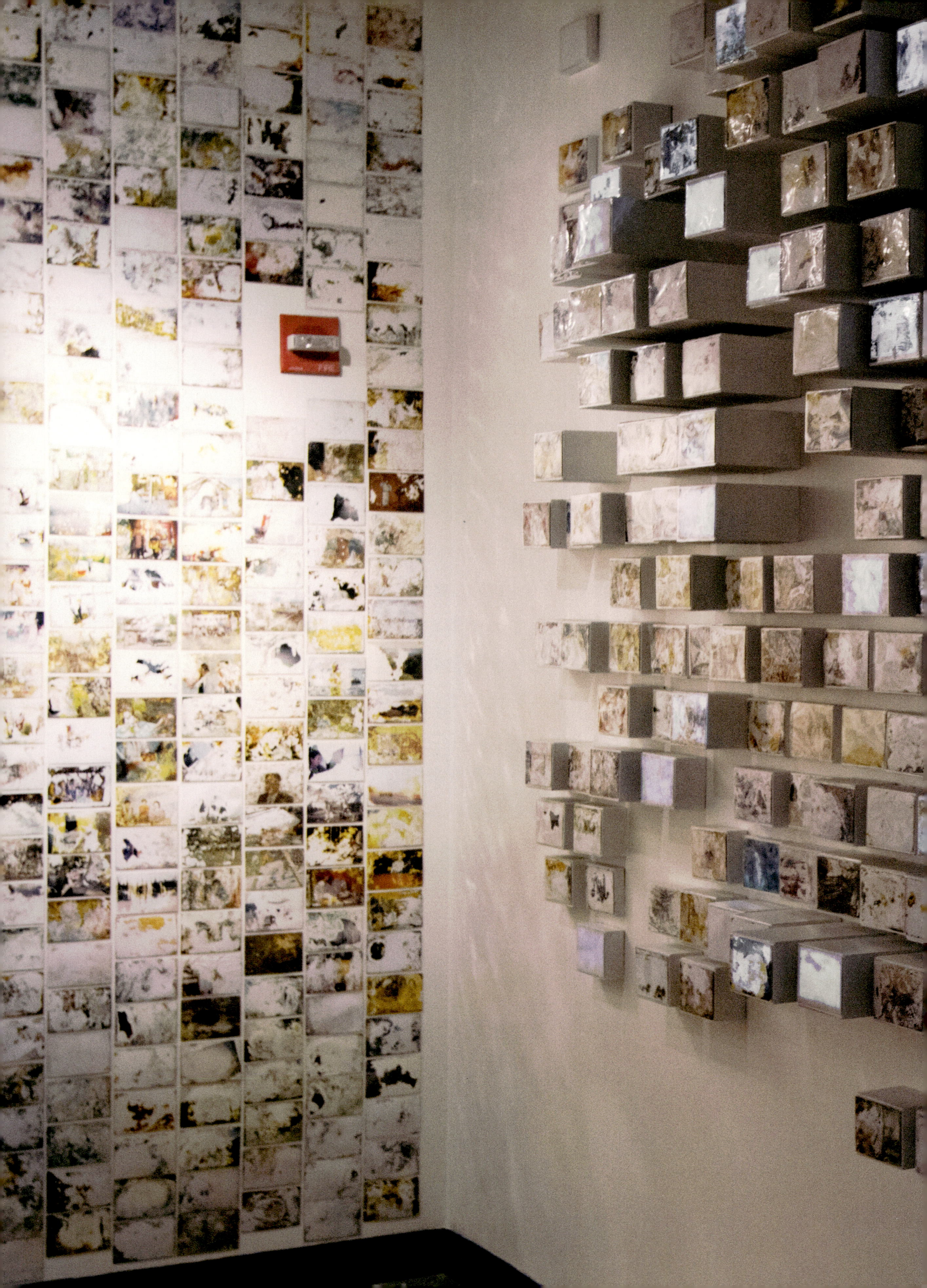

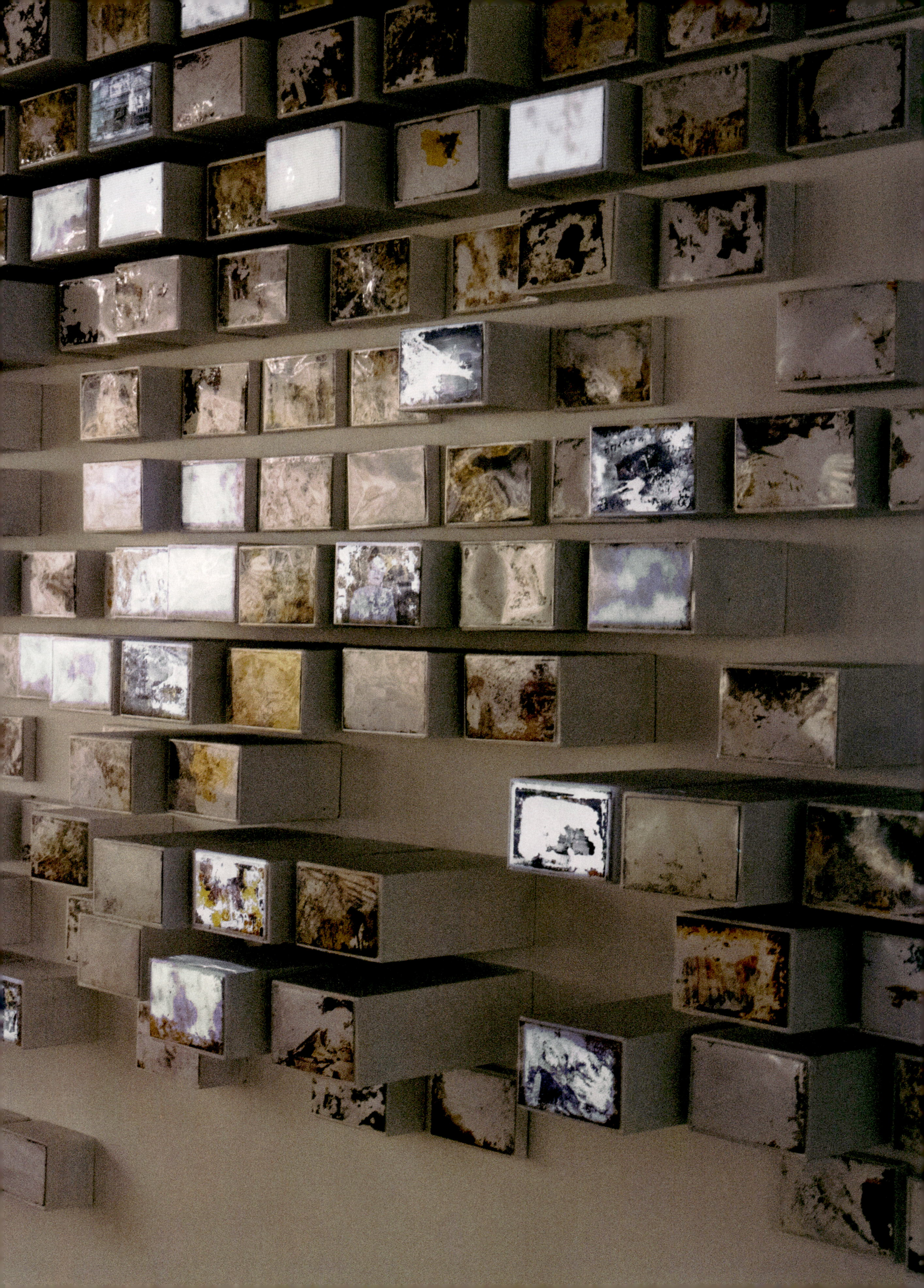

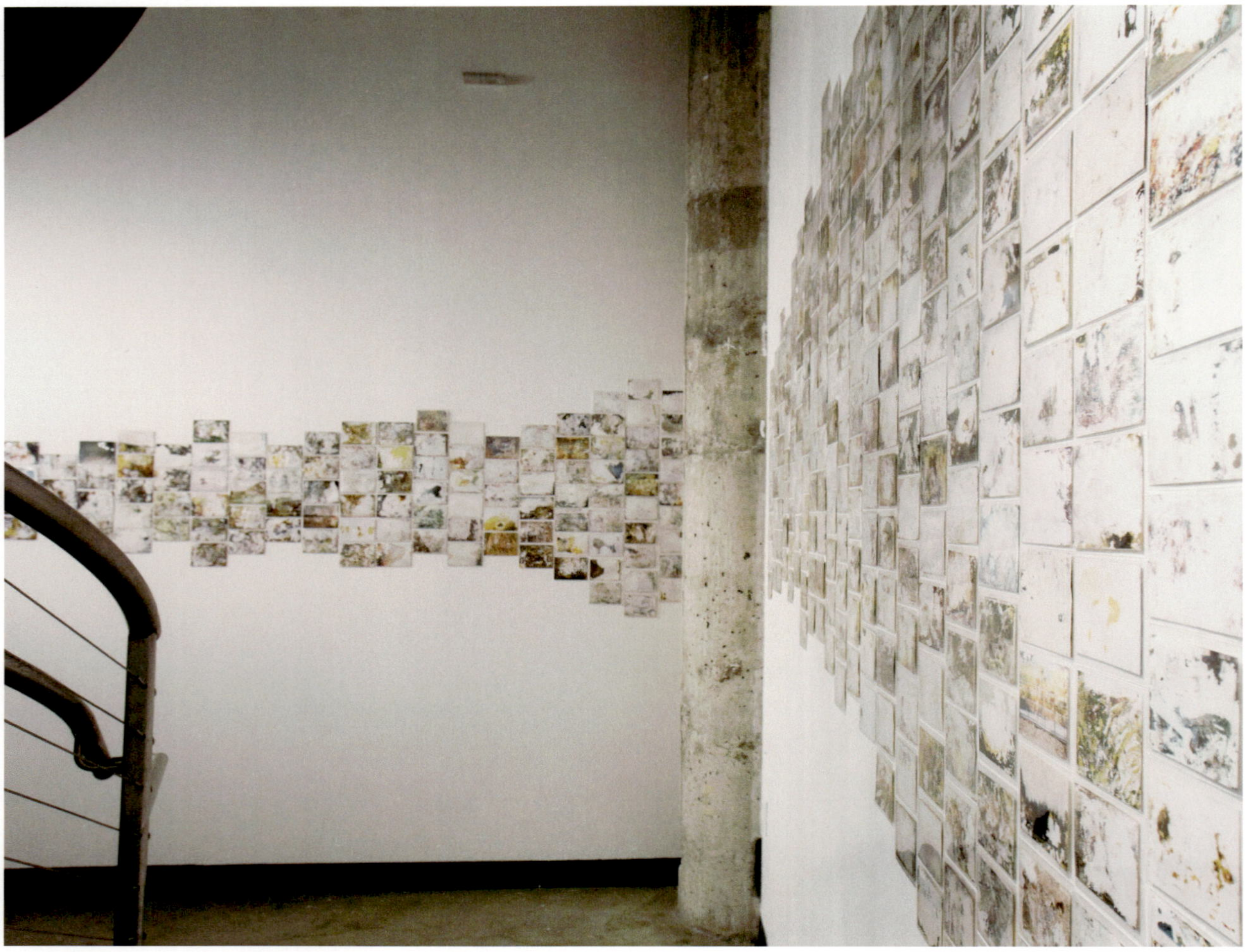

What did you think at first when you see the Lost & Found photo?

東京からサンフランシスコに届けられたLost & Foundプロジェクトの写真を初めて目にした時は、涙が止まらなかった。写真とは、いとも簡単に地理的・言語的・文化的な差異を飛び越えて我々に迫ってくる表現なんだ。誰もが、写真を見て何かを感じとることができる。出産、結婚式、卒業式の写真。休日の団らん、旅行、野球の試合で撮った写真。親友、母親、父親、きょうだいと一緒に撮った写真。夕食、愛犬、部屋の写真。そんな、何千もの写真を見ながら、それらが抱える数多くの思いと記憶に圧倒されたよ。捉えようのないほどの大きさで起きた地震と津波の悲しみを、とても個人的な、人間的な尺度で、このプロジェクトは伝えてくれたんだ。

When I first saw the photographs from the Lost & Found project after they were delivered from Tokyo to San Francisco, I cried. Photographs are such a universal language that transcends differences in culture, language, and geography Everyone understands photographs. Baby photographs, wedding photographs, graduation photographs. Photographs of holiday gathering, photographs of vacation, photographs of baseball games. Photographs with a best friend, photographs with a mother, father, brother, sister. Photographs of meals, photographs of dogs, photographs of homes. Seeing thousands of these photographs, and thinking about what memories and feelings each single one contained is overwhelming to say the least. It really brought the immense scale of the earthquake and tsunami disaster down to such an intimate, human scale.

3.
観客の反応は、どのようなものでしたか？
Could you tell me how the audience's response was like?

サンフランシスコの人々は、これらの写真に大きく心を動かされていたよ。写真を見て涙を流すひとも多く、みな個々の写真をとても長い間見て、たとえイメージがほとんど判別できなくても、そこに何が写されているのかを見極めようとしていた。もちろん彼らもTVで災害の写真や映像を見ていたのだろうけど、それらの流された家族写真を見た時ほどに、大きく心を動かされたことはなかったそうだ。繰り返しになるけど、写真は思想も国境も軽々と超越する、自

由な表現なんだ。家族の写真や家庭風景、旅行先での写真などを見れば、とても個人的かつ感情的に、それらの写真に共感を覚えることができる。そして、これらの何千もの思い出を失うということが、どれほど辛いことかを理解できる。

The audience's response in San Francisco, CA has been very moving. Many people cried at seeing all of the photographs, and spent a lot of time looking at individual photographs, trying to make out what the image was amongst all of the parts that were washed away. People remarked that although they saw photographs and videos of the tsunami disaster on television, many had not felt the emotional impact in such a powerful way until they saw this collection of washed away family photographs. Again, because the language of photography is so universal and international, many people could relate to seeing photographs of family, of home, or vacation on a personal, emotional level, and also understand how hard it must be to lose these treasured memories.

4.
ムネマサとの思い出を教えて下さい。
Could you tell me your memory with Munemasa?

ムネマサは、Lost & Foundという、とても勇気ある重要なプロジェクトを遂行している。さらに多くの国で、これらの写真を展示することが必要だと僕は思ってる。津波が起きたのは二年以上も前のことだけど、いまだに多くの人がどのように生き、どのように暮らしを立て直すのかと途方に暮れているはずだよね。ムネマサは、そんな思いに寄り添いながら、責任感を持ってこのプロジェクトに接してる。彼は、山元町の人々にとって最善のことを行い、そこで今も続く生について、世界の反対側にいる我々に気づかせてくれるんだ。

Munemasa is doing brave important work with the Lost & Found project, and its really important that he continues to share these photographs on an international scale. Although the tsunami occurred over two years ago, so many people are still trying to find ways to survive and rebuild their lives. Munemasa approaches this project with a deep level of respect and responsibility. He just wants to do right by the people of Yamamoto, and to help raise awareness of life continuing in this part of the world

展示8
2012.9.20 – 10.28
ローマ現代アート美術館
ローマ、イタリア

ローマでは、ニューヨークのジェイクさんの友達でキュレーターをやっているアナリッサさんが、年に一度の写真祭FOTOGRAFIAで展示を企画してくれた。展示する場所としては、特別にコンテナを準備してくれていた。それは津波で流されたコンテナがカナダに流れ着き、その中から見つかったハーレーダビッドソンをダビッドソン本社が無償で修理することになったというニュースがあったからだった。偶然ではあるが、そのバイクは山元町から流されたものだった。そのコンテナで一緒に展示作業をしてくれた人に、星さんが質問したことがあった。「なんでこんなに手間をかけてぼくらに協力してくれるの？」答えはとてもシンプルだった。「ハートだよ」

The Eighth exhibition
2012 9.20-10.28
Museum of Contemporary Art of Rome,
Rome, Italy

In Rome, Jake's friend Annalisa, a curator, organized an exhibition at the city's annual photo festival Fotografia. They prepared a special venue inside a shipping container, having been inspired by the news of a container – holding a Harley-Davidson – being taken by the tsunami and later washing up in Canada. Harley-Davidson generously repaired the motorcycle for free and returned to its owner who – by sheer coincidence – was a man from Yamamoto-cho. At the container-venue in Rome, Hoshi-san asked one of the helpers, "Why do you support us when it's so time-consuming?" The answer was very simple: "My heart says so."

海外からの声 04　アナリッサ
Voice 04 Annalisa

1.
Lost & Foundプロジェクトを手伝うことになった理由は？
Why did you decide to help the Lost & Found project?

友達のジェイク・プライスがニューヨークから連絡をくれて、Lost & Foundについて教えてくれたの。とても感動して、力になれることが嬉しかった。手伝うかどうか考える必要もなかったわ。このプロジェクトに心を動かされて、断るなんてもっての他だった。私の人生においてとても貴重な体験となるとすぐに判った。そして、その予感は的中したの。

When my friend Jake Price contacted me from NY telling about the Lost & Found project I was very touched and pleased to take part of the project. I didn't even have to think about accepting or not, I was so touched by the whole project that I couldn't refuse. I knew it was going to be something very important in my life. And so it was.

2.
初めてLost & Foundの写真を見た時、どのように思いましたか？
What did you think at first when you see the Lost & Found photo?

初めてネット上で写真を見たとき、イメージの力に衝撃を受けたことを覚えてる。それから実際にそれらを目の前にして、手に取ることが出来たとき、写真の親密さにひどく心を揺さぶられたの。大自然の力でほとんど消えそうになりながらも、まだ紙面上にのこる人々の表情からは、彼らが培ってきた暮らし、その物語を想像せずにはいられなくて、胸を打たれたわ。

When I first saw the photos, through the internet, I was shocked by their power, when I saw them physically and I was able to touch them I was overwhelmed by their intimacy, by the faces almost erased by the strength of nature, but still there, being able to imagine the stories of those families. Very touching.

3.

観客の反応は、どのようなものでしたか？

Could you tell me how the audience's response was like?

展示はローマの国際写真フェスティバル、FotoGrafia XIの一部として開催されたの。観客は、Lost & Foundに圧倒されていたわ。多くの人は、それらが本物の写真、実際の家族写真だとは気づいていなかった。もしかしたら、信じられなかったのかもしれないけど。多くの人が、Photoshopで加工された写真、もしくはスキャンされた写真だと思っていたみたい。それらが本物の写真だと知ったときは、みんな胸を打たれた様子だった。すぐにプロジェクトに興味をもった人々は、箱に入れられた写真を一枚一枚、時間をかけて見ていたわ。箱には4000枚程の写真があったのにも関わらず。何度も来てくれた人もいた。フェスティバルのディレクターは、フェスティバルにおいて最も重要な展示になった、と言ってくれたの。個人的には、それは展示と言うより、もっと大きな枠組みをもった取り組みなんだって思ったけど。

The exhibition took place within a larger photographic contest, during the Festival of Roma. The audience, though, was completely taken by the Lost&Found project. Many people didn't understand they were real images, original family pictures, or perhaps I should say they could not believe it. Many people thought they were retouched with photoshop, or scanned etc. When they understood they were original they would be visibly touched. Many other people understood at first and spent a long time in the "container", looking at every single picture (there were almost 4000 images inside the container). There were people who went back to see them various times. The director of the festival told us it was the most important "exhibition" of the festival (even though I don't like to call it an exhibition, it was much more).

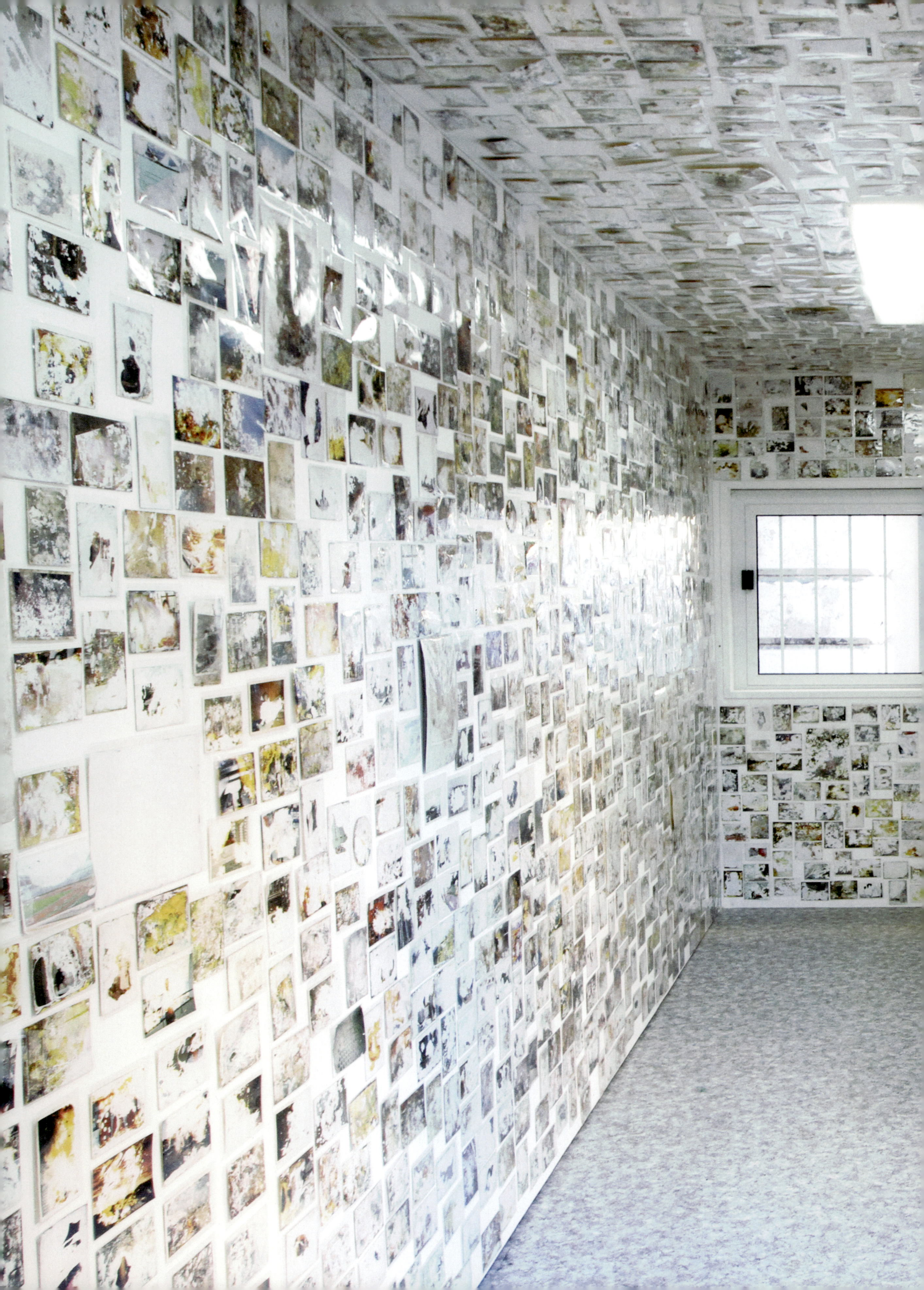

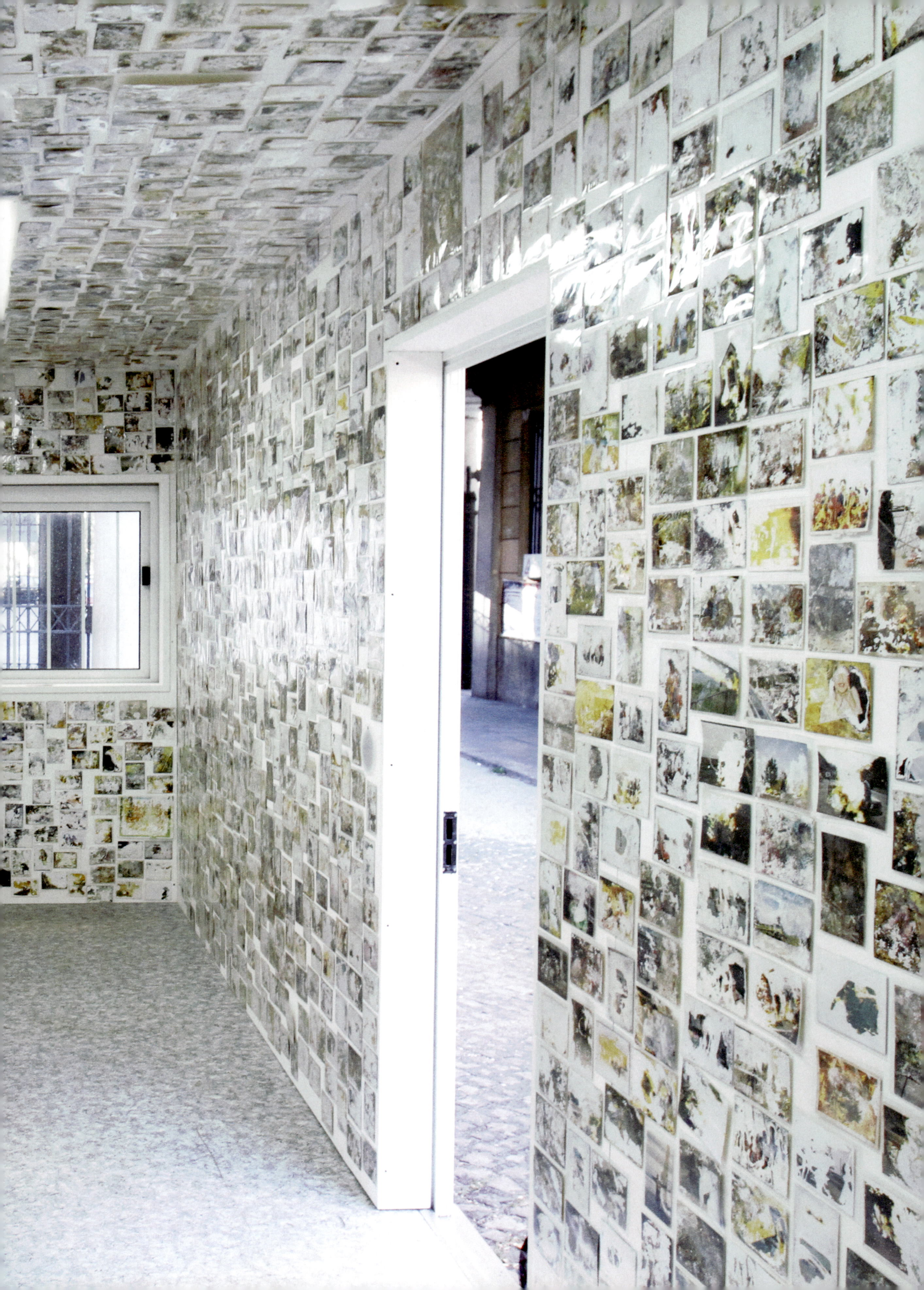

4.
ムネマサとの思い出を教えて下さい。
Could you tell me your memory with Munemasa?

ムネマサとの出会いは素晴らしいものだったわ。彼とカズト（星さん）には、すぐに親近感を覚えた。彼らが実際にローマに来て、設営などを一緒にできたことは大きかった。沢山の笑いと物語を共有できて、新しい友達の絆ができた。また会えるかしら！ムネマサの思いがあったからこそ、このプロジェクトはとても大きな、大切なものになったんだと思うの。

Meeting Munemasa was amazing. I felt immediately very close to him and Kazuto. It was fundamental that they came in Rome and we worked together on the hanging etc. We shared laughs and stories, I feel like we now have new friends, and I wish to see them again! Munemasa's idea is why this project became so important!

共通の感想

このように最初の東京展のあと、展示は海外のいくつかの場所を巡ることになった。まずはロサンゼルスそしてニューヨーク、メルボルン、もう一度ロサンゼルス、サンフランシスコとローマ。その間に台湾に行き、ベトナムにも立ち寄った。展示をするごとに、知り合った人が友達を紹介してくれて様々な場所に行くことになった。全ては人のつながりと、プロジェクトに対する協力で進んでいった。そのなかでいろんな国の人とプロジェクトを通じて話し合ってきた。フランス人、アメリカ人、台湾人、ベトナム人、オーストラリア人、インドネシア人、イタリア人、オランダ人、ドイツ人。運良く、ひとりのギャラリストをのぞいて全員がいい人たちだった。そしてみんな口を揃えて言う言葉があった。「あんなに大変なことが起きたときに写真を返そうと思いつくなんて、とても日本人らしいね。確かに写真を持ち主の手

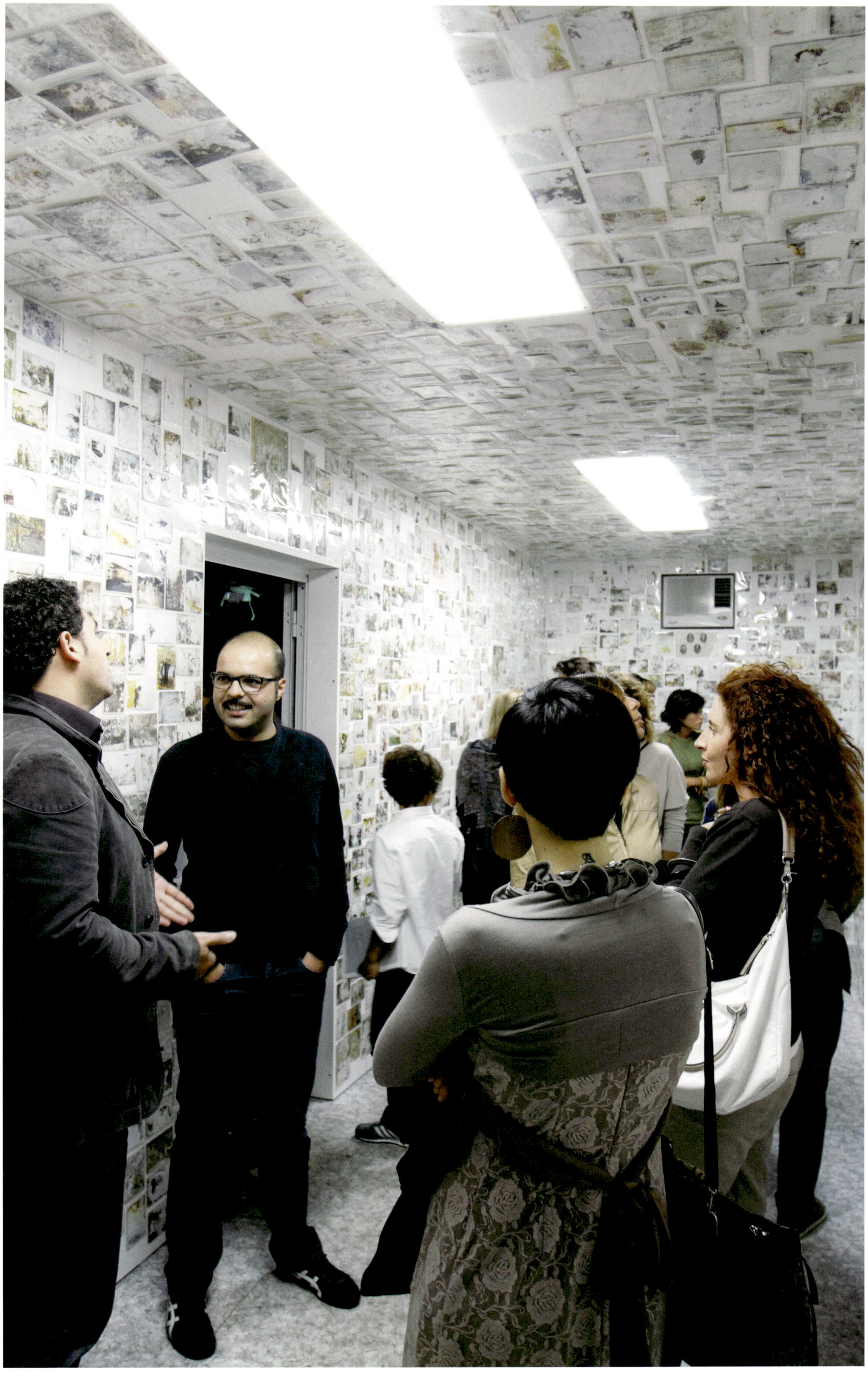

に戻すっていうのは大事なことだよね」外国では多くの人が集まり、手間をかけてシステムを組み写真を返していくなんてあまり想像がつかないことらしい。インドネシアの大学の先生と話す機会があったときに質問したことがある。「スマトラの地震で津波が起きたときには写真はどうしていたんですか」「いろんな国やNGOやボランティアから支援があった。まずは救助とけが人に対する医療、それから食料や安全な場所への避難。そういうものがあったけれど、写真を返すための活動なんて一度も聞いたことがないよ。君たちはとてもいいことをしたね」と彼は言った。

People's Responses

After presenting the exhibition in Tokyo, I traveled to several places around the world: Los Angeles; New York; Melbourne; back to LA; San Francisco; and finally Rome. During that time, I also visited Hong Kong and Vietnam. Every exhibition drew new supporters, who then provided opportunities to exhibit in other places. The project progressed as a result of people's goodwill and generosity. I spoke about the project in many countries with a range of people: French, American, Taiwanese, Vietnamese, Australian, Indonesian, Italian, Dutch, and German… and almost everyone was supportive. They all said, "It's very Japanese to attempt to return the photographs to their owners in the wake of such a catastrophe. It's such an important thing to do." In other countries, our epic task of returning the photographs seemed peculiar, especially because what we doing seemed so insignificant, particularly given the challenges and the number of people involved. At one time, I asked an Indonesian college professor, "What about the photographs when the earthquake happened in Sumatra?" He replied, "We received tremendous support from many countries and NGOs: firstly with rescue and medical support for the injured, and later with food and shelter. We received a lot of help but we never spoke about recovering photos. You are doing a great thing," he said.

運営費

展示を続けていくにはそれなりのお金が必要だった。結果的に展示会場に対する経費は、開催場所の人たちの協力でかからなかったものの、写真の輸送費、現地までの交通費と滞在費が必要だった。最初はこん

なにいろんな場所でやるつもりもなかったので、自分のお金でやりくりしていけばいいかなと考えていた。そんなときダメで元々で応募した、三菱商事復興支援財団の助成金を獲得することができた。このおかげで1年間いろんな場所で展示をしていくことが可能になった。本当に多くの人の手を借りながらプロジェクトは進んでいった。

Running Cost

We needed a considerable amount of money to fund the traveling exhibition. Thanks to the generosity of people in each city we didn't have to cover the cost of the venues but we still needed money for shipping, transportation, and accommodation. I hadn't planned to exhibit in so many places and had thought that I would be able to cover the expenses myself. Fortunately we received a grant – rather unexpectedly – from the Mitsubishi Corporation Disaster Relief Foundation and with that funding I was able to take the exhibition to many places. The project moved forward with the help of many people.

コミュニケーション

展示を通していろんなコミュニケーションが生まれていたように思う。ただぼくは、質問や取材に答える以外にはあまり話す必要はないんじゃないかと考えていた。まあ、ぼくが英語が話せないというのもあるけど。大事なのは展示を一緒に見に来た友達や、家族がそれぞれに話をすることにある。人はいつか居なくなる、そしてそれは誰の身にもやがて訪れる。

Communication

Throughout each exhibition, many relationships were established, but I felt that it wasn't necessary for me to speak up unless I was asked a question or being interviewed. One reason for my hesitation was my poor English skills. The most important thing was that visitors talked about the images with one another, as well as with their friends and family members. One day we will all be gone – eventually the time comes for everyone.

寄付金

寄付金

HABANA
REPÚBLICA de CUBA

HABANA
REPÚBLICA de CUBA

寄付金

ハート

例えば、友達の身に悪いことが起きたとき、ぼくらは直接問題を解決することができなくても何か友達のためにできることはないだろうかと考える。そして機会があれば行動する。きっと写真洗浄に手を貸してくれた人も、展示を手伝ってくれた人も、ポスターを購入したり募金をしてくれた人も、みんなそんな気持ちだった。ぼくらのやっていることが何かを大きく改善することはなくても、いつか大震災によって引き起こされたつらさが和らぐことを、本当に多くの人が願っている。文字にするとちょっと胡散臭いけれど、2年間たくさんの人たちと関わってきた実感として、人の気持ちには距離も国境も文化も何も関係ない。そういった応援の気持ちを募金として少しずつ集めて、仮設住宅や小学校へと届けていった。少しでも何かの役に立っていてくれたら嬉しいなと思う。そしてこの本の印税も寄付金として山元町に送るつもりだ、東日本大震災から時間が経ってなお、関心を持っている人がこの本を買ってくれたんじゃないかと想像している。その応援の気持ちもちゃんと届けることを、ここで約束しておきたいと思う。

Heart

If something bad happened to our friends, we would think about supporting them, even if we couldn't solve the problem immediately. We take action whenever we have the chance. Over the course of two years, many people came to help us: some volunteered to clean the photographs or to assist at the exhibitions; others bought the posters and donated their money to the project. I think they all shared the same willingness to support others. What we were doing didn't change the big picture, but everyone involved hoped that one day, the hardship that people suffered as a result of the earthquake would be eased. It sounds brash, but after working with so many people over the course of two years, I now know that people's feelings can be communicated across borders, cultures, and any other kind of divide. We raised funds and successfully delivered the money to the temporary housing communities and elementary schools in the affected areas. I hope that the money will be used to make those people's lives better. The royalties from this book will also be donated to Yamamoto-cho. It's been a long time since the Great East Japan Earthquake, but I hope there are people who can sympathize with what we have done, and will purchase this book. I will deliver all of the reader's support to the town, I promise.

写真

写真についてずっと考えてきた。高校を卒業した後写真学校に入って勉強をしてきたし、今ではそれが仕事になっている。作品をつくって写真集も出版した。目の前にあるものを解釈し、調理して提出することが写真の能力だと考えていた。しかし、それは大きな悲劇を前に、何の役にも立たなかった。写真には何の価値もないように思えた。しかし本当にそうだったろうか。全てを失ったときにまで、人はそんなに価値のないものを求めるだろうか。他人の価値のないもののために、多くの人が膨大な単純作業を淡々と進めるだろうか。ではいったいそこにあった写真の価値とは何だ。震災から2年間、写真を洗い、複写し、返し続けてきた。そしてその写真の一部をいろんな人に見てもらうことで共有し、コミュニケーションを生み続けてきた。写真を瓦礫の中から集めた人、写真を探しに来た人、写真を持ち主に返そうとした人、写真の展示を見た人が感じたことには共通の意識があった。写真の価値とは記憶の価値に近いものだ。しかもそれはプライベートな写真の場合、いいときの記憶と結びついている。なぜなら人は楽しいとき、誰かと共有したいものと出会ったとき、忘れたくないものがあるときに写真を撮る。そしてアルバムには、人生のよかった記憶のダイジェストが残る。その価値は誰かを失うときに最も強くなる。ある日、人は死ぬ。もう話すことはできないし、ありがとうを言うことも喧嘩をすることも謝ることも何もできなくなる。それが寂しくて悲しくて、別れるのも忘れるのも嫌で、少しでも距離が離れるのを遅らせるために、人は何度も写真を見て思い出す。何度も何度も見ているうちに、やがてその不在に慣れ、ちゃんと別れられるようになっていく。

そのとき写真は、急な別れの緩衝材になる。ぼくらは別れるのが苦手だ。だからいろんなものを使ってそれを先延ばしにする。写真というものは、そこでとても有効にその力を発揮する。また、誰かに見せるために撮られた写真は、撮影者が伝えたいと考えるもののために、その記憶の一部を共有する。たとえば、ぼくが役に立たないと感じた大震災の写真たちは、直接誰かの助けになることはなくても、数が多かっただけに様々な人のところに届いた。基本的に、写真にはその光景の前後やフレームの外側は写ることがないから、写真を見た人の経験と想像力に補完されて、そこに写る事実を形成する。その事実の大きさは、人を行動させる動機になり、食料や燃料を運ぶ人や、瓦礫を片付ける人や、写真を洗う人など多くの協力を生んだ。今になって思えば大震災をいち早く撮影した撮影者の思いは、しっかりと届いていたのかもしれないと思う。地震が起きたときは、ぼくが感情的になり役に立たないと決めつけただけだった。というよりも、写真が記憶に近いものならば、それを見せることは記憶を話すことに近いものであって、そもそも最初から直接役に立つことはない。けれど、そこに説得力がちゃんとあるならば、その思いは誰かを動かす力になれる。写真は真実を写しはしないし、完全な客観性をもつこともないけれど、撮影した人の思いを記憶して運ぶ。それは写真の基本的な機能だと思う。今はもう、写真が役に立たないなんてことは思わなくなった。

Photography

I have been thinking about the meaning of photography for some time. After completing high school I studied at photography school, and now work as a photographer, as well as making personal works and publishing a book. I took what was in front of me, cooked and served it to the people - that's how I describe what I've done with photography. When faced with an enormous tragedy, photography proved to be of no use. I felt it was completely useless, but is that really true? Why did people search for such useless things even after they had lost everything? How did so many people end up helping with our basic and time-consuming work? What was the value of all those photographs that moved so many people? Two years after the earthquake, we have cleaned, digitalized, and returned photographs to their owners. By sharing some of the photographs in exhibitions, we have helped to form new relationships. There were people who collected photographs from the debris, people who came to us to find their photographs, people who gave us photographs with the hope of their owners finding them, and people who came to see the exhibitions. They all seemed to share a common awareness: the value of a photograph equates to that of the photographer's memory. Family photographs almost always represent good times. People take photographs when they are happy, when they see something they want to share, or when they have something they don't want to forget. Summaries of people's best memories are filed away in their personal albums. Photographs can give an acute sense of loss when people lose someone close. All people die, one day. The deceased cannot talk anymore, nor can they thank you. They cannot fight, nor can they apologize. They cannot do anything. As the bereaved feel sad and lonely, they refuse to forget and be separated from the deceased, and in order to remain close, they look at photographs over and over again. They gradually get used to the absence, and then one day they accept death. At such times, photographs can act as a mediator. Personally, I am not good at farewells and use any possible method to delay the moment. I think that photography can be the most effective way to do so. Photographs that are taken with the intention of being shown to others carry fragments of the memories the photographer had hoped to share. The photographs which I dealt with from the affected areas may have looked useless at first, and may have not have helped people directly, but their sheer quantity meant that they reached out to many people. A photograph cannot accurately depict what happened before or after the moment, nor what was outside of the frame. People use their imagination to fill in the missing parts, and shape their own versions of reality. The power of that reality can lead people to take action, which in our case meant groups of volunteers delivering food and gasoline, clearing up the debris, and cleaning of the photographs. Looking back, the purpose of the photographers who shot the devastated areas after the earthquake was effectively delivered to the viewers. When it all happened, I was too emotional and jumped to the conclusion that those photographs were useless. However, if photographs are closely related to memories, showing a photograph can provide a similar experience to sharing memories, both of which are too personal to immediately affect others. But, if photographs can share memories, they have the power to influence and move people very intimately. Photographs do not present reality, nor do they have complete objectivity, yet they encapsulate the photographer's feelings and share them with the world. That is the most important function of photography. I have come to realize that photography isn't useless.

おわりに

長々と写真について書いてきたけれど、ぼくが写真にこんなにも固執する理由を簡単に説明しておこうかと思います。ぼくの父親は

２００２年の３月に自殺しています。場所は職場の物置みたいなところでした。連絡をもらい、ぼくは前日に父が死んだ場所へ向かいました。頭が真っ白になるという言葉がありますが、まさにそんな感じの状態で何かを考えようにも何もちゃんと像を結ばないような状態です。言葉で説明するのは難しいですが。でも、ぼくはそのときカメラと三脚を持っていきました。理由はありません、そうすべきだと思ったわけでもありません。ただ、そうしないと失われてしまうと感じた、というのが近いように思います。現場につくと、頭が真っ白ながらも体はとてもてきぱきと動きました。三脚を立て、カメラをセットし、フィルムを装填し、フレーミングしてピントを合わせ、露出計で光をはかり、絞りとシャッタースピードを決めてシャッターを切りました。我がことながら、体って自動的に動くもんだなと思ったことを覚えています。薄暗い場所に朝の光が入り込み、妙にきれいに見えました。敷いてあった毛布にはタバコの焦げあとがあって、最後の一服だったのかなぁと思いました。その物置は会議室の隣にあって、そのときはちょうど会議が行われているところでした。そこに自殺した職員の息子がやってきて、一言も喋らずに大きいカメラでバシバシ写真を撮り始めるんだから、きっと奇妙な光景だったと思います。それからずっと、なんであんな時なのに写真を撮ったんだろうなぁと思うようになります。何のために、誰のために撮影したのかわからなかったからです。まあ、でもそれは自分のためで、何か大事なことだったんじゃないかと思ったのですが、それが何なのか全然わからなかったんです。その疑問が広がって、なんでみんなこんなに写真を撮るんだろう、ということに繋がっていきました。正直に書きますと、いろんなことに一生懸命手を貸してきたのは、この１０年にわたる個人的な疑問に通じる部分があったからじゃないかなぁと、今では思います。ぼくはあのとき、写真にすることで現実を全部受け止めるのを保留したんですね、それから時間をかけて受け入れていったんだと思います。これは

楽しい写真でも同じだと思います。写真にして留め、それを引き延ばすことで、後になっても少しはその時の楽しさを味わうことができます。こう思うと、家の引き出しや携帯電話に入っている何気ない写真が、とても大切なものに思えてきませんか？

In Conclusion

I've written a rather long text on photography, and now I would like to briefly explain why I cling to photography so desperately. My father committed suicide in March 2002. He did it in the storage space at his office. When I received the news, I headed to the place where he had died the day before. It was the first time that I really understood what people meant by one's mind going blank. My thought process stopped completely and my thoughts disappeared like mist as I tried to grasp at them. I still cannot adequately explain my state of mind at that point in time. I brought a camera and tripod with me to the site. There was no particular reason for that and I didn't think it was right thing to do, but I just thought that if I hadn't brought them then something would be lost forever. My mind was still blank when I arrived at the site but my body moved effortlessly. I set the tripod and camera, loaded a roll of film, framed, focused, checked the exposure with the light meter, chose the aperture and shutter speed, and pressed the shutter release. I remember thinking how automatically my body moved, even though my mind seemed so disconnected. The place was dim, but a ray of morning light was coming in, and it was simply beautiful. I found a small cigarette burn on the blanket that had been put on the floor. Perhaps that had been his last drag. The storage space was located next to the company's meeting room, and they were having a meeting that morning. At the same time, the son of the man who had just committed suicide had come and started taking photographs without a word... It must have seemed very bizarre to them. For years after that, I had been thinking about how and why I photographed such a situation. I never understood my motivation. I didn't know for what or whom the photographs were taken. I guess it was for my own sake, maybe it meant something very important but I never really grasped what was at the core of my actions. That question lingered and I started to think about why people take so many photographs. I now realize that the reason why I helped the others, rather desperately, through the project was that I hoped that I could maybe find an answer to the question I have been faced with for the past ten years. Back then, I refused to accept the reality and I dealt with my refusal by taking photographs. That prolonged the mourning process and enabled me to slowly face the facts. It took a very, very long time. I think the same thing can be said for people's happy photographs too. We keep happy moments by taking photographs. That way we can stay connected to the moments for even longer and can remember and relive the enjoyment of each one. If you think this way, then perhaps the seemingly meaningless photographs in your drawers or on your cell phones may become very precious, don't you think?

追伸

２０１３年はずっとこの本を作っていた。今まで起こったことを思い出しながら文章を書いて写真を選んだ。本の中身がほぼ完成したころ、ずっと一緒にプロジェクトをやってきた星さんが死んでしまった。今はいろんなことが思い出せるけど、この先どんどん記憶は曖昧になっていくんだと思う。そして残った写真を見ながら記憶を再生するようになっていくんだと思う。星さんとは思い出サルベージの現場で出会った。自分の専門分野以外の能力が欠けている偏った人間が多い中で、星さんの明るさと気遣いがみんなをまとめていた。被災地だからと暗くならずに、ボランティアには楽しく作業をして帰ってもらって山元町を好きになってほしいと言っていた。ボランティアばかりやっている大学生たちの人生を本気で心配していた。困ったことがあればなんでも力になろうとした。そして自分の辛いことは一切表に出さなかった。星さんがいなければ、思い出サルベージとこんなに関わり続けることもなかったし、LOST & FOUND PROJECTをスタートさせることもなかったと思う。東京から山元町にやってきたぼくらは、地元でやって良いことと悪いことの判断がつかなかったので、ことあるごとに星さんに相談した。例えば、写真を洗浄して持ち主に返そうとしていた時、何度も話題になったのは個人情報をどう扱うのかという問題だった。簡単に言えば、プライベートな物である写真を返却するためとはいえ他人に見られることを嫌がる人はいるだろう、ということだ。津波に家を流されてほとんど戻る物がない時に写真を探しにくる人がいて、さらに今判断せねばどんどん写真が劣化していくだろうという状況があって、ぼくらには手段があった。目の前に探している人がいて、きっとどこかには見られたくない人がいるという時に、ぼくらは目の前の人に協力することを選んだ。縁がある人のために動くというのは、人間として自然なことなんじゃないだろうか。こう思える

ようになったのも星さんと話し合ってきたおかげだ。そしてそれはLOST&FOUND PROJECTでも同じことだった。持ち主がわからないとはいえ、写真を山元町から持ち出すことが果たしていいことなのかどうかは誰にもわからなかった。ダメージが酷い写真を捨てたくなかったというのもあるし、寄付金を集めたかったというのもある。けれどぼくは東京と山元町を往復する中でだんだん感じるようになっていた違和感をどうにかできないかとも思っていた。当時東京に入ってくる情報は、どんどん作り物めいていっているように感じた。家族や友達を急に失う気持ちというのは1年や2年で簡単に納得できるようなものじゃない、表面的にどんなに元気に振る舞ってもそれはずっと心の中にあるはずだ。少なくともぼくの父親が自殺した時は、3年間は辛さが変わることはなかった。そしてその思いを考慮せずに応援したとしても、すれ違いが増すばかりじゃないかと考えた。津波に流された写真を見てもらうことで、その気持ちの差を少しでも埋められると思ったし、それは必要なことだと思った。星さんに相談すると、いつも最終的におれたちは悪いことをやろうとして活動しているわけじゃないんだし、やれるだけやって怒られたらちゃんと謝ろうという結論になった。いつだって応援してくれる友達だった。ぼくも含めて、星さんに関わったみんなのカメラの中には星さんの写真が何枚も入っている。どれも楽しそうな写真ばかりだ。これからみんなの写真を集めてアルバムでも作ろうかと思う。残された写真はいつだって楽しかった記憶を思い出させてくれる。その楽しそうな顔を見て、笑えるときもあるし、寂しくなるときもある。どんな気持ちになったとしても写真はある方がいい。この本に載っている写真は、比較的イメージが残っているものを選んだので、また持ち主が見つかればいいなと思う。

Postscript

I was working on this publication for the majority of 2013 and as I selected photographs and wrote text, I remembered what had happened over the past few years. When this book was almost complete, Hoshi-san, who had been working closely with me on the project, passed away. I can still vividly remember so many things about him, but I guess those memories will slowly fade away over time. When that happens, I will look at the remaining photographs to remember him and what we shared. I first met Hoshi-san at the Memory Salvage workshop. Everyone specialized in something yet were clueless in everything else. It was Hoshi-san, always kind and cheerful, who kept us together. He always hoped that the volunteers would not be too solemn about being in the affected area, and that they would have fun in Yamamoto-cho and have happy memories of the town by the time they left. He worried about the future of the college students who were volunteering in the town for a long period of time. He was always willing to help others. He never spoke of his own difficulties. If it wasn't for Hoshi-san, I wouldn't have become involved in Memory Salvage for such a long time, and we would never have launched the Lost & Found Project. In Yamamoto-cho, I was a newcomer from Tokyo. I couldn't figure out what was acceptable and so every time a problem came up, I would consult with Hoshi-san. Many people who had lost their home and most of their belongings in the tsunami visited us in the hope of finding their photographs. In order to return the photographs to the owners in the best possible condition, we needed to take care of the photographs right away, otherwise they would have continued to deteriorate. There were people who came to us in search of their photographs; yet on the other hand, there were people who might get offended by what we were doing. We chose to help the people that came to us, and it was through the series of conversations with Hoshi-san that I came to think that way. We faced the same dilemma when we started the Lost & Found Project. None of us could decide whether or not it was a good thing to take the photographs away from Yamamoto-cho, even though their owners had not yet been found. Additionally, even though some photographs were severely damaged, we didn't want to discard any of them; and we were also hoping to raise funds to support the town. I also wanted to find a solution to the odd feeling I had been having as I traveled back and forth between Tokyo and Yamamoto-cho, as the news of the affected area being broadcast in Tokyo, was beginning to seem fictionalized. For those affected, the pain of losing friends and family was not something that would pass after a year or two. Even though people appeared positive on the surface, the sadness would remain with them forever. In my case, when my father committed suicide, the pain stayed with me for three years. If we tried to cheer people up in the affected area without acknowledging their feelings, the psychological distance between Tokyo and the affected area would grow. I believed that by presenting the photographs that had been swept away by the tsunami, that distance could be reduced. As I discussed this with Hoshi-san, we reached the conclusion that we should do what we could, and if people got angry at our actions, we could apologize. We were not doing anything wrong. He was such a good friend, and always encouraged me. The cameras owned by the people who worked with Hoshi-san, including mine, contain many images of Hoshi-san. In all of the photographs, we look happy. We are now thinking about gathering those photographs and making an album for him. Photographs always bring back happy memories. Looking at the happy faces in the photographs, we sometimes feel joy; we sometimes feel sadness. Regardless of the feeling they provide, it's always better to have photographs, rather than none at all. For this book, we chose photographs that still hold their images relatively well. We hope that through this publication we can connect more people with the photographs they lost.

Reverie: Lost and Found

写真が朽ち果てた時に失われる、とはどういうことなのか？そして、その時に見えてくるものとは？２０１１年の３月に日本の東北地方でおこった地震とそれに伴う津波によって流され、瓦礫と共にそこに残され、自衛隊などの手によって再び集められた７５万枚ものスナップ写真は、この疑問を考察する機会を与えてくれている。まず何よりも、ここで展示されている写真は災害の証であり、この場合の災害とは人間の近視眼的判断（単に政府の政策ミスだけではなく、私たち近代社会の住居や電気等に対する欲望）によって悪化してしまった天災のことである。私たちが生活する現代では、もはや単純に、自然と文化、政治をそれぞれ切り離すことはできないようである。これらの写真は生き延びたものの、その多くは風化し、浸食され、ほとんど完全に消えてしまった状態で戻ってきた。場合によっては残ったイメージから顔や体の一部が覗く事があり、そのありふれた眼差しはそれがごく当たり前であるが故に心を締めつける。人々は誰かに向かって微笑みかけているが、その微笑みを向けられた人の場所は私たちが占めている。その微笑みを受け入れることは、これらの人々の私生活と共にこれらの人々を覆い尽くした災害の証拠に立ち入ることを意味している。しかしこの災害のより大きなメタファーは写真そのものによって呼び起こされたものではなく、紙の上に残った、あたかも細菌や病によって浸食され写真というものの肉体が攻撃を受けたかのように思えるイメージによるものである。そしてまるでこれらのイメージの残滓が、かつてはビヒモス（ヨブ記に登場する巨獣）のように世界を席巻した表現手段の成れの果てのように感じざるをえない。コダック社は最近破産宣告をしたが、それは私たちがかつて知っていた写真というものがデジタルの津波によって洗い流されたということを強調している。日本におけるこの天災は、あたかも写真におきている技術的、商業的

な事態をも象徴するもう一つの姿のようだ。しかし、もしこれがある種の写真の終わりを意味するとしたならば、その死とされるものがこれ程までに美しかったことはない。無理矢理抽象画にされてしまった平凡なスナップショットの神秘的な美しさは、これらの写真の痛々しさを和らげている。しかしこのような罪悪感を伴う美の感覚は、これらのイメージをひとまとめに眺める、つまり個別のイメージではなくインスタレーションとして全体を眺めることによって初めて感じることができる。この状況では、個々の写真は括弧付きの「写真」となり、日本での具体的な出来事（なぜここにこれらの写真があるか、そして１万９千人もの命が奪われ、現在でも復興への戦いが続いていること）に関することだけでなく、別の観点を提供してくれている。例えば、私たちはこれらの写真を自分たちにも馴染みのある喜びについての証明、つまり写真を撮り、同時に撮られる喜びについての証明として見ることもできる。全ての写真と同じように、スナップショットとは撮影された対象の存在の痕跡を残すものであり、それはその対象が実際に存在したことを証明し、それを記憶しているものであり、その対象が消え去った後にもそれが存在したことを示すはかない護符のようなものとして残る。このことは写真を撮る者にも、撮られた者にも真実である。言い換えれば、写真を撮る者は愛する者の存在を記録するためだけではなく、それを忘れたり、同時に忘れられたりする事に対する恐怖を和らげるためにスナップ写真を撮影するのである。私たちが写真を撮り続けるのは、視覚的な手段を使って「私はここにいた！」という証を求める渇望である。このことこそが私たちがなぜそうやって魅了されながら写真を眺め、時にはこのように眺めるものがない、他人の欲望の残滓以外に何も残っていない時にでも写真を眺めようとする理由なのだ。彼らのように、私たちも死の可能性を否定するために写真を撮り、写真によって時間の流れを止め、私たち自身を過去にとどめようとするが、その行為自体がある種の小さな死刑宣

告となり、いつか来る終わりを予言する。写真を眺めるのと同じように、写真を撮るということは過ぎ去った時間の存在を証明するだけではなく、時間が過ぎ去ることは避けられないということも証明している。その対象が何であれ、そして今となってはその対象が判別できなくなっていたとしても、全てのスナップ写真はこの逆説的なメッセージを具現化したものであり、生と死の間のどこかで私たちを宙づりにしながらも、生と死を同時に語ろうとするのである。だから、これらの日本の写真がこのような交錯した感情を生み出すことは疑いようがない。片方で、それらは死や苦しみ、喪失と破壊について物語っている。そしてもう一方で、それらは生への肯定、そしてそれら自身が引き受けた運命すらを乗り越える可能性を示唆する。これらの写真は、どのようなものであれ、どのような形で生み出されたものであっても、写真は何よりもまず信仰の告白であるということを思い出させる。私たちは人生の永続性を確保するために、様々なたくらみを見逃すことを選択し、時間を超越するという写真の可能性について、深い信仰を受け入れたのである。そしてこの短い時間のなかでそれを分かち合うことで、私たちもまた彼らと同じ人間であることを確信する。そしてたとえ心の中だけであったにしても、「これは私にも起こりうることなのだ。私たち全てに。」※と呟くに至るのだ。

※ 原文[there, but for the grace of God, go I.]は英語のことわざ

ジェフェリー・バッチェン（写真史家）

Reverie: Lost and Found

What is lost when a photograph is ruined? And what is to be found? These photographs, some of the 750,000 snapshots gathered by Self-Defense forces from the wreckage left behind by the earthquake and tsunami that swept over eastern Japan in March 2011, offer an opportunity to reflect on such questions. First and foremost, the photographs presented here are a testimony to a disaster, a natural disaster that was in this case exacerbated by shortsighted human decisions (not just by failures of government, but also by our modern society's voracious appetite for housing and electricity). It seems that in our current epoch, it is simply no longer possible to divide nature from culture, or politics from either. These photographs have survived but they come to us weathered and scoured, many of them with their images almost completely obliterated. Occasionally faces or portions of bodies peep through the wreckage, offering glimpses of ordinariness made all the more heartrending by their banality. We see people smiling at someone whose place we have usurped. In accepting that smile, we intrude on their privacy, yet further evidence of the catastrophe that has overtaken these people. But the greater metaphor for this catastrophe is conjured by the look of the photographs themselves, with the image on each piece of paper seemingly eaten away, as if by a fungus or disease. One can't help but feel that the flesh of photography itself is under attack here, as though these few damaged remnants are all that survive of a mode of representation that once bestrode the world like a behemoth. Kodak's recent decision to declare itself bankrupt only adds to the sense that photography as we once knew it is no more, swept away by a digital, rather than an oceanic, tsunami. A Japanese disaster has become a surrogate for this other, technological and commercial one. But if this is the end of a certain kind of photography, then never has that death looked quite so beautiful. This beauty, a kind of imposed painterly abstraction, making otherwise unexceptional snapshot images seem ghostly and mysterious, ameliorates the otherwise painful meanings of these particular photographs. But the guilty pleasure we feel before such beauty is only possible when we look at these images en masse, when we can repress the individual pictures and see only the installation. In that situation, photographs become "photography," with the inverted commas a rhetorical invitation to forget the specifics of events in Japan (forget why these photographs are here, forget the 19,000 deaths and the millions who are still struggling to recover) and consider other possible ways to regard this ensemble of pictures. We could choose to see them, for example, as valiant declarations of a familiar desire, the desire to photograph and be photographed. Like every photograph, the snapshot is an indexical trace of the presence of its subject, a trace that both confirms the reality of existence and remembers it, potentially surviving as a fragile talisman of that existence even after its subject has passed on. This is as true for the photographer as for the photographed. In other words, it could be said that photographers take snapshots, not just to record the appearance of loved ones, but also to allay their own fears about forgetting and being forgotten. It is the need to provide witness to existence in general--to declare "I was here!" in visual terms--that surely drives us to keep on photographing, rather than the intrinsic qualities of the picture that results. This is also why we look at such pictures, always with fascination, and even when, as here, there is nothing much to see, nothing but a residue of the desires of others. Like these others, we too take photographs in order to deny the possibility of death, to stop time in its tracks and us with it. But that very same photograph, by placing us indisputably in the past, is itself a kind of mini-death sentence, a prediction of our ultimate demise at some future time. Photographing, like looking at photographs, certifies times past but also time's inevitable passing. Every snapshot, no matter what its subject matter, no matter if that subject matter is now illegible, embodies this same paradoxical message, speaking simultaneously of life and death even while suspending us somewhere in between. No wonder, then, that these Japanese photographs induce such mixed emotions. On the one hand, they speak of death and suffering, of loss and destruction. But on the other, they offer us an affirmation of life, even the possibility of a transcendence of the very fate they themselves embody. They remind us that photography, whatever its quality, place of origin or mode of production, is, before all else, a declaration of faith. We adopt a fervent belief in the capacities of photography to transcend time that chooses to overlook its various artifices in the interests of securing for ourselves a life everlasting. By looking at these photographs, we outsiders affirm and bear witness to that faith. In sharing it for just this brief moment, we declare our common humanity and are moved to murmur, even if only to ourselves: "there, but for the grace of God, go all of us."

Geoffrey Batchen

謝辞

本書を刊行するに当たり、「思い出サルベージ」や「Lost & Found」の活動を通じてご協力いただいた方々に感謝いたします。名前を残していかれない方もいらっしゃったので、ここにある名前は全員ではないかもしれませんが、この本に書いてあることは多くの人が力を合わせてきた結果なので、全ての人に感謝しております。

Acknowledgements

I am grateful to everyone who helped us with Memory Salvage and Lost & Found. As some people didn't leave us their details, the list below is not complete. Without all of your support, this publication would not have been possible. Thank you very much.

荒木悠	安部悠子	横山なぎさ	幾留恵美子	橋田樹徳
イザイクルミコ	伊東浩	横山貴洋	幾留健大朗	橋本千裕
いしたにまさき	伊藤美羽	岡島ひとみ	幾留浩一郎	橋本定昌
いなづか行雄	伊藤ゆうじ	岡部明洋	旗手浩	橋本悠佑
カンミソン	伊藤咲織	岡本敬三	亀井祥史	郷古涼佑
ケンちゃん	伊藤泰子	荻原宏美	菊池東太	玉川博之
チョウカンウ	井上直司	下坂敦俊	吉岡正文	錦澤大介
トム岸田	井上尚人	加藤建	吉沢幸美	近藤麻紀
ナガスミリカ	井田貴美子	加藤孝	吉沢平吉	金慶美
ビラールニロファール		加藤春日	吉田寛	金原聖子
フジモリメグミ	井田幸治	加藤哲	吉田喜彦	金子暁
ミズカイケイコ	稲毛美紗	加納善子	吉田彩	金子和
ヤマシタナオト	稲留宏之	皆川博	吉田秀秋	金千瑛海
やまだまさゆき	宇田周平	岳綾子	吉田敦	金谷雅子
ライトボウ千秋	栄藤泰	額田節生	桔梗理恵	駒込雄太
阿部美和	永久保佳宏	梶山だいすけ	久保山智香	熊野弘久
阿部礼子	永住薫	関根さゆり	久保田祥平	熊野北久斗
飴屋美咲	永瀬道子	関本英太郎	久野崇文	迎優
鮎原靖典	永田恒和	丸橋透	及川まりこ	原岡友里
安達千季	榎本香織	丸山マリアナ	宮崎俊英	原田エリ
安田真奈己	遠藤綾乃	丸山人詩	宮崎香菜	原田博紀
安藤毅	遠藤正則	岩永安行	宮川江梨	古関万人
安藤久美子	遠藤正太	岩上優介	宮田充宜	古川あきら
安部めぐみ	横溝光太郎	幾留愛	魚崎嘉仁	古川章

戸津ヒロタカ	佐藤宏美	山田陽子	小木真	星名ののか
戸田雄輔	佐藤久美	山内悠	小野ヨシ子	星名恵子
後藤由紀子	佐藤元樹	山本健	小野泰正	星名豊
後藤さん	佐藤朱理	山本暁	小林愛	星野公昭
後藤孝子	佐藤純	山本穂高	小澤仁美	星裕紀
工藤秀昭	佐藤勝紀	山本峰生	庄司昌彦	星和人
工藤和美	佐藤瑞希	山本邦夫	庄田多江	正慶真弓
工藤光嗣	佐藤典子	四家正紀	松井恒明	正直加奈子
工藤晃子	佐藤雄一	市原裕昭	松井くにお	清水まゆみ
工藤裕美	佐藤京子	志賀真人	松岡衛	清水幸子
江幡弘道	佐伯慎亮	志村	松原	清水桜子
江本祥多	佐々木徹	志村麻衣	松山宗子	清水俊吉
溝口佑爾	佐々木麻矢	児玉美恵	松尾孝弘	清水俊太
溝上幾子	斎藤亮	持家学	松本淳	清水由起子
行武宏訓	坂哲二	宍戸理衣	松本早野香	清水和子
香山知子	坂本謙一	柴田邦臣	松本哲	清沢緑
高橋英哉	坂本新治	手塚雅美	松本雄地	生井久美
高橋正広	笹原利江子	種村しゅん	松本雄地	西丸雅之
高橋ちぐさ	笹口さおり	種村京子	新井紀美代	青山孝司
高橋佳子	笹口悦民	周立紅	新井啓介	青木秀平
高橋希	三浦麻子	周立紅	新井孝杆	斉藤竹史
高橋淳子	三坂修二	秋本裕史	新井隆弘	石井克尚
高橋尚紀	三宅淳	渋谷善光	新藤祐一	石井直仁
高橋知江	三宅則男	緒方亜衣	森田一平	石井直仁
高橋里江	山形明夫	小橋ユカ	森嶋剛	石井勉
高橋朗	山元兵助	小山昂志	森尾博昭	石元秀明
高山真吾	山口華代	小山晋	森本徹	石原基希
高山裕康	山口由貴	小川好則	深田健吾	石原博史
高藤りゅうせつ	山口穣	小倉快子	真田大輔	石原良子
高木朝成	山中智衛	小倉直子	須賀健介	石川泰典
合田真奈美	山田峻輔	小池友梨恵	須藤一夫	石谷直子
黒河正志	山田将之	小堤雅彦	杉本達應	石田博志
黒崎智康	山田真央	小島昇	菅原威史	石田カズ子
黒田光一	山田達也	小島梨乃	菅野幸恵	石毛大介
今野照夫	山田鎮二	小嶋三樹	成宮淳一	赤崎圭輔
佐古裕	山田由加	小木幸絵	成瀬新也	赤錆健二

折田明子	大島哲	田辺恵久	冨田直希	鈴木とおる
千葉尚彦	大藤直子	田邊恵理	武田一也	鈴木晃広
川村剛史	大内斎之	渡辺実	武藤裕也	鈴木純平
川部亮子	大野弘美	渡辺実花	平松恵理子	鈴木晶子
川並京介	大矢万由佳	渡辺真知子	米澤恵	鈴木泉
浅井肇	大塚幸代	渡辺裕之	片山玲子	鈴木唯
浅見智徳	大塚滋	渡邊博史	保井元	鈴木陽子
浅田政志	大塚正喜	土佐いづみ	保坂信幸	鈴木隆一
船曳達也	大鶴倫宣	土蔵亜由美	保良康平	鷲尾和彦
前田太郎	谷津美歌	島津朋彦	望月圭	國島美華子
倉上陽子	谷藤貴志	東城孝昌	北川航志	榮藤泰
相原愛	丹野ゆみ	東田真由美	北川正明	澤井誠
相澤繁	地頭所和徳	棟居李奈	北村可奈子	齋藤真由美
村松弘敏	竹内弘真	湯沢梢	北澤みゆき	種田優子
村上岳	竹内万里子	藤井敏男	北澤道夫	塚下真紀
村上慎吾	中山雅貴	藤原光一	本郷明美	塚原敬史
太田悦子	中山由希子	藤森和哉	木下史朗	枕本友里
大橋勝美	中山祐子	藤村広平	木皿信也	福井はる菜
大橋悠美香	中村まさ比呂	藤田健介	木村俊裕	福田弘
大空真由美	中村弥生	藤本総子	門藤勇樹	福島亮
大熊彩子	中田綾子	藤本智士	野間恒毅	福嶋美代子
大熊匠	中島昌吾	徳光智子	野瀬香織	諸田知直
大江幸子	中嶋輝	徳竹亮志	野瀬智弘	逸見由紀子
大山光二郎	中嶋灯奈	内村英恵	野村直子	飯村誠一郎
大山和子	中能泉	内池秀人	野村洋	時川英之
大山和子	中鉢欣秀	内藤由樹	野澤由利子	服部哲
大西潤子	中澤健	南出健吾	矢島郁子	Andy Yamada
大西緑	長山萌	南波有希	矢島慎一	Annalisa D'angelo
大西累互	長尾敦子	二瓶隆幸	柳沢和美	Annette Booth
大川潤子	鳥潟雄一	馬場夕紀子	柳迫僚	Ariel Goldberg
大沢	椎名洋介	柏原健助	有泉令	Chiara Capodici
大谷啓代	鄭晶晶	柏葉隆也	落合友子	Chigusa Saga
大坪輝世	田代光輝	箱崎忠宏	林敏弘	Fiore
大坪順潔	田中重充	畑智章	鈴村綾子	Hartmut Woerrlein
大庭佐知子	田中達郎	比嘉幸則	鈴木信行	Hinton Miyuki
大島康志	田中裕子	尾田信介	鈴木仁	Hiro Kamizono

HyunSook Yun	Kristian Haggblom	Mark Baugh-Sasaki	Xavier Arnaudo	Kio Griffith
Ivan Vartanian	Mina Haggblom	Mayumi Hamanaka	Yumiko Arnaudo	Erika Abe
Jake Price	Koyuki Haggblom	Moana Kidd	Taizo Arnaudo	Hiroki Shirota
Jun Hiraoka	Papa of Kristian	Sean McFarland	Yoko Senesac	
Kari Orvik	Shane Haggblom	Seloua Luste Boulbina		
Kelli Yon	Mama of Kristian	Taro Hattori	Carlos Tanaka	
Kevin B. Chen	Lesley Martin	Toshiyuki Imai	Masatomo Hashimoto	

思い出サルベージで
関わった全てのみなさま
Everyone who supported Memory Salvage

LOST & FOUND PROJECTの準備に
力を貸してくれた全てのみなさま
Everyone who assisted with
the preparation of the Lost & Found Project

東京の展示に関わった全てのみなさま
Everyone who supported
the exhibition in Tokyo

ロサンゼルスの展示に
関わった全てのみなさま
Everyone who supported
the exhibition in Los Angeles

ニューヨークの展示に
関わった全てのみなさま
Everyone who supported
the exhibition in New York

オーストラリアでの展示に
関わった全てのみなさま
Everyone who supported
the exhibition in Australia

北海道の展示に関わった全てのみなさま
Everyone who supported
the exhibition in Hokkaido

サンフランシスコの展示に
関わった全てのみなさま
Everyone who supported
the exhibition in San Francisco

ローマの展示に関わった全てのみなさま
Everyone who supported
the exhibition in Rome

展示にきてくれた人たち
Everyone who visited to the exhibition

NPO法人ゆにふりみやぎ
ニフティ㈱
㈱もずや
㈱旅日記
陸上自衛隊第10師団
富士フイルムイメージングシステムズ㈱
写真でつながるプロジェクト
（旧写真救済プロジェクト）
キヤノンマーケティングジャパン㈱
㈱ホットリンク
㈱ロックオン

三菱商事復興支援財団	坂元ダイスキ鎮魂祭　実行委員会
CIPA	山元町立山下中学校
日本財団	山元町立坂元中学校
赤い羽根共同募金	大妻女子大学
山元町役場	京都大学グローバルCOEプログラム
㈱ワコム	「親密圏と公共圏の再編成をめざすアジア拠点」
ホーチキ㈱	東北大学地域復興プロジェクト「HARU」
BYB	静岡大学
一般社団法人ヒューマンタイズ	日本写真芸術専門学校
プロペット㈱	青山学院大学ボランティア・ステーション
プロテックス	アルバムエキスポニッポン
trimdesign	
BANG! Design, inc.	and you.
チバフォート	
新美㈱	
ソフトバンクモバイル㈱	
理想科学工業㈱	
日本ヒューレット・パッカード㈱	
東近江市商工会議所	
コトナリエ	
りす会 +moi「あらいぐま作戦」	
湖南グループあらいぐま作戦＠茅ヶ崎	
（海辺のあらいぐま）	
あらいぐま作戦 in 山口周南	
（りす会山口支部）	
ハートプロジェクト	
ハートプロジェクト静岡	
ハートプロジェクト長崎	
ハートプロジェクト向笠	
武蔵小杉さかい歯科医院写真洗浄ボランティア	
MM思い出返し隊	
岩沼　思い出再会ひろば	
気仙沼復興協会写真救済部「思い出は流れない写真救済プロジェクト」	
新地被災写真複製プロジェクト	
子どもも大人もみんなで遊び隊	
中浜いもに会～笑顔でお茶のみすっぺ～実行委員会	

津波、写真、それから　—LOST & FOUND PROJECT

著者：高橋宗正
2014年2月14日初版発行

デザイン：寄藤文平 + 鈴木千佳子（文平銀座）
英訳：宮城太

発行人：姫野希美
発行所：株式会社赤々舎
京都府京都市下京区堀川五条東入中金仏町215-6 増田屋ビル
TEL：075-371-8025　http://www.akaaka.com
印刷：株式会社オノウエ印刷
製本：新日本製本株式会社
©2014 Munemasa Takahashi
©2014 AKAAKA ART PUBLISHING, Inc.
ISBN 978-4-86541-012-9
本書の無断転写、転載、複製を禁じます。

Tsunami, Photographs, and Then　—LOST & FOUND PROJECT

Munemasa Takahashi
First Edition February.14.2014

Design: Bunpei Yorifuji + Chikako Suzuki (Bunpei Ginza)
Translation: Futoshi Miyagi

Publisher: Kimi Himeno
Publishing house: AKAAKA ART PUBLISHING, Inc.
Masudaya Building, 215-6 Nakakanabutsu-cho, Higashi-iru, Horikawa-Gojo
Shimogyo-ku, Kyoto, 600-8332 Japan
TEL: +81-75-371-8025　http://www.akaaka.com
©2014 Munemasa Takahashi
©2014 AKAAKA ART PUBLISHING, Inc.
ISBN 978-4-86541-012-9

All rights reserved.
No part of this publication may be reproduced or transmitted in any form or by any means,
electronic or mechanical, including photocopying,
recording or by any information storage and retrieval system
without written permission of the publisher.
Printed and bound in Japan

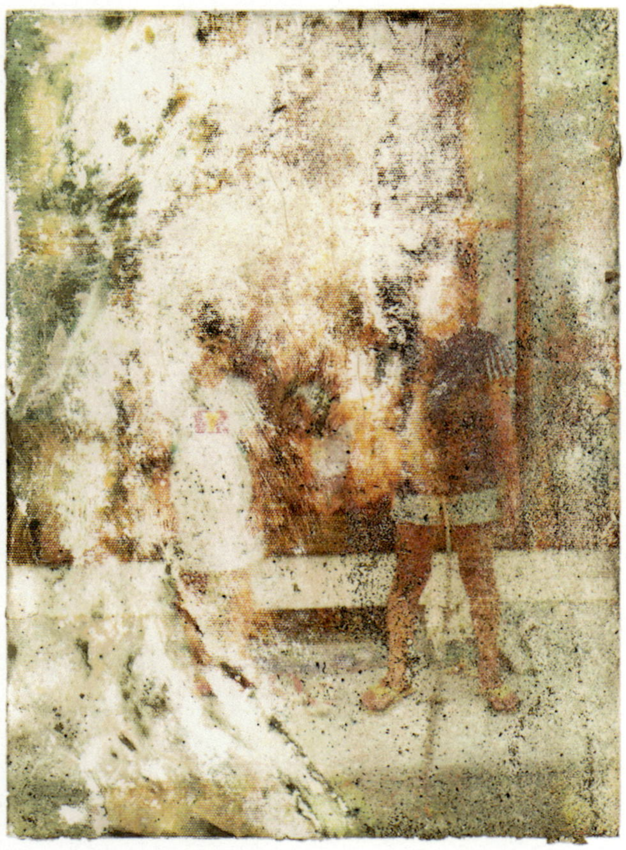
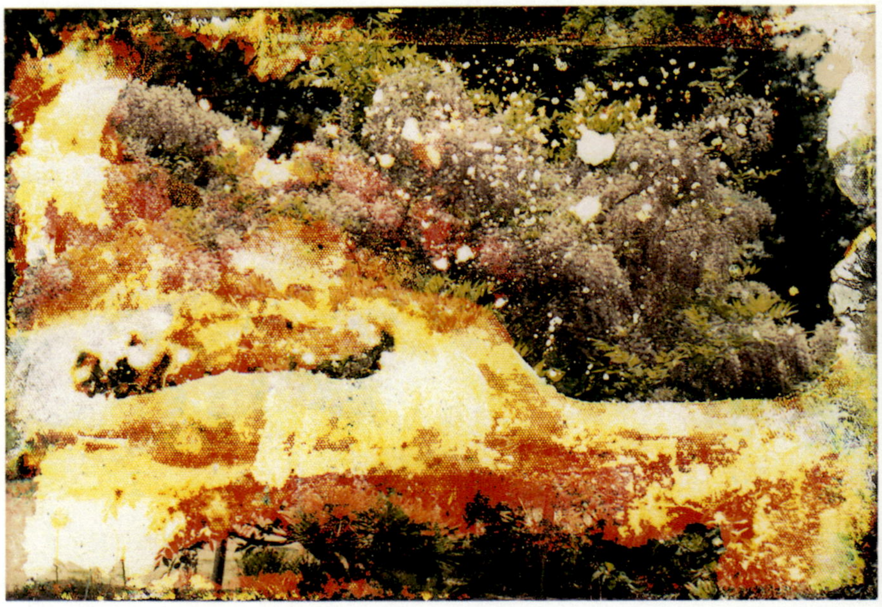

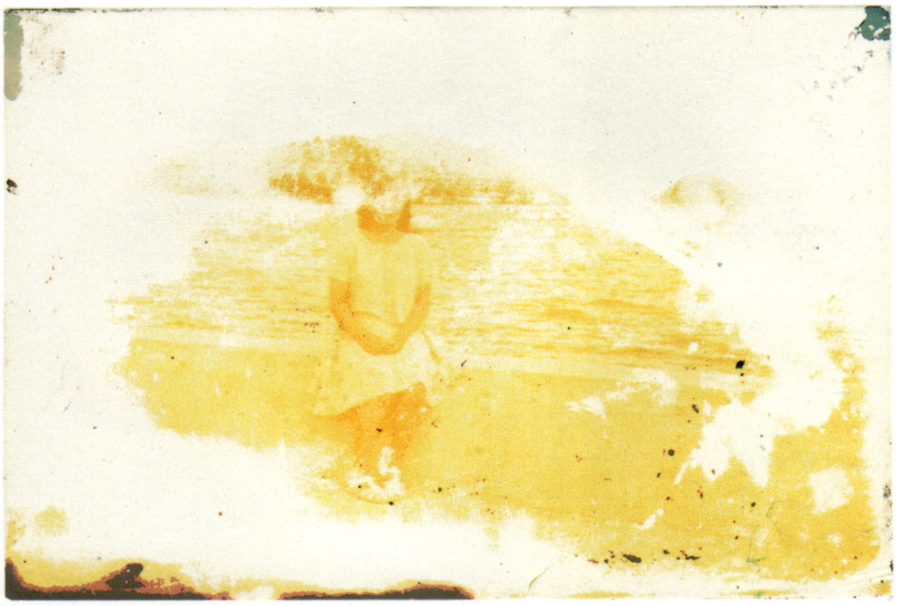
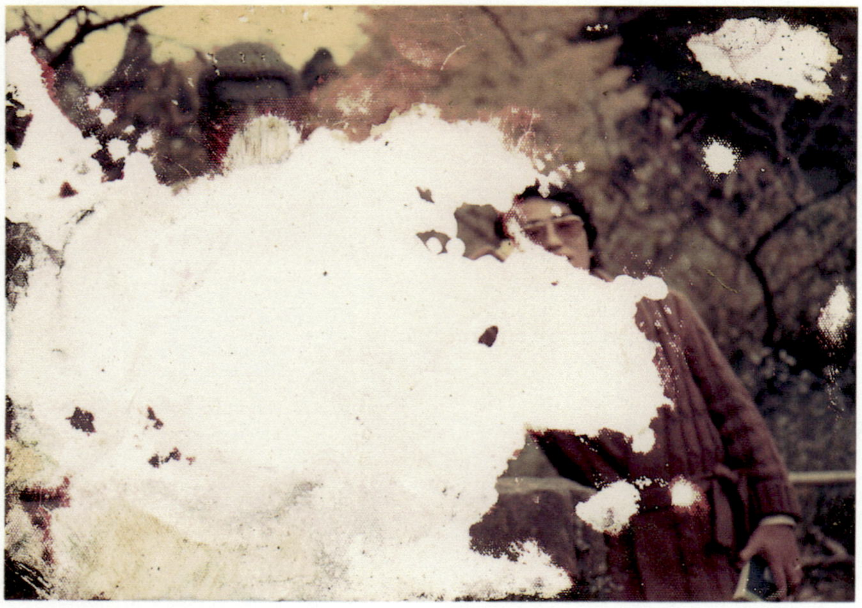
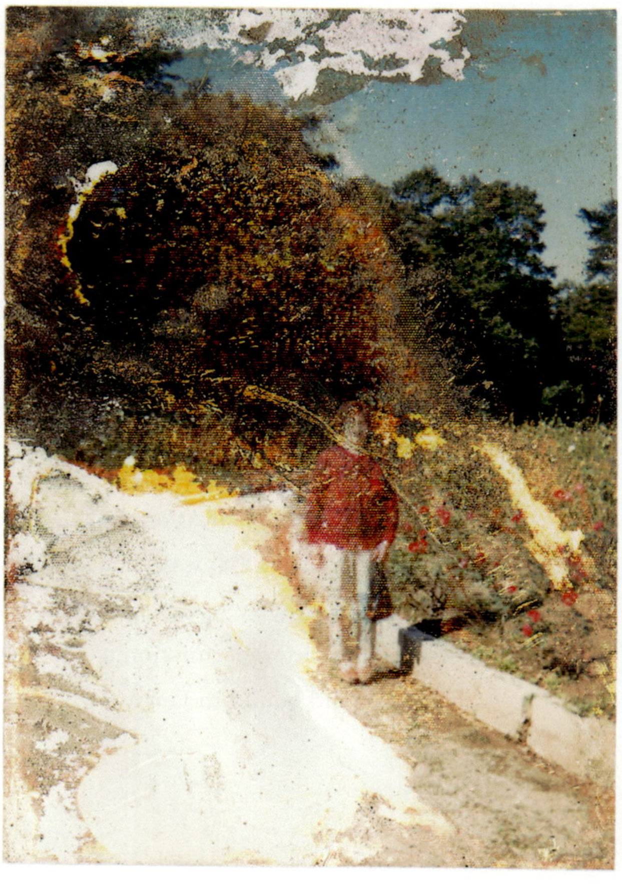

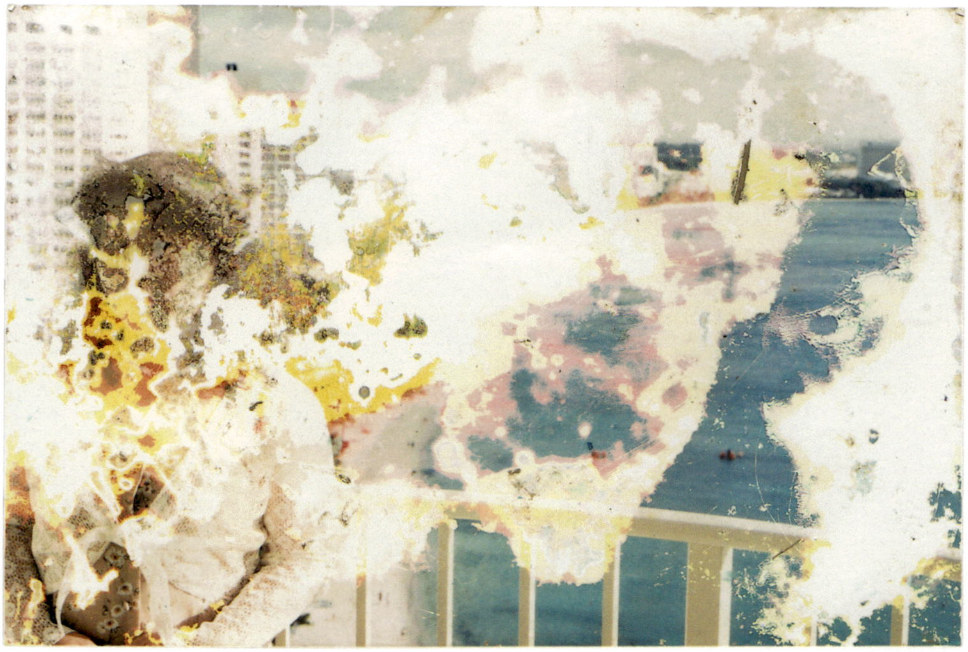

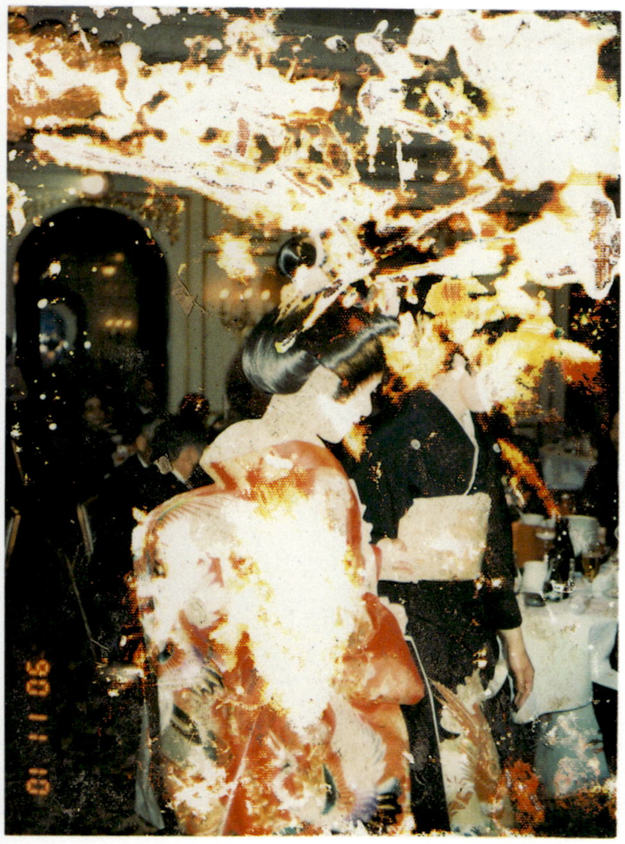

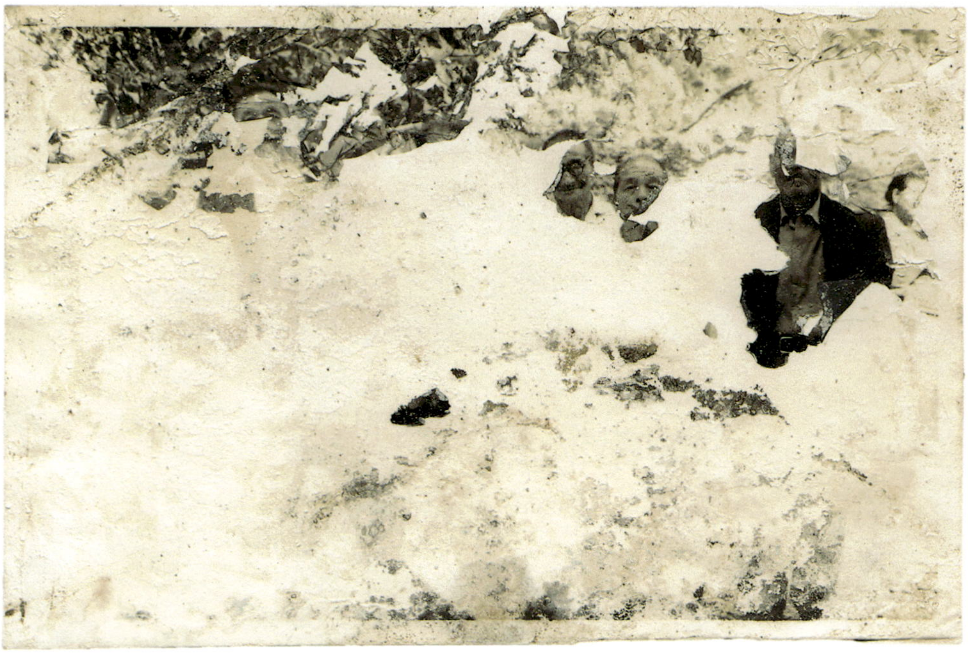

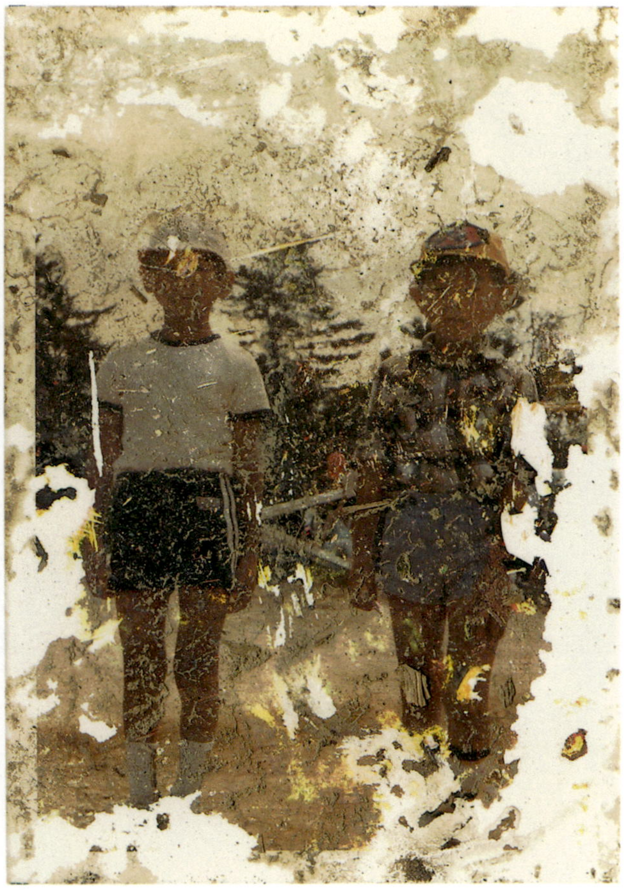

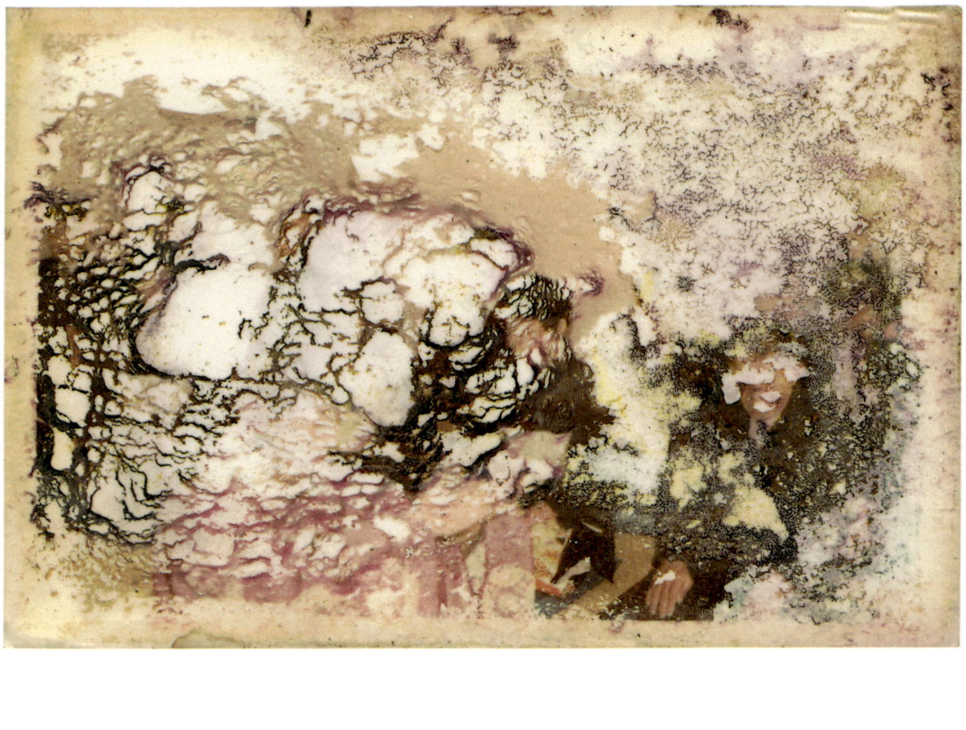

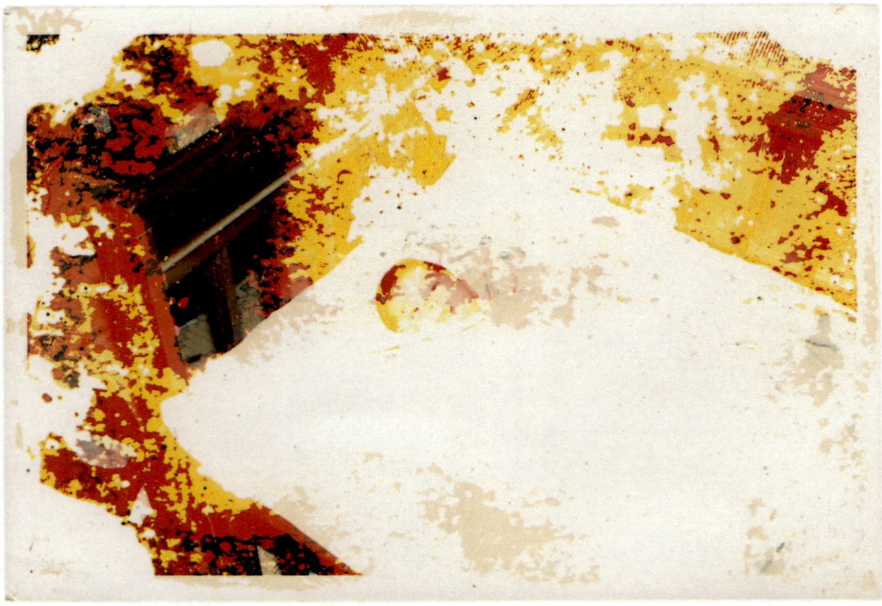
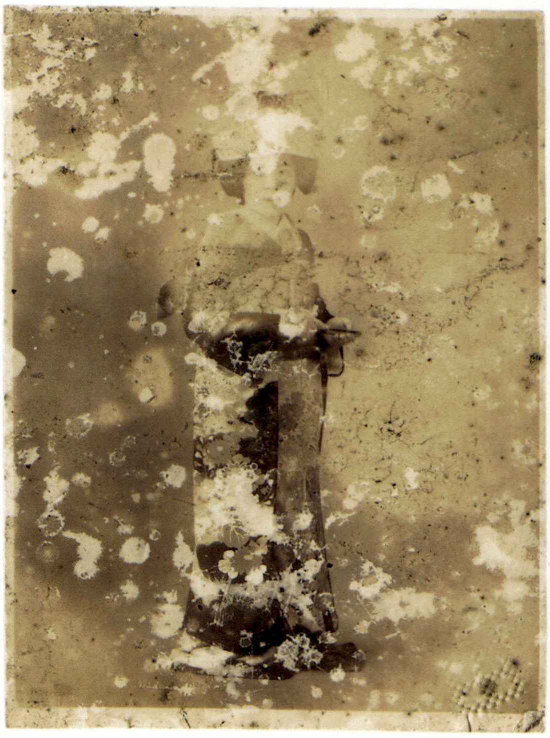
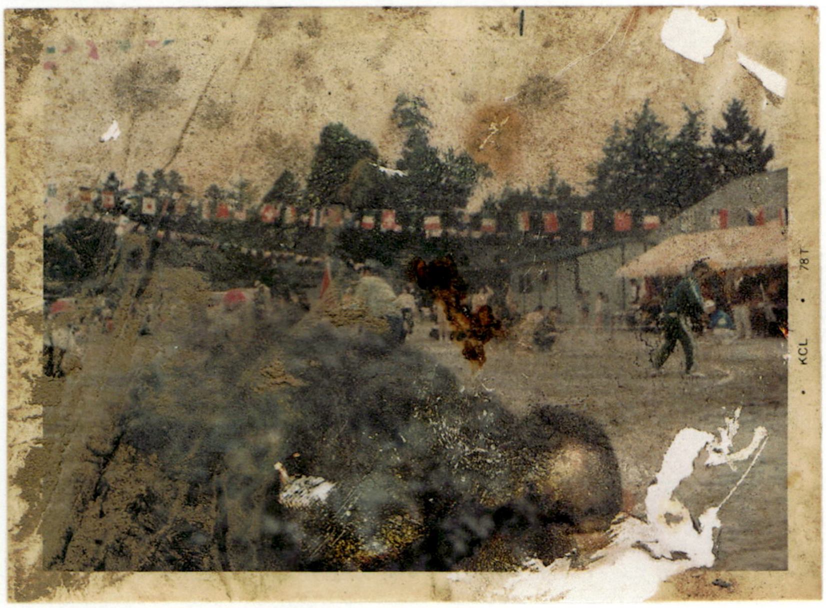
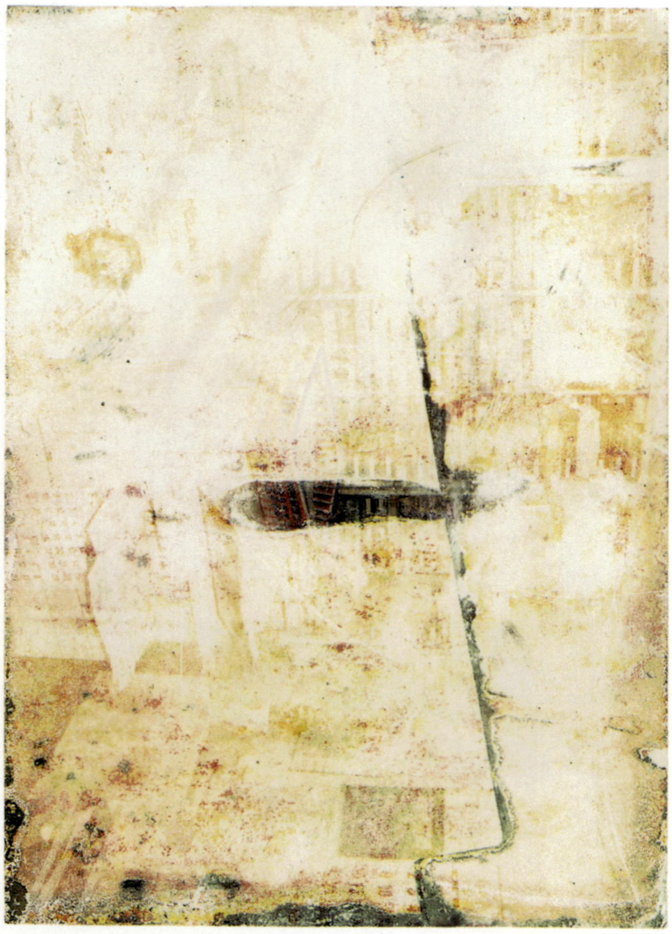
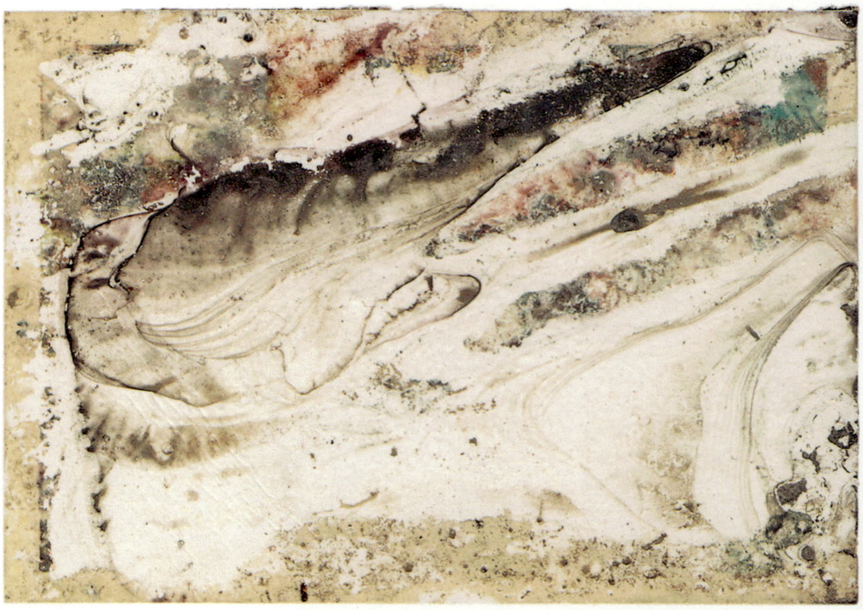
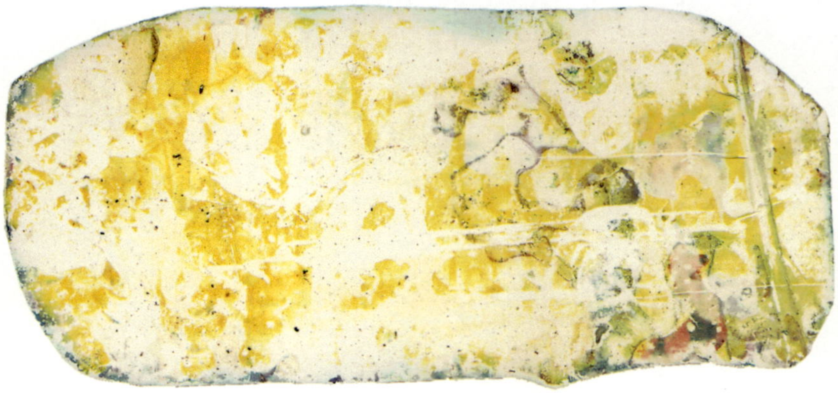

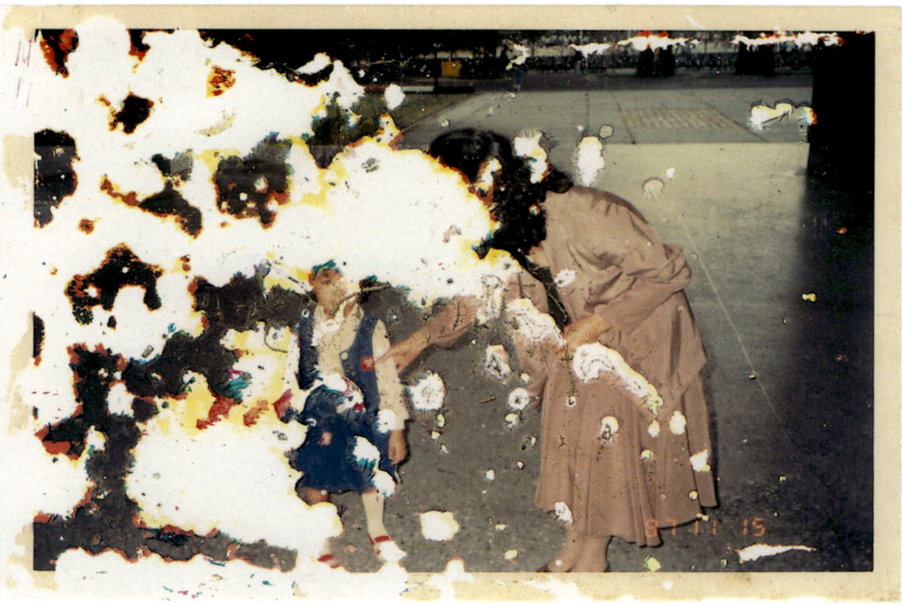

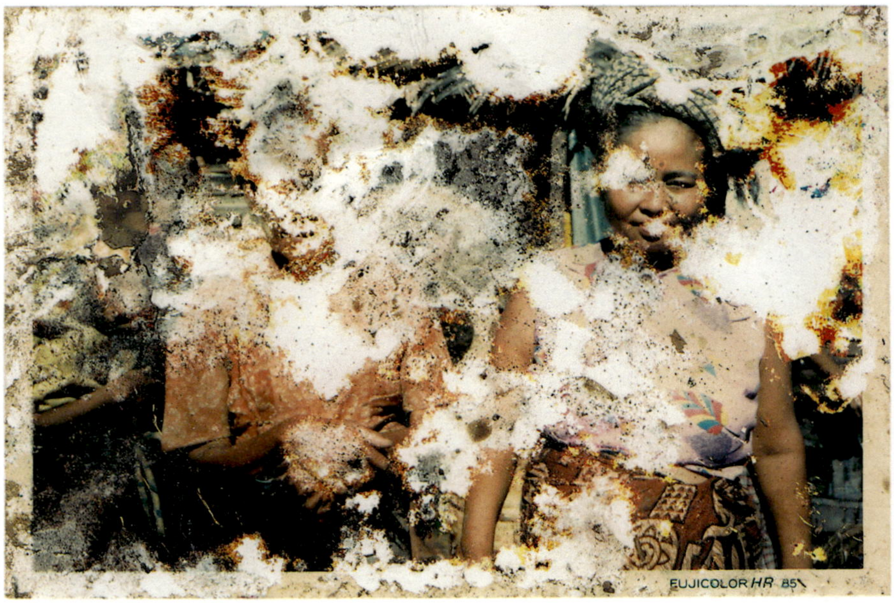
FUJICOLOR HR 85

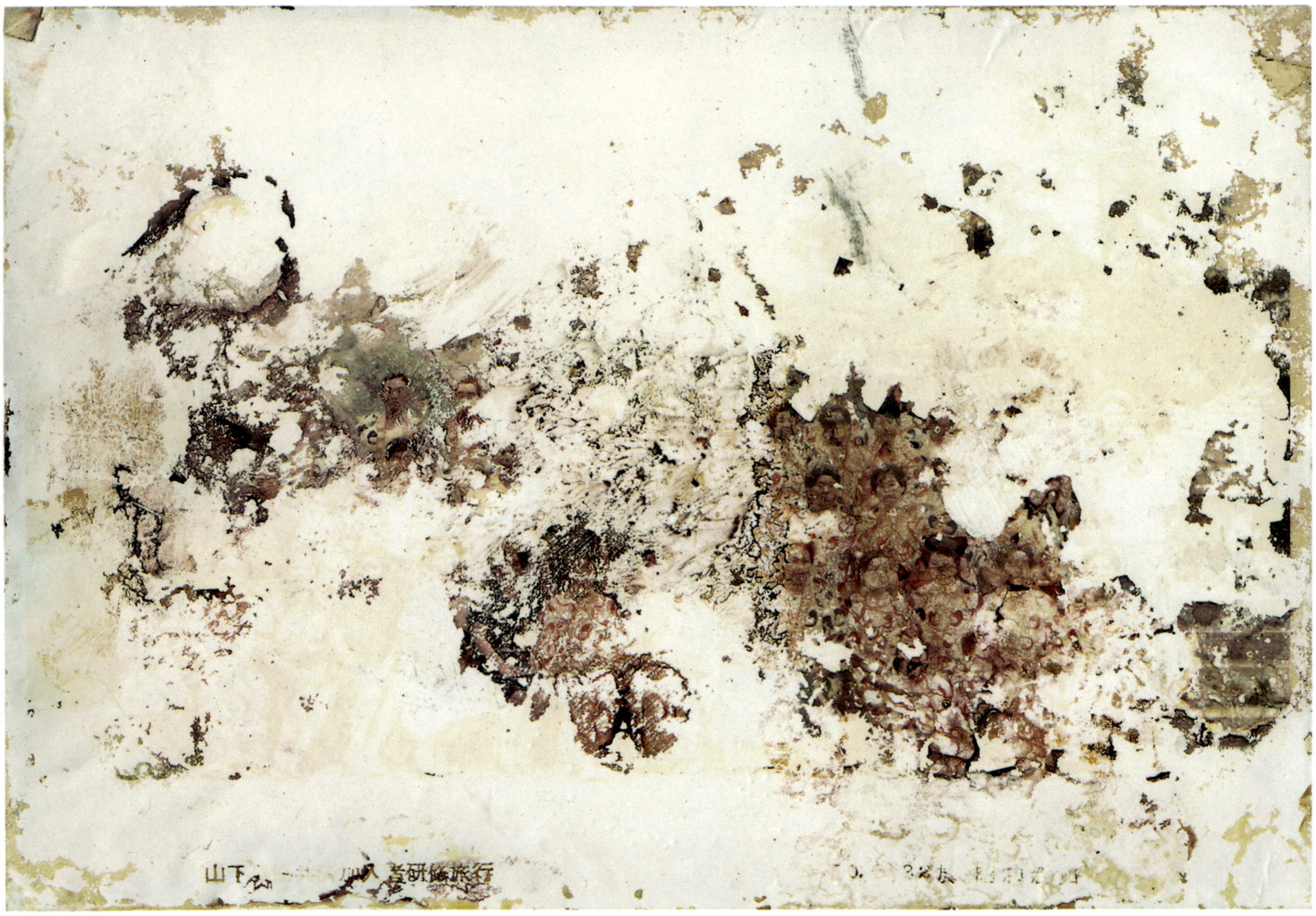
研修旅行

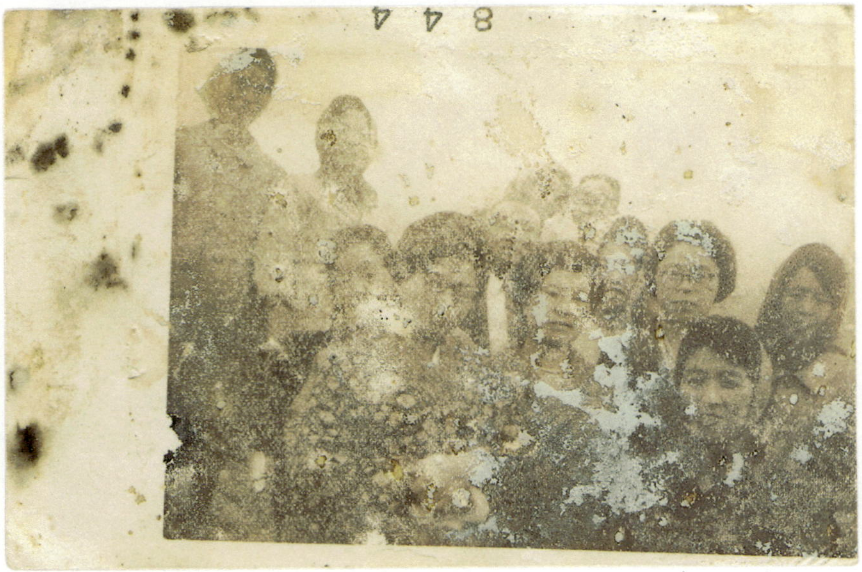
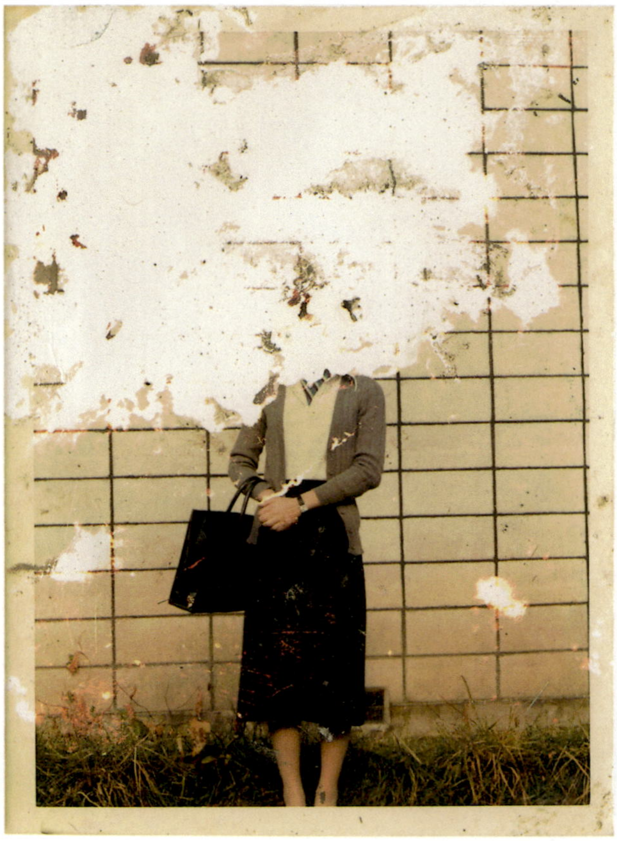
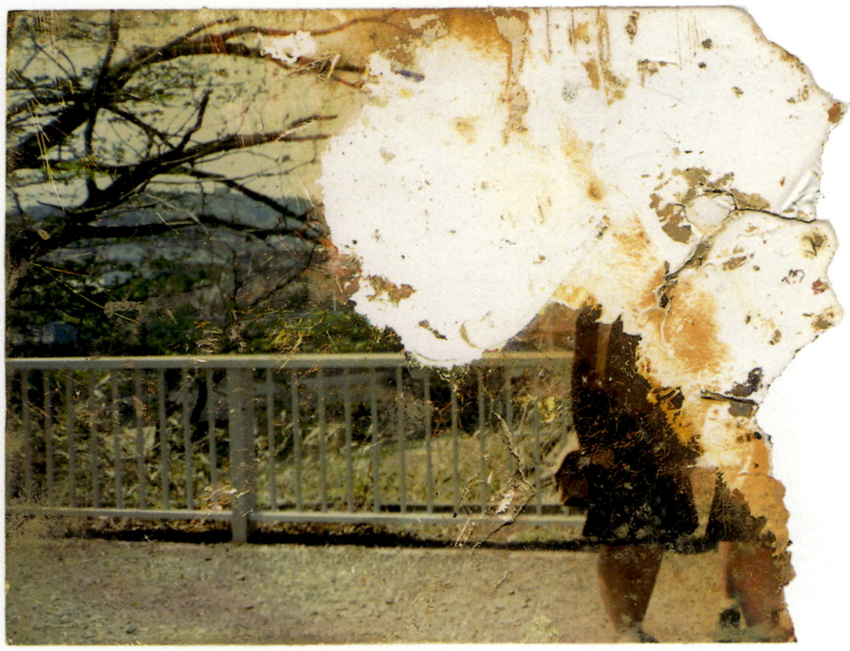
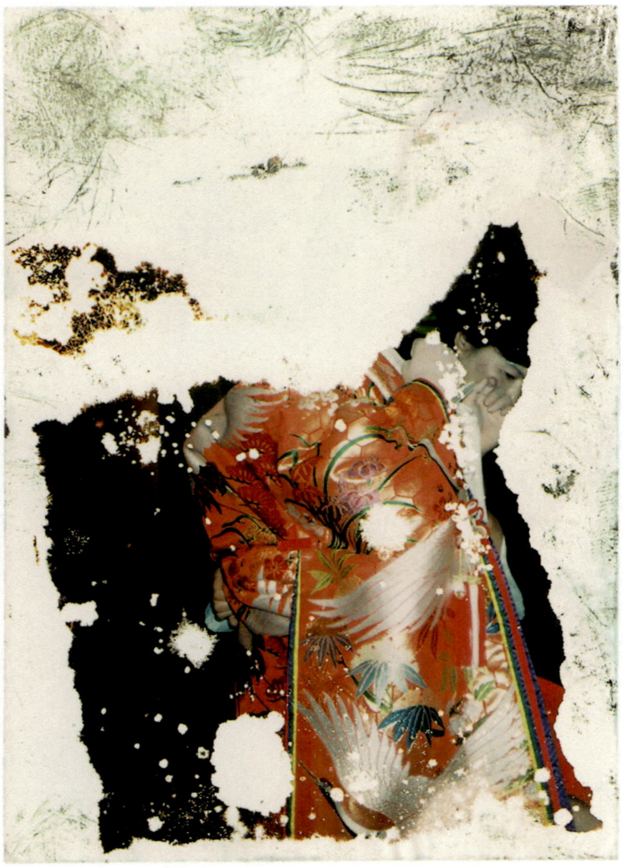
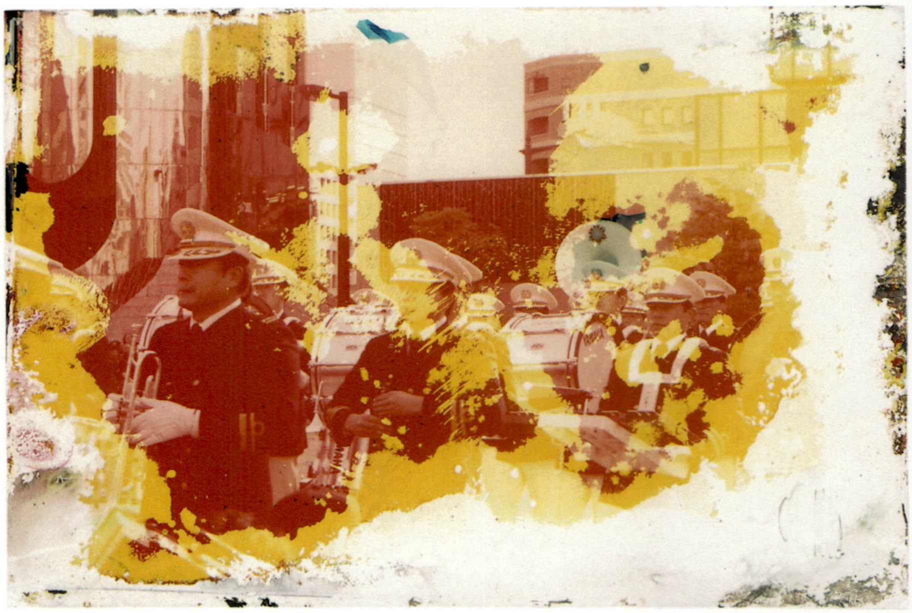

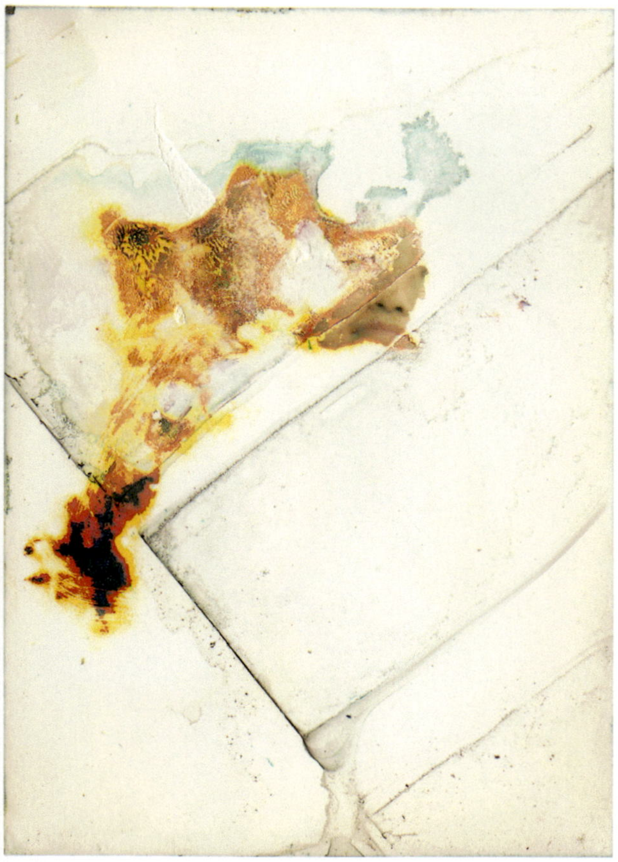

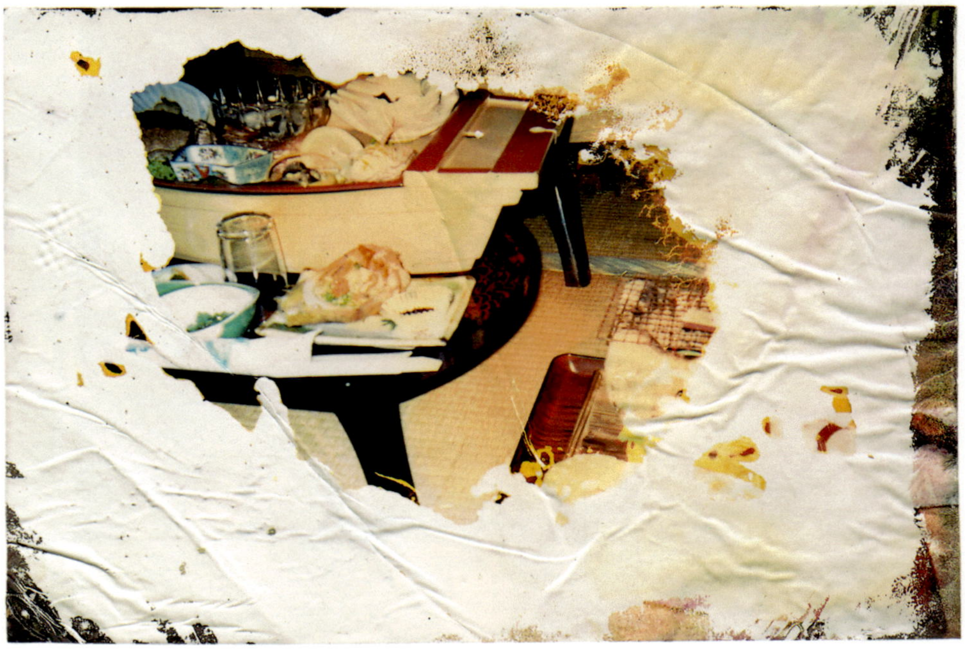

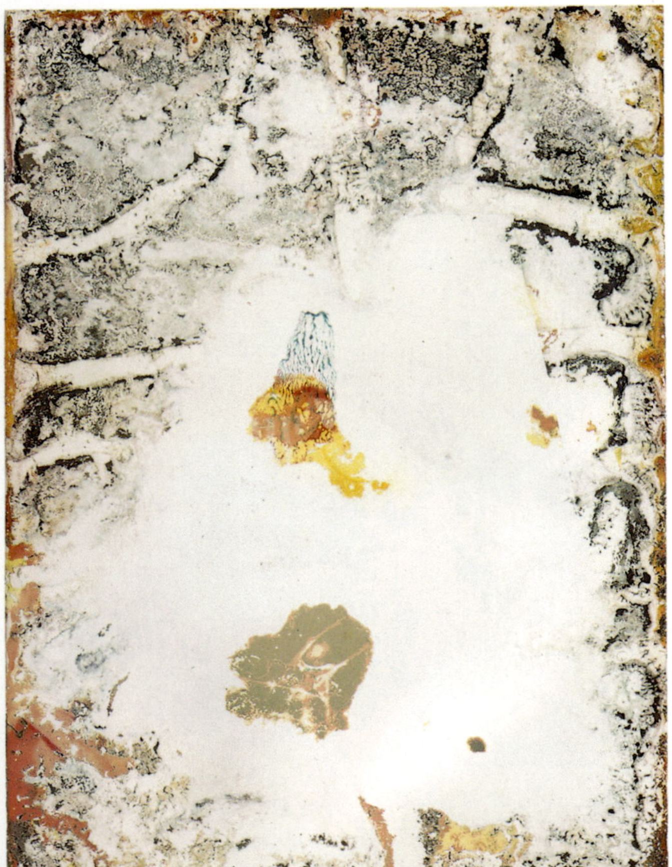

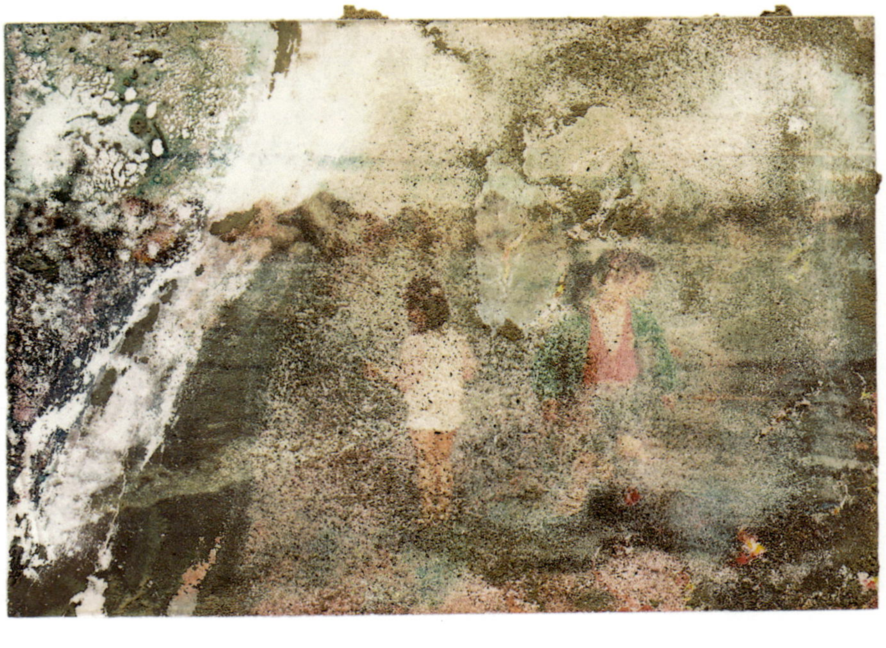

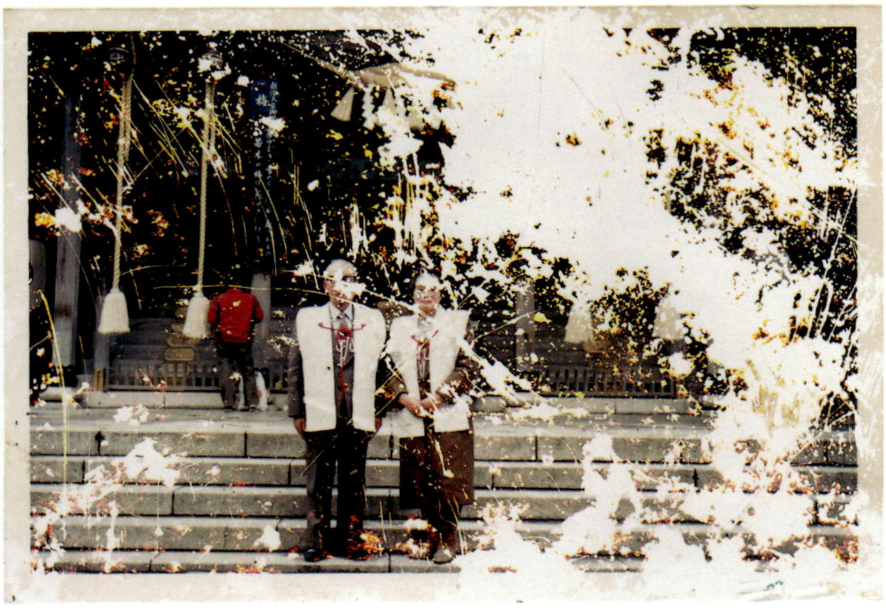

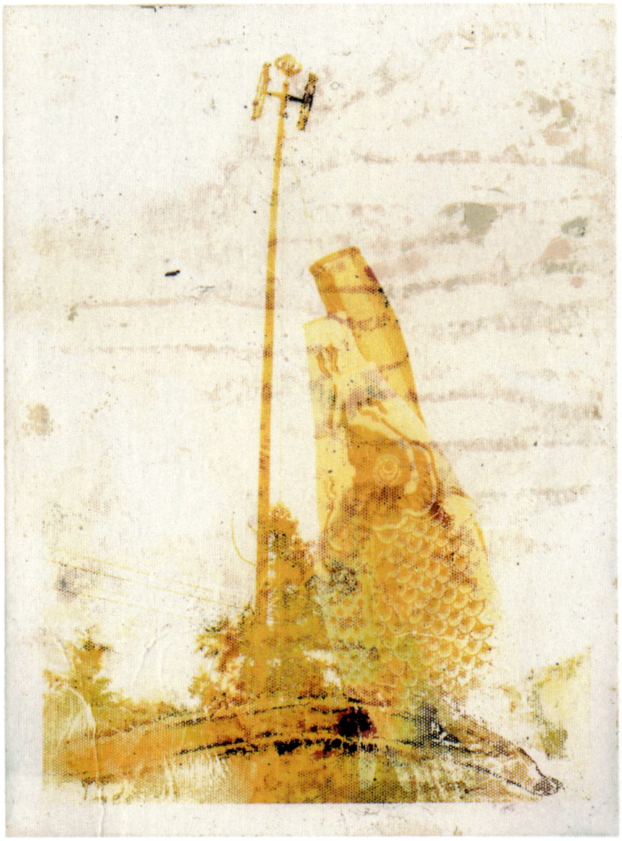

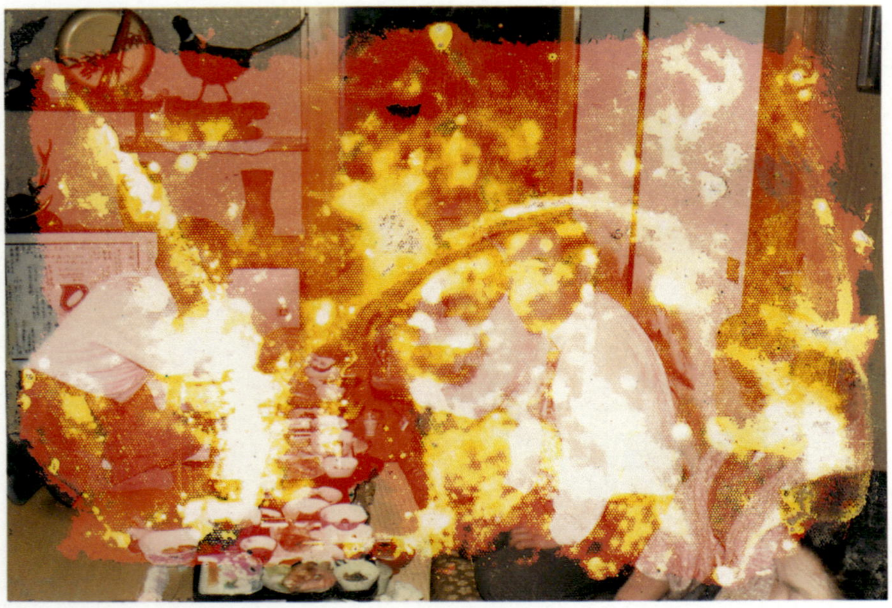

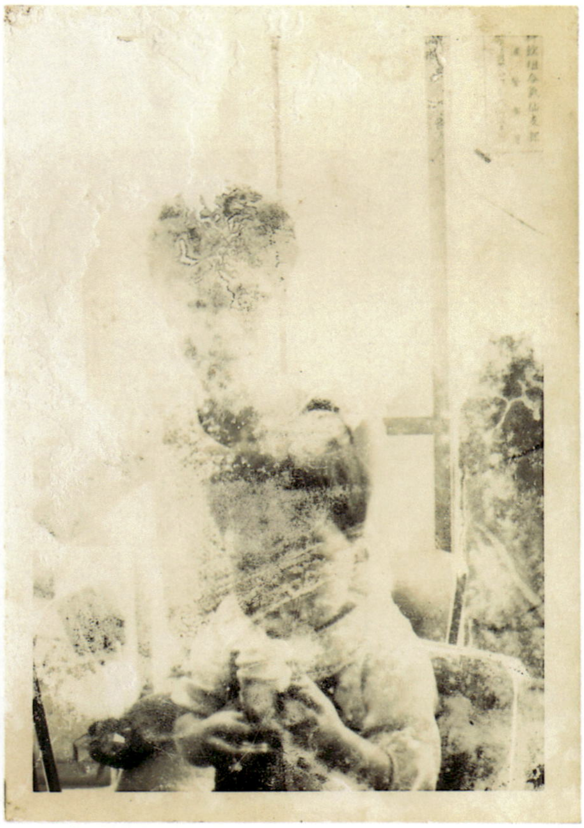

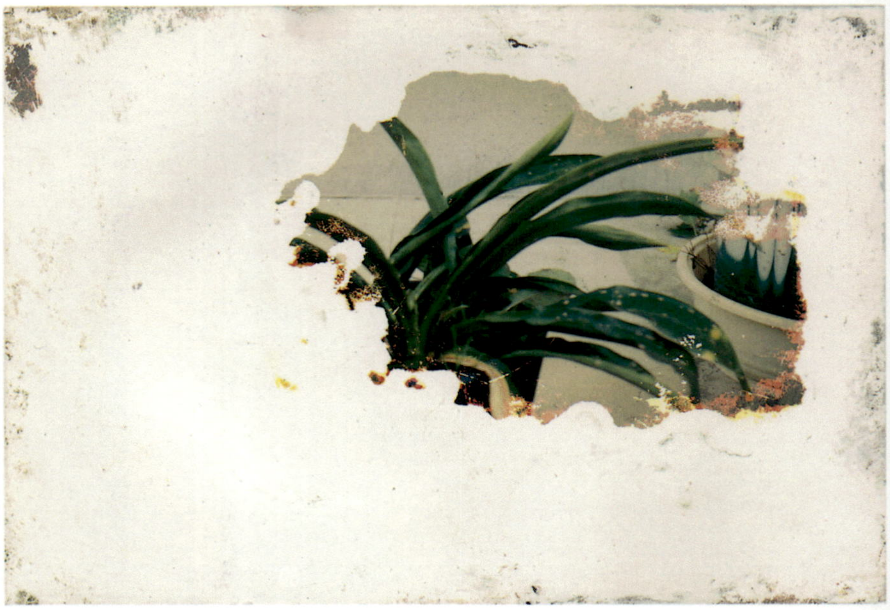

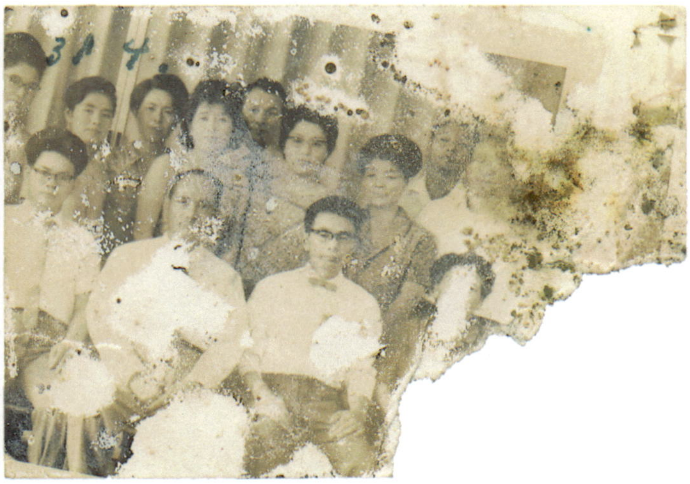

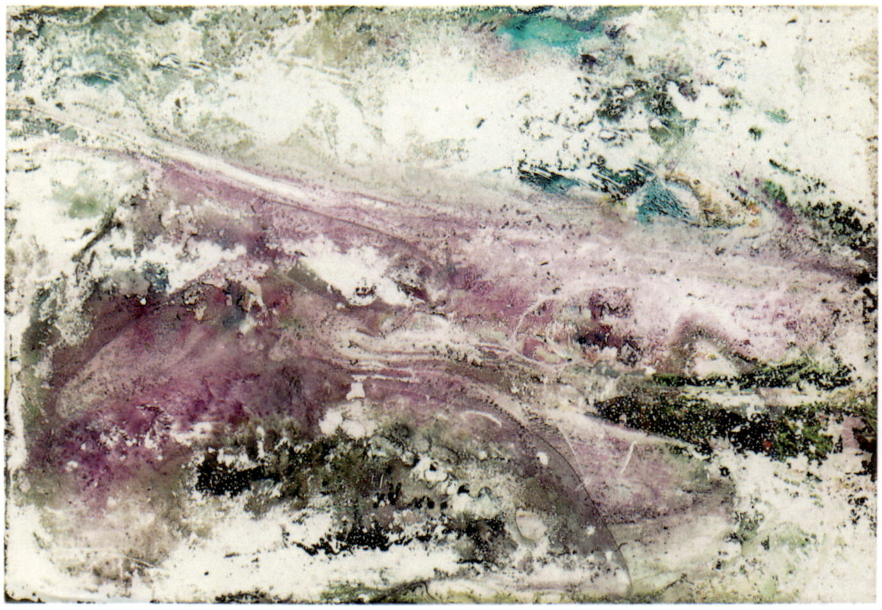

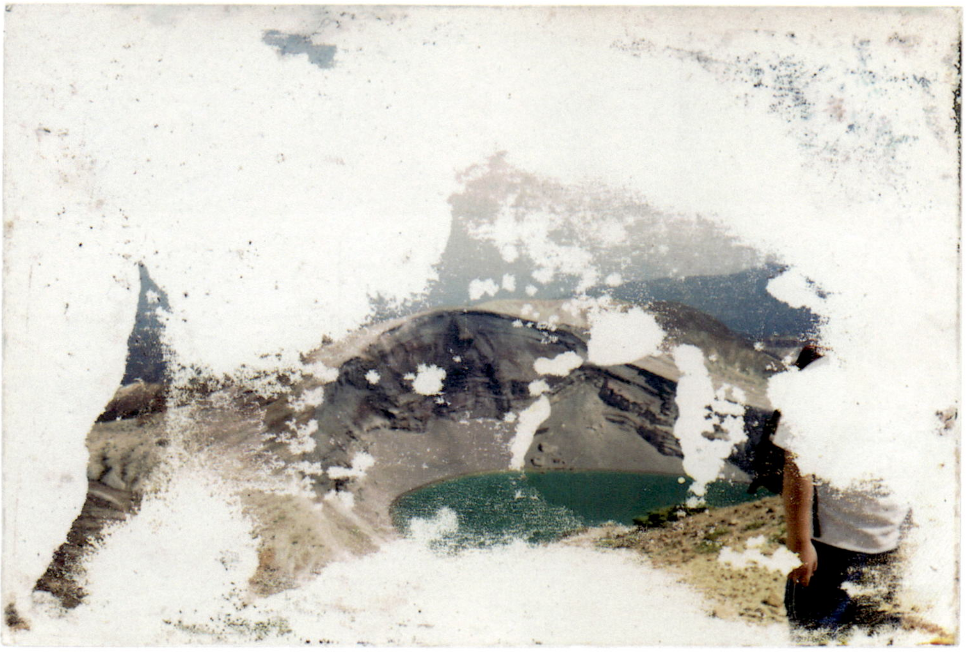

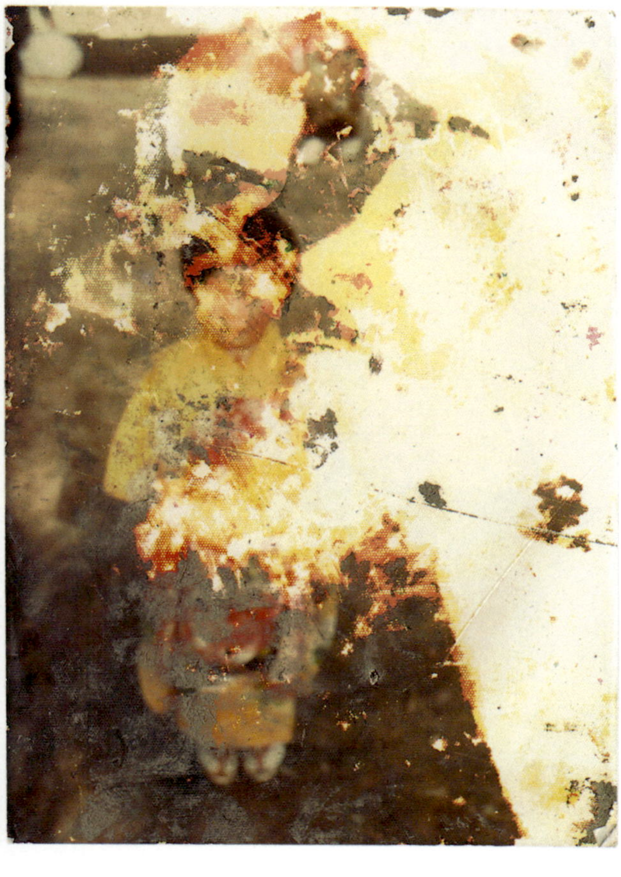

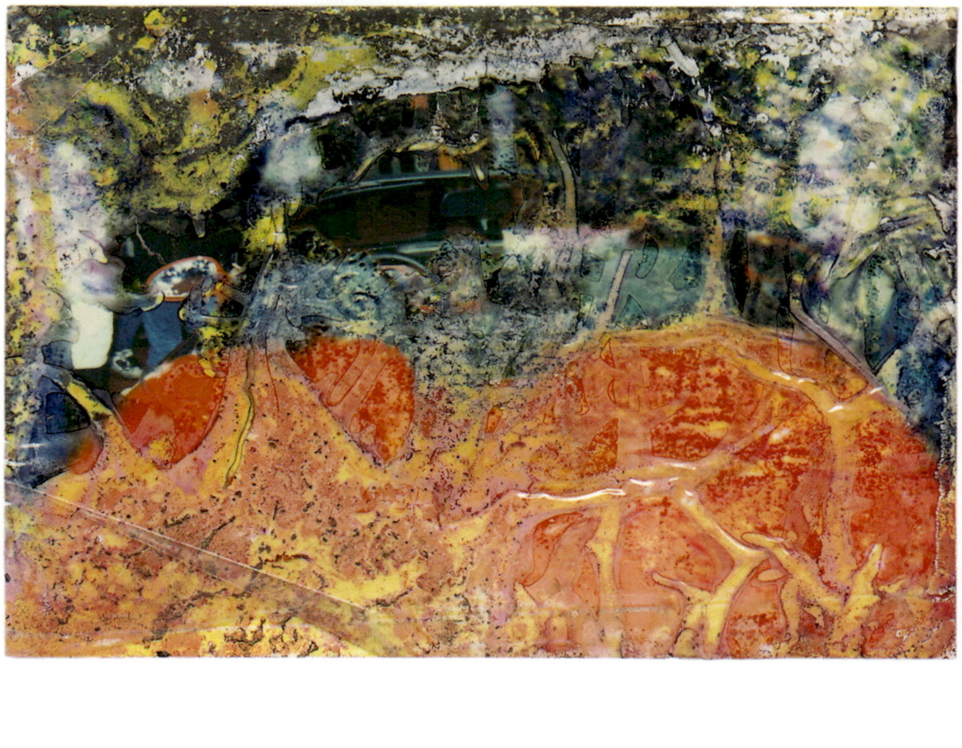

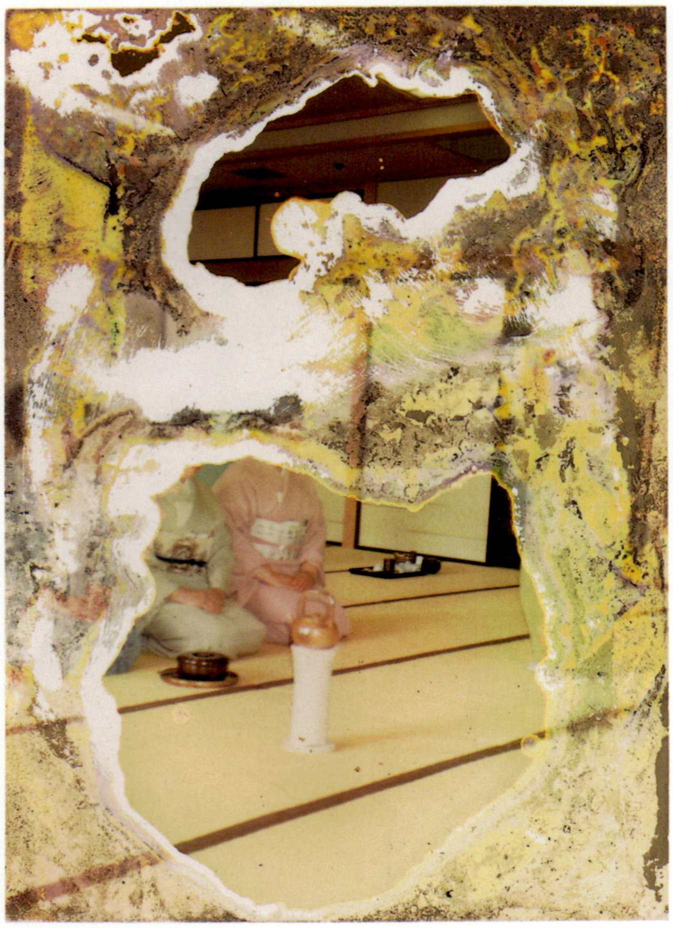
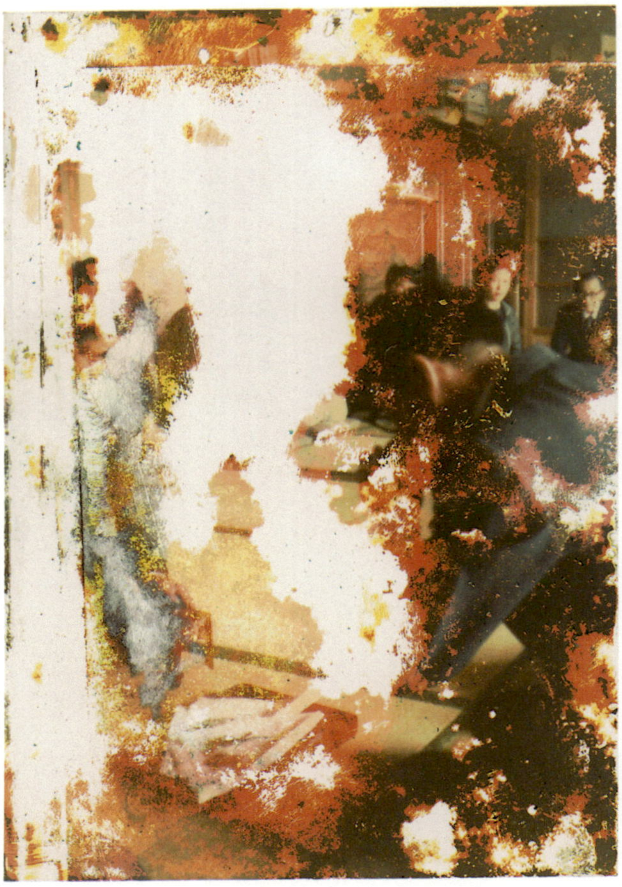
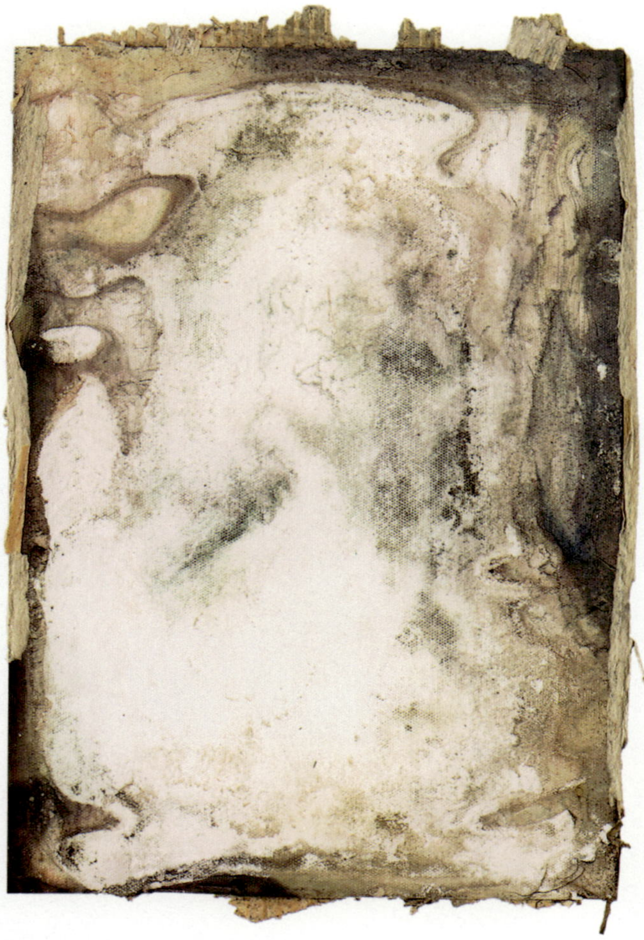
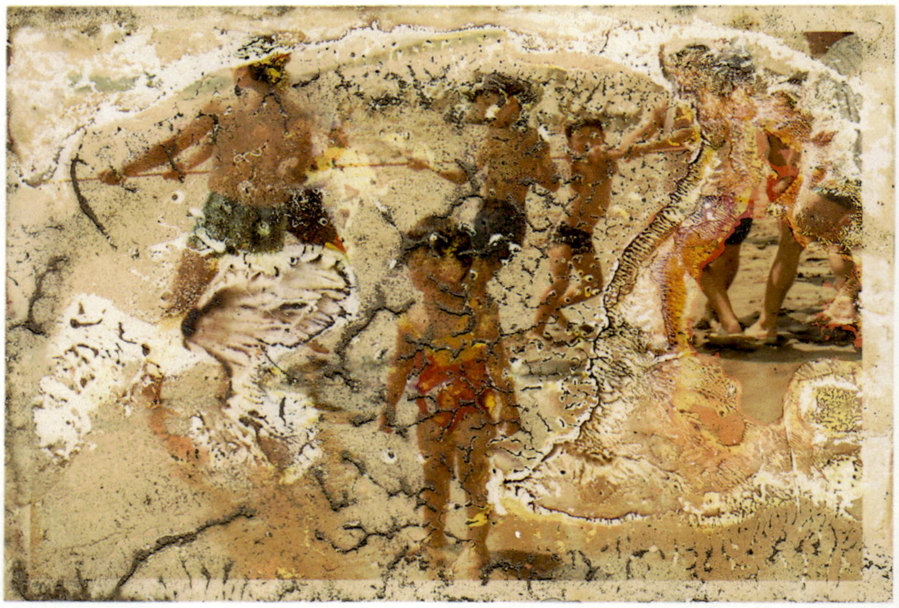
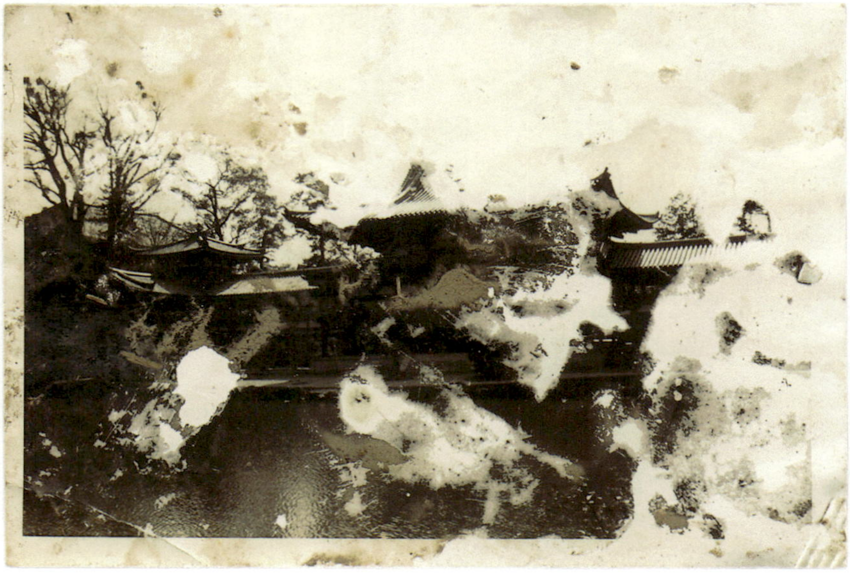

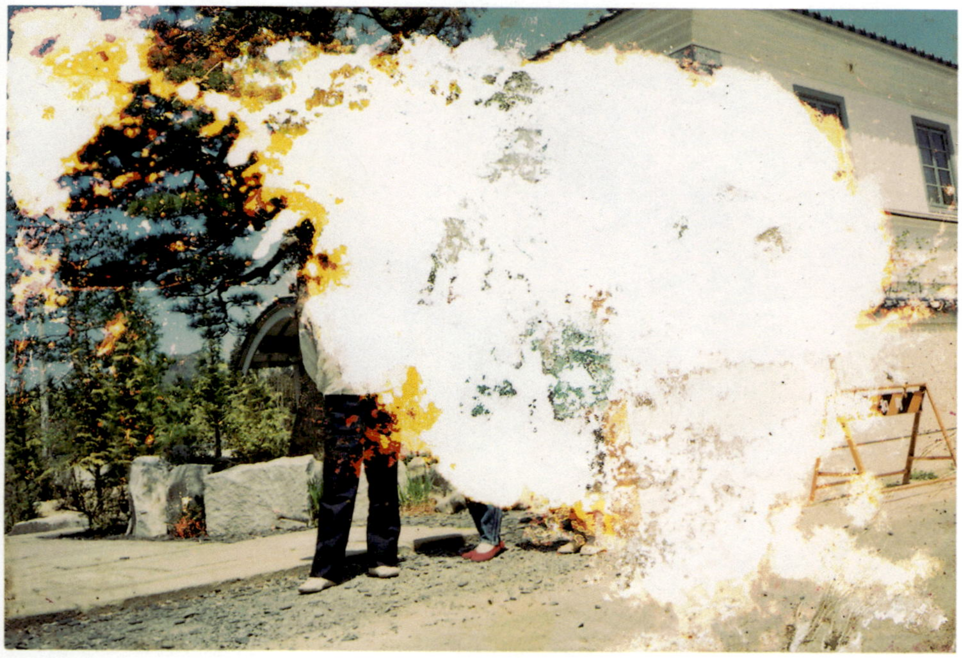
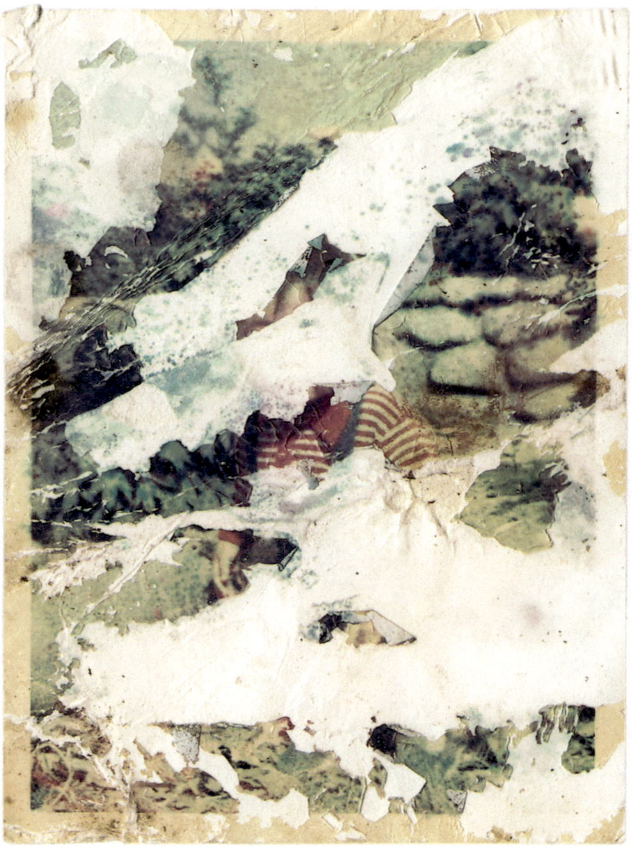
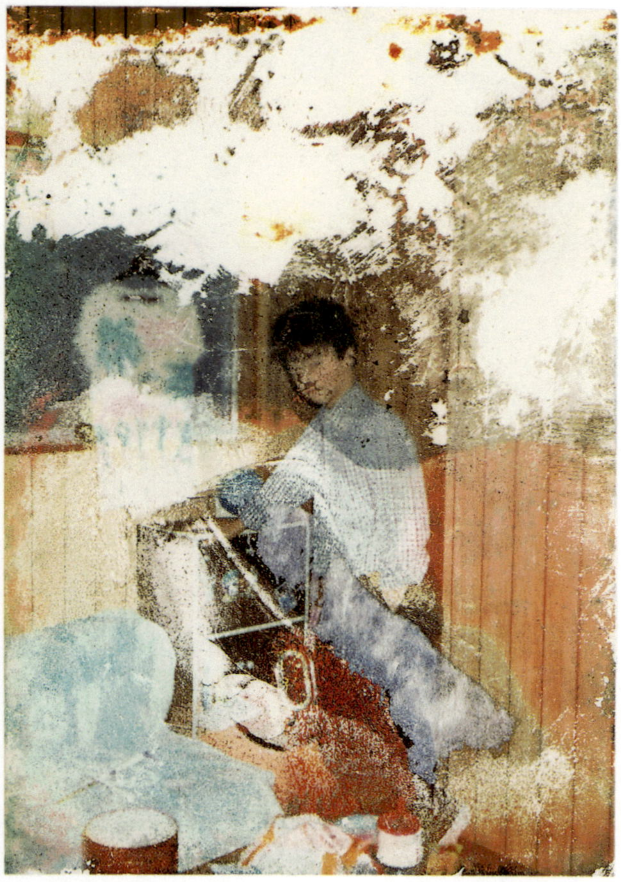
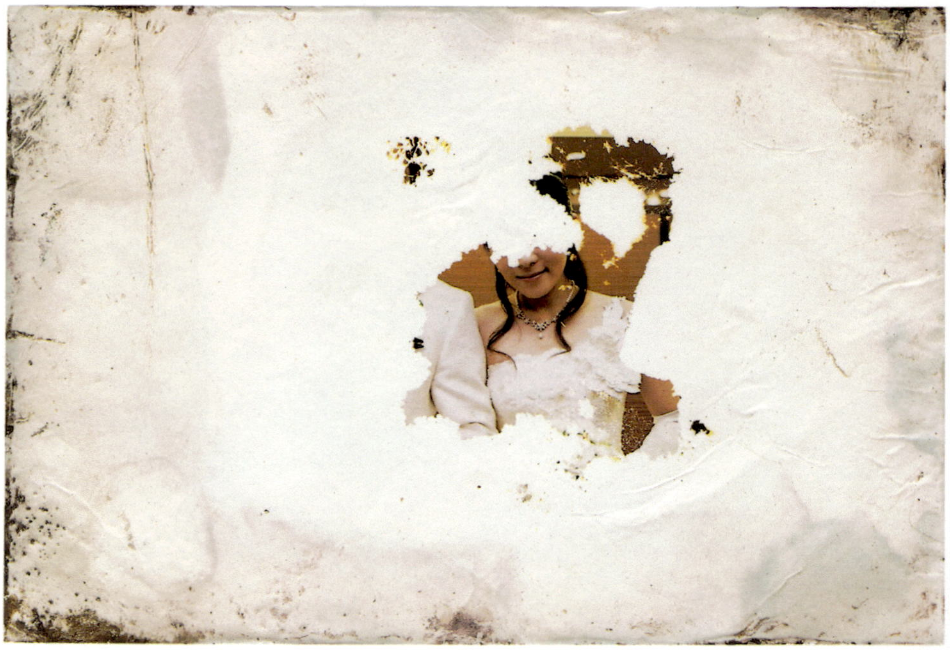
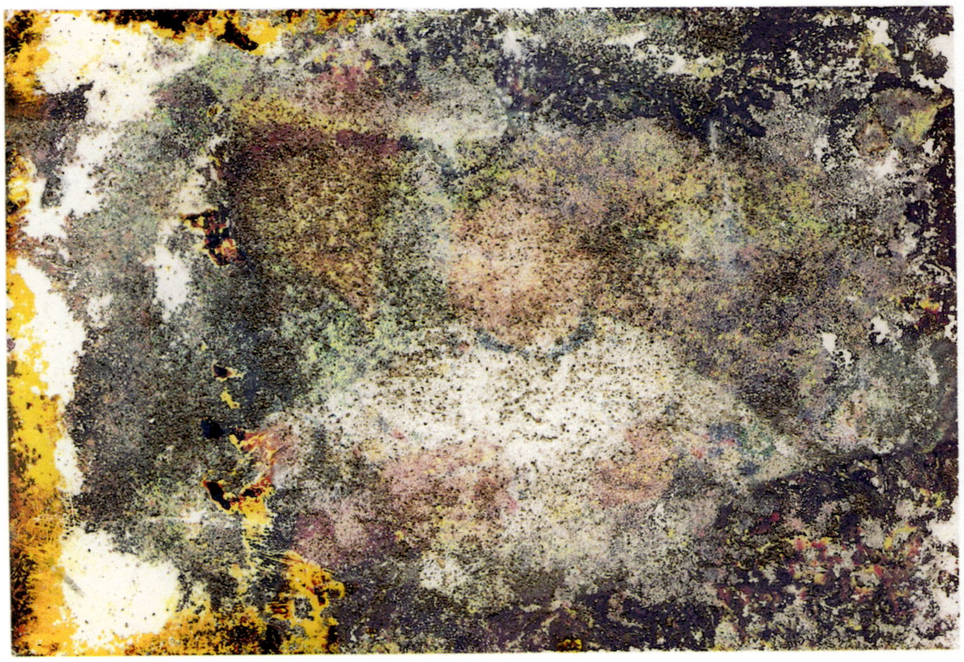

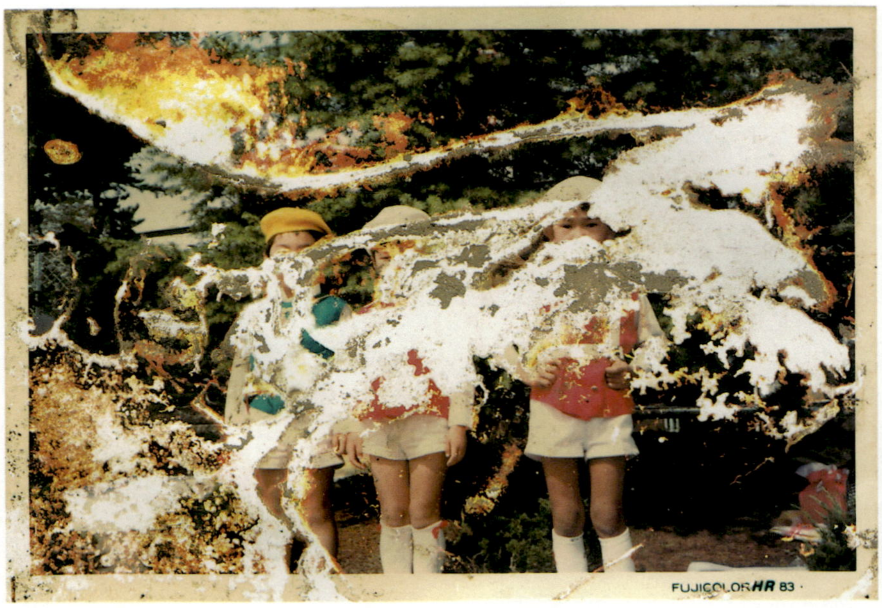
FUJICOLOR HR 83

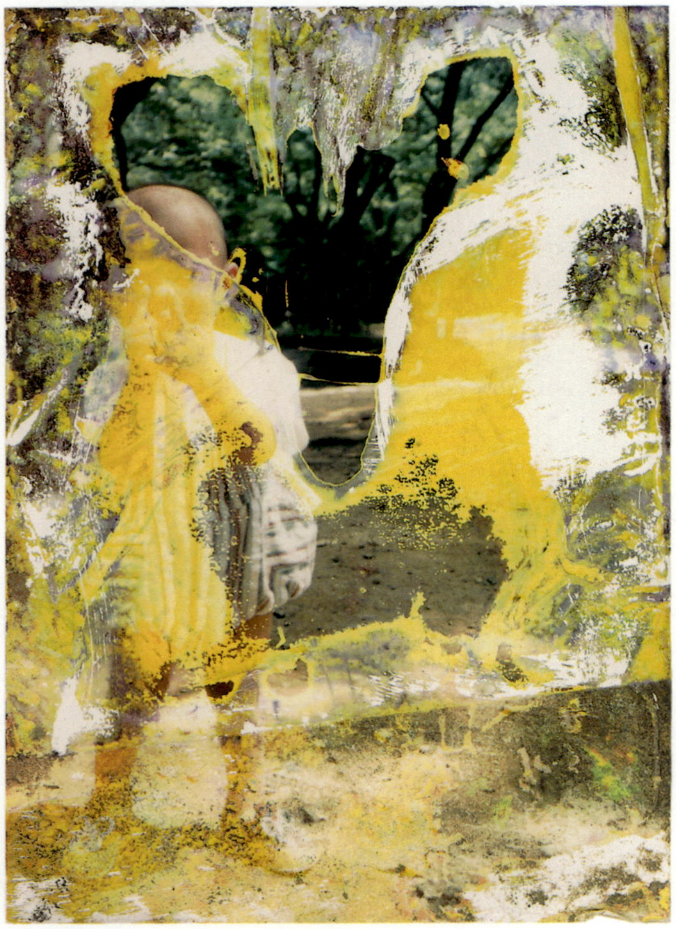

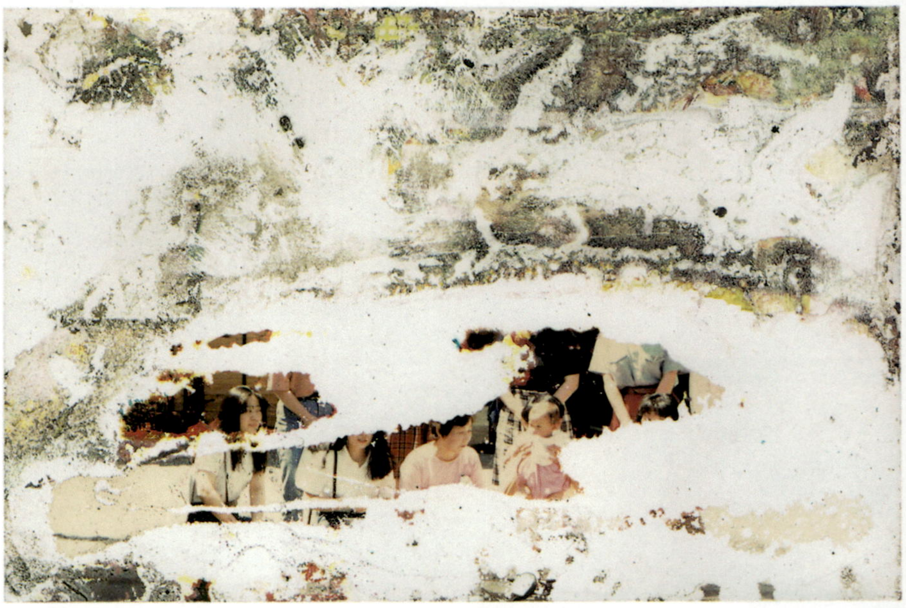

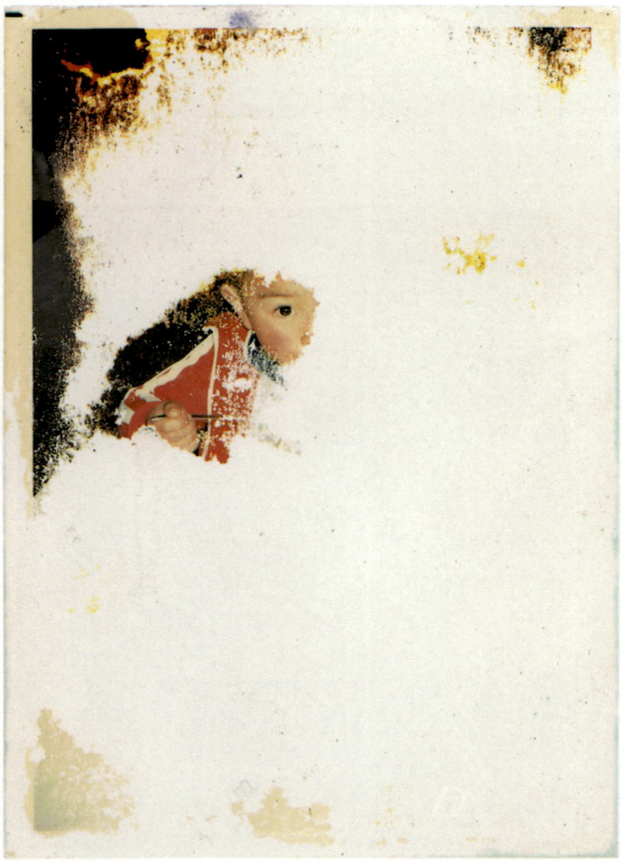

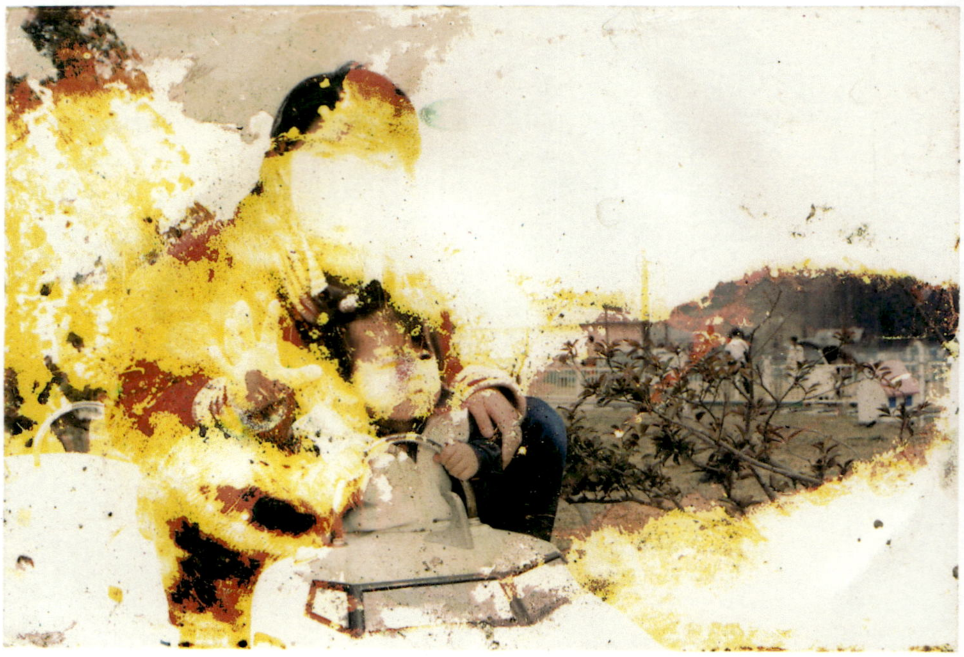

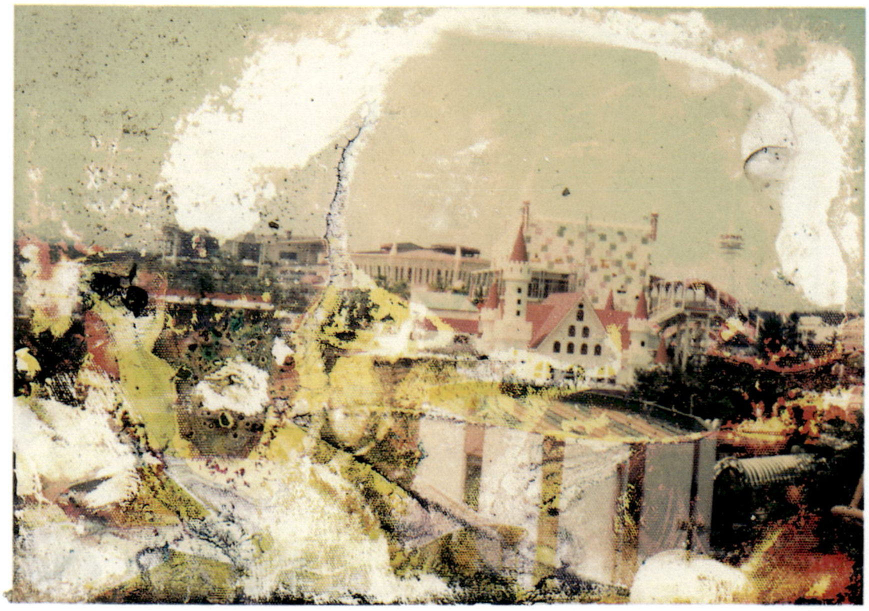
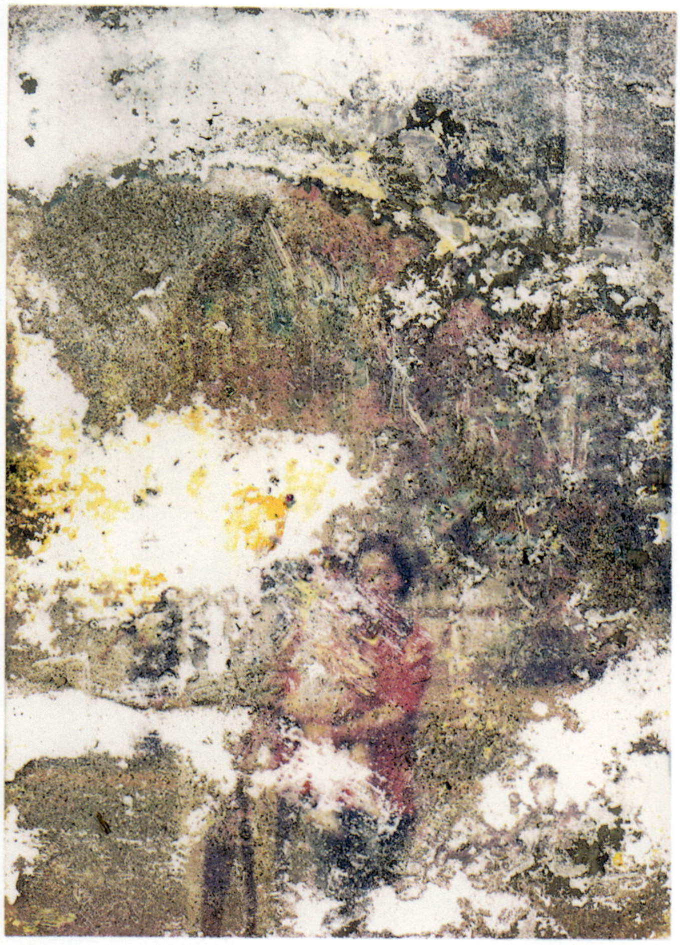
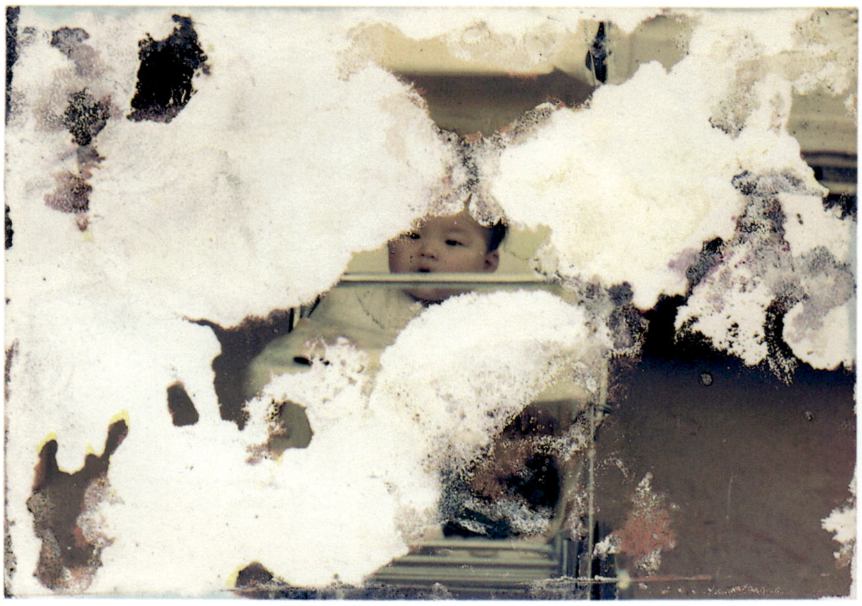

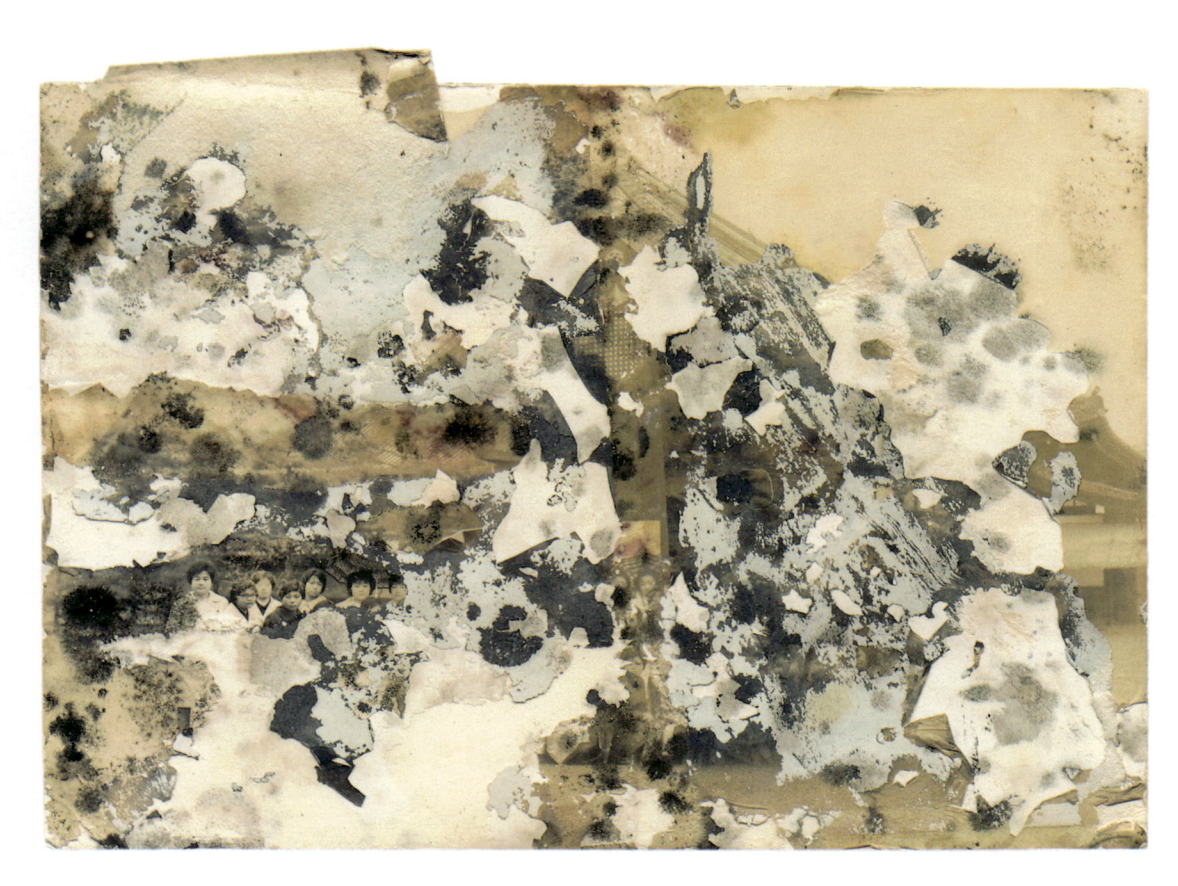

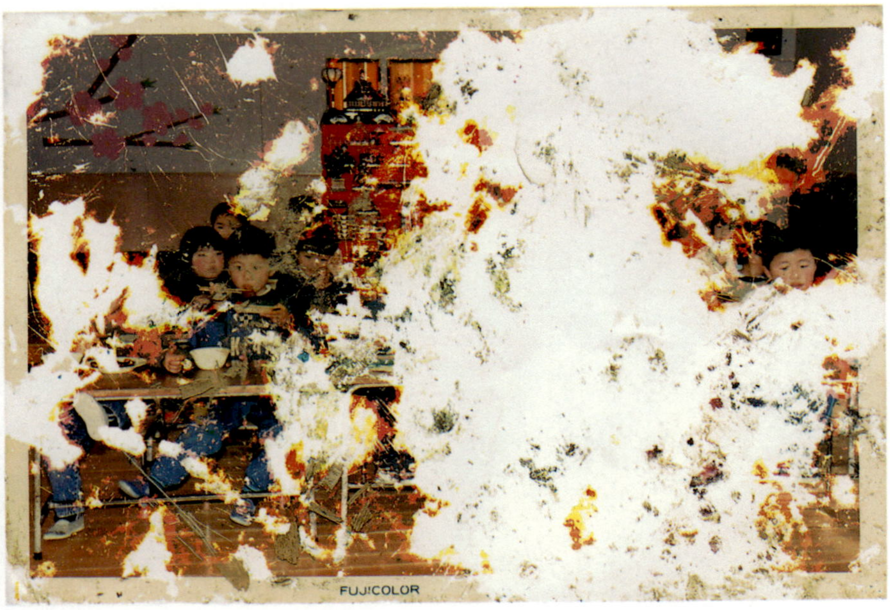
FUJICOLOR

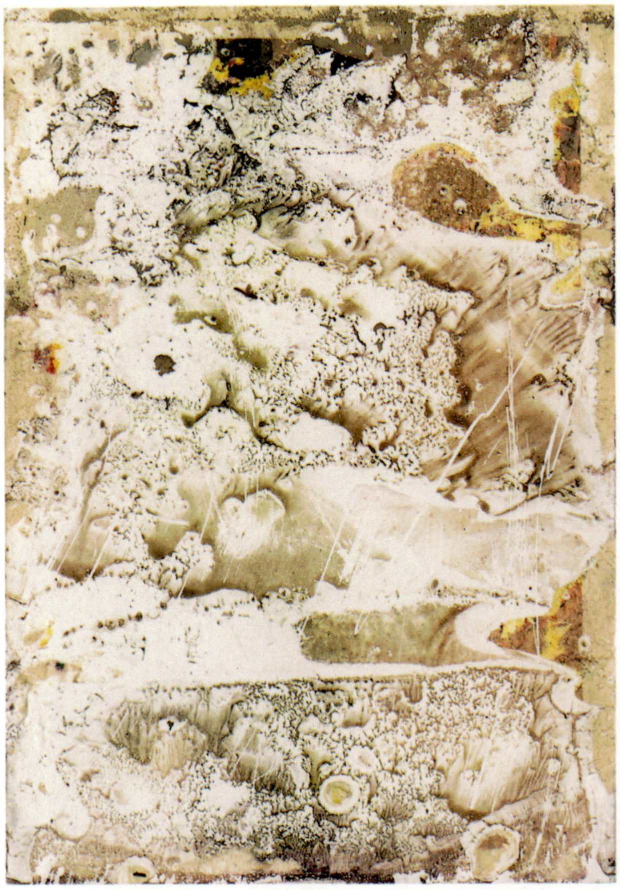

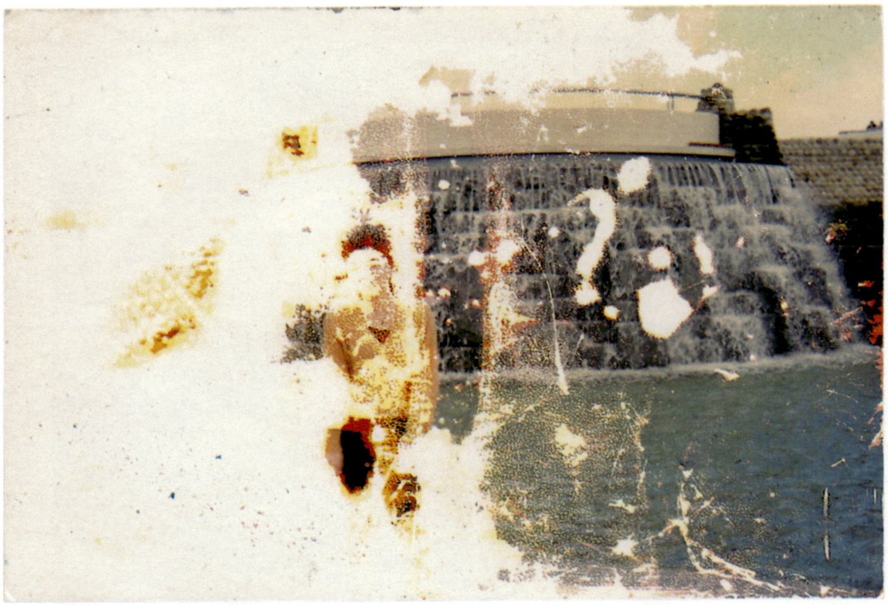

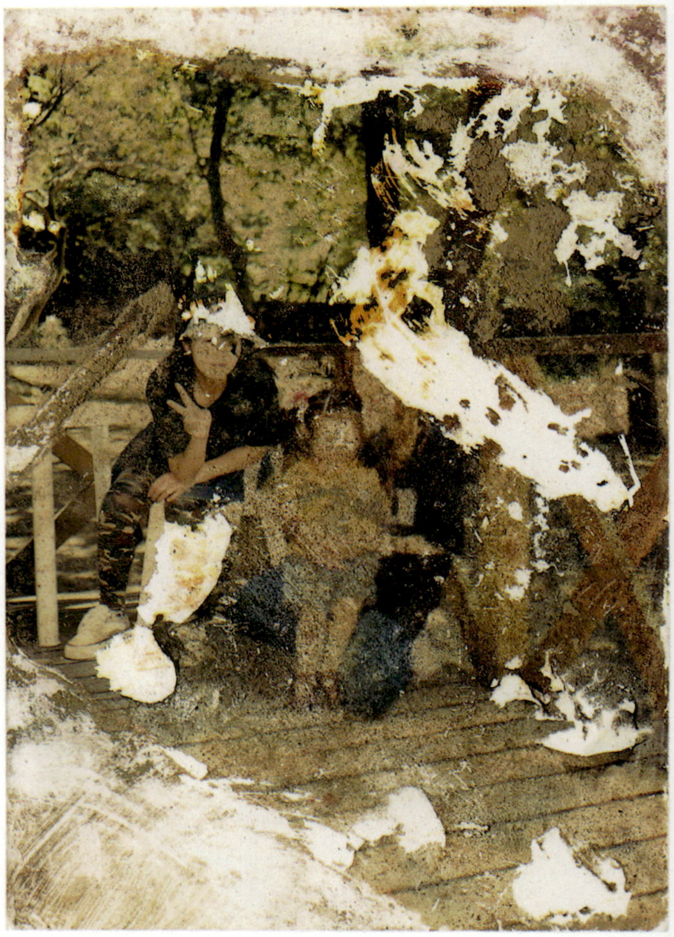

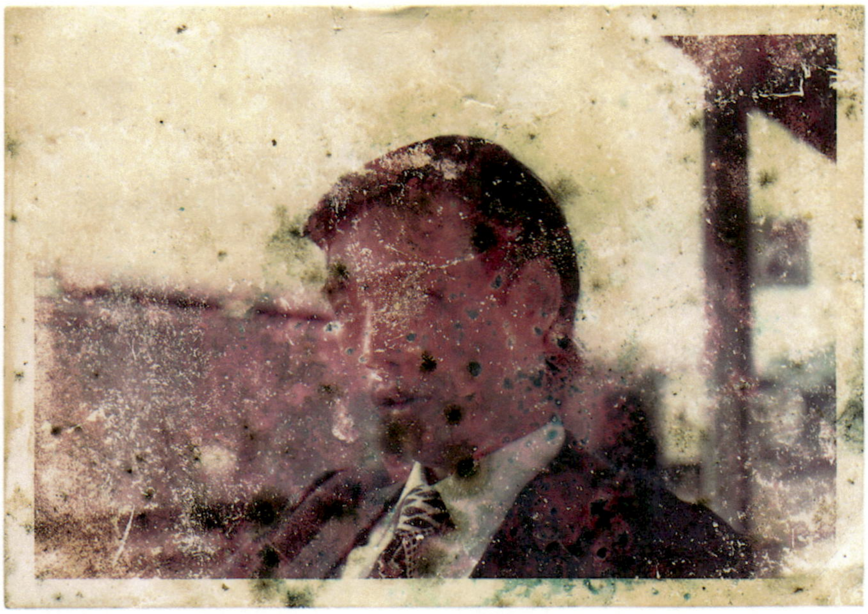

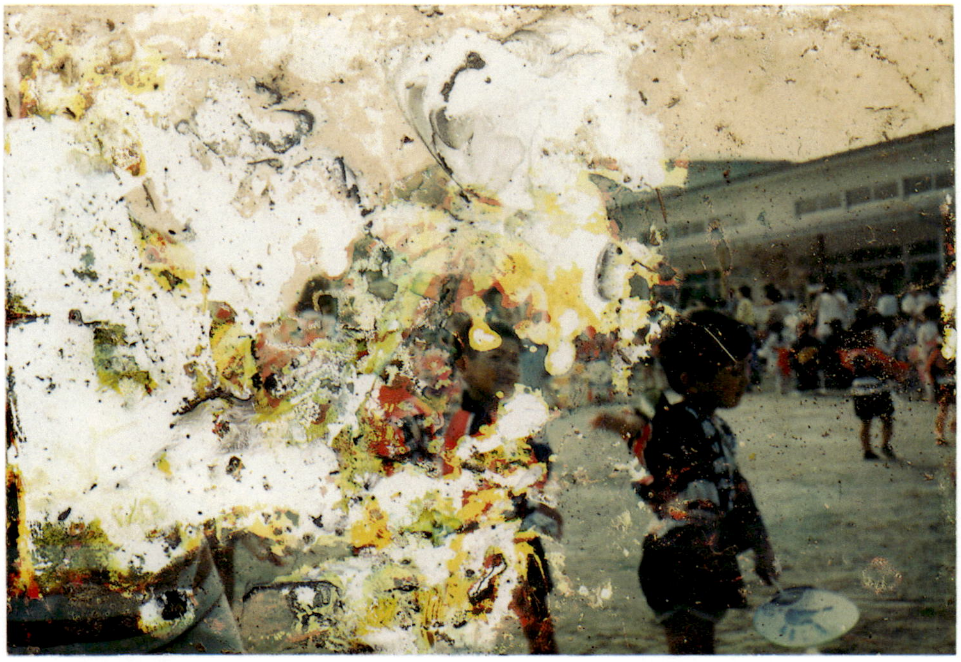
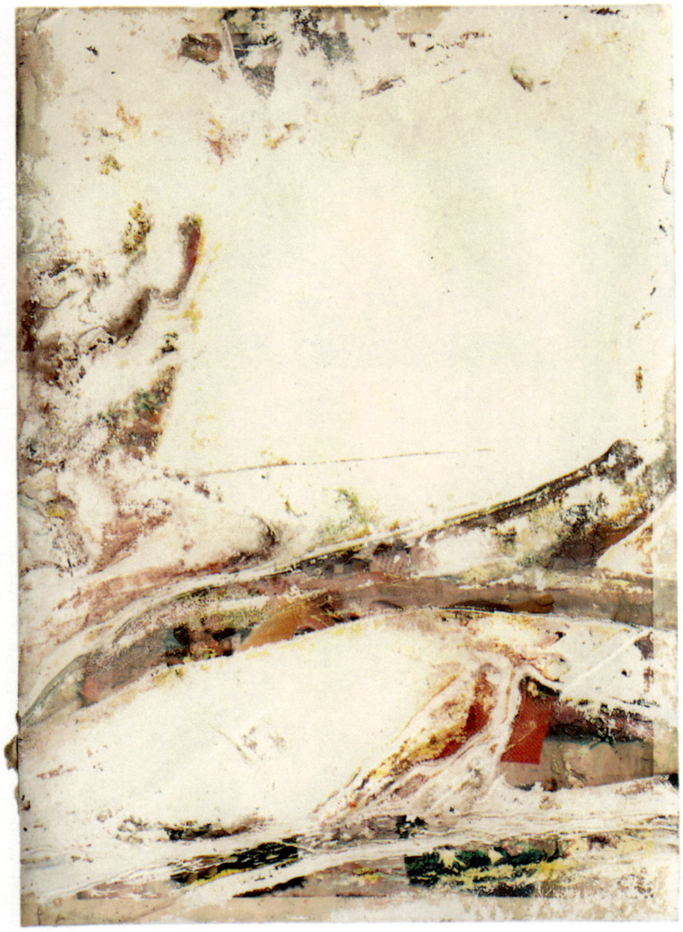
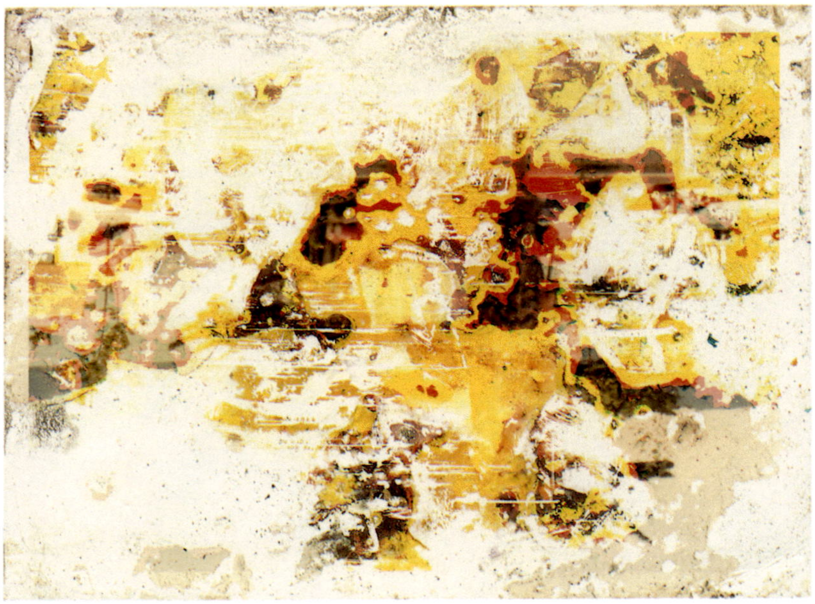
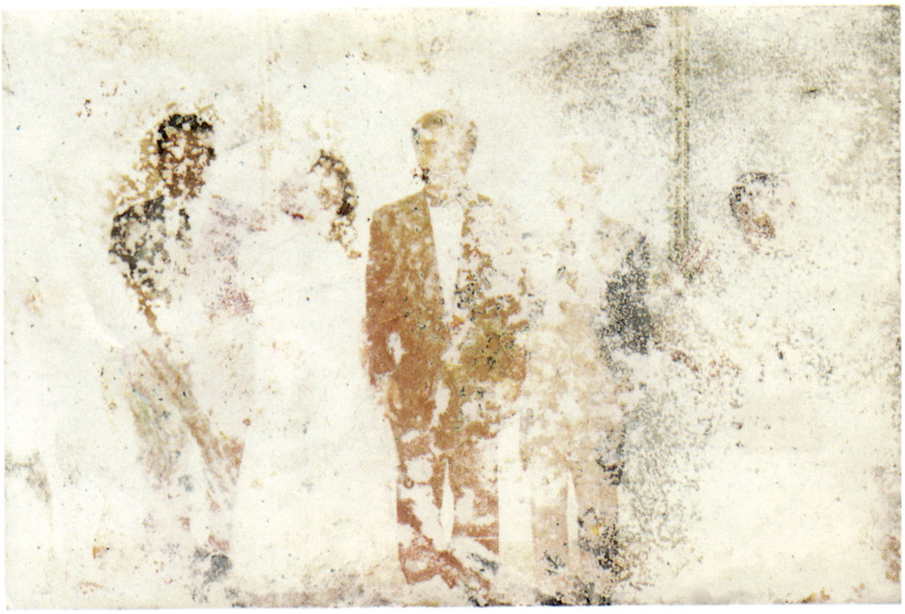

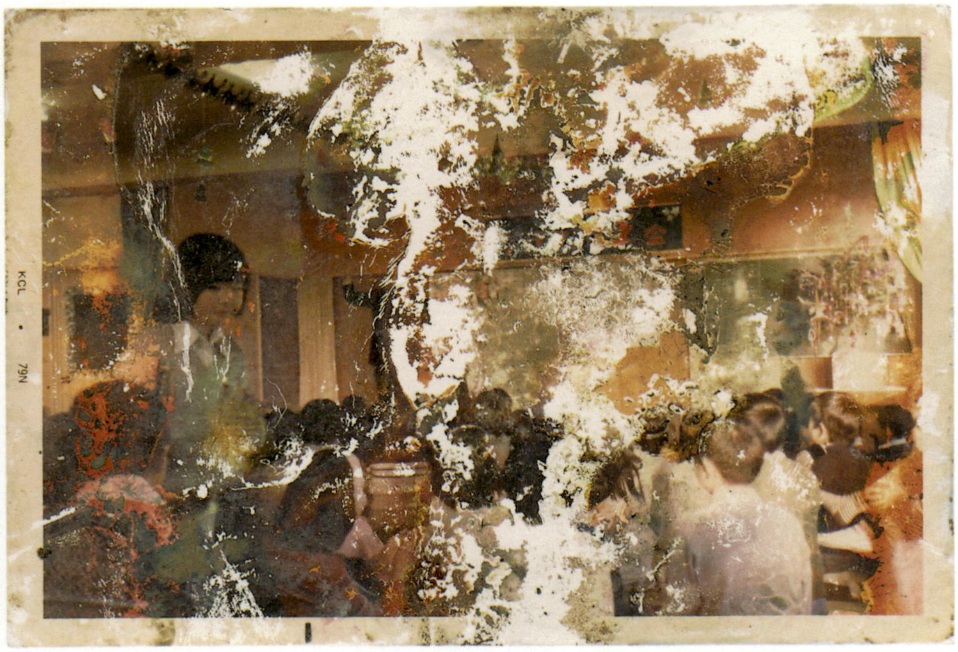

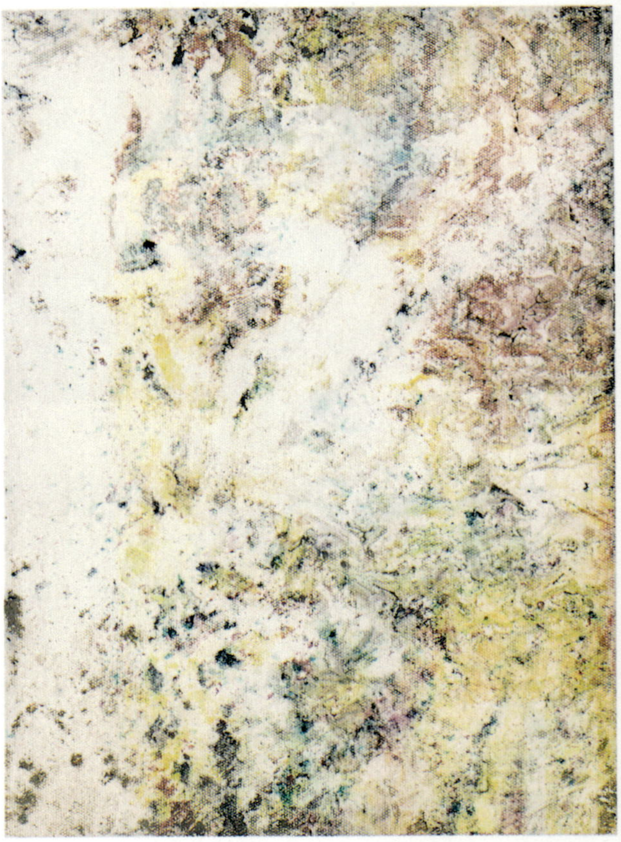

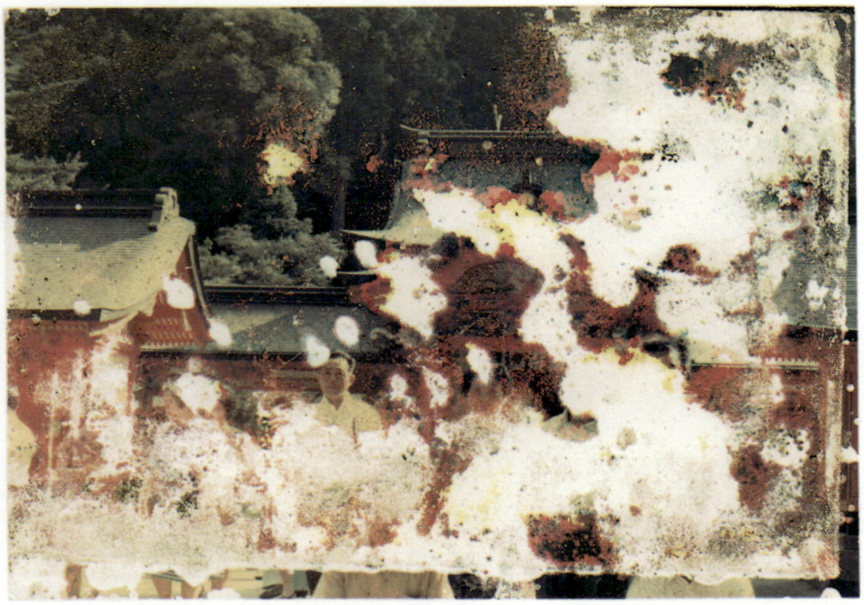

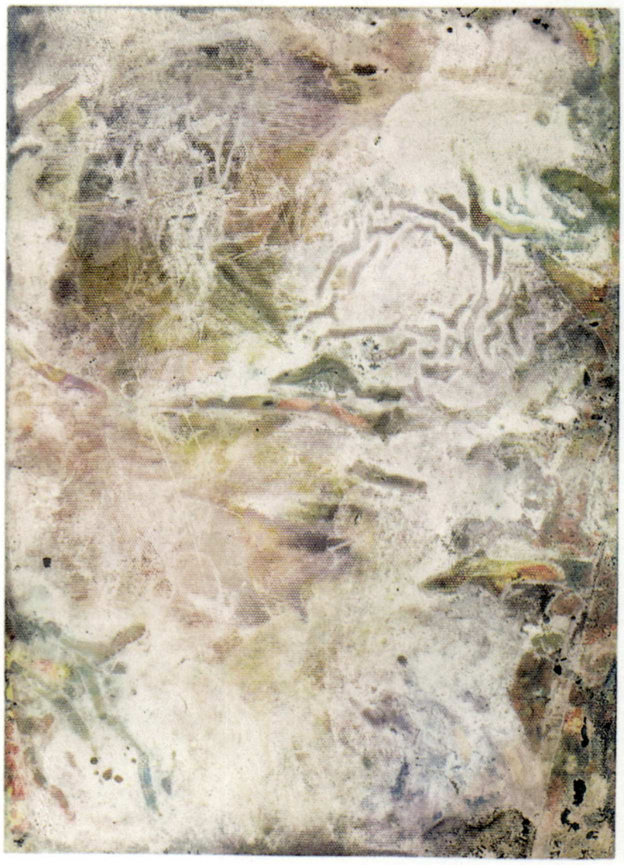

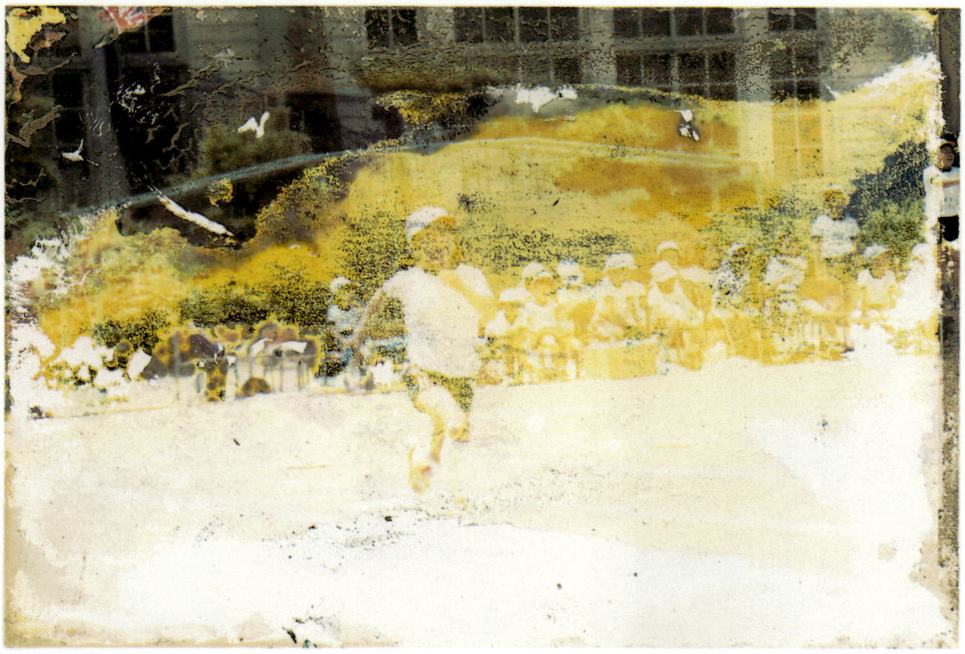